W9-CCF-068

Performance and Femininity in Eighteenth-Century German Women's Writing

"Palgrave Studies in Theatre and Performance History" is a series devoted to the best of theatre/performance scholarship currently available, accessible and free of jargon. It strives to include a wide range of topics, from the more traditional to those performance forms that in recent years have helped broaden the understanding of what theatre as a category might include (from a variety of forms as diverse as the circus and burlesque to street buskers, stage magic, and musical theatre, among many others). Although historical, critical, or analytical studies are of special interest, more theoretical projects, if not the dominant thrust of a study, but utilized as important underpinning or as a historiographical or analytical method of exploration, are also of interest. Textual studies of drama or other types of less traditional performance texts are also germane to the series if placed in their cultural, historical, social, or political and economic context. There is no geographical focus for this series and works of excellence of a diverse and international nature, including comparative studies, are sought.

The editor of the series is Don B. Wilmeth (EMERITUS, Brown University), Ph.D., University of Illinois, who brings to the series over a dozen years as editor of a book series on American theatre and drama, in addition to his own extensive experience as an editor of books and journals. He is the author of several award-winning books and has received numerous career achievement awards, including one for sustained excellence in editing from the Association for Theatre in Higher Education.

Also in the series:

Undressed for Success by Brenda Foley
Theatre, Performance, and the Historical Avant-garde by Günter Berghaus
Theatre, Politics, and Markets in Fin-de-Siècle Paris by Sally Charnow
Ghosts of Theatre and Cinema in the Brain by Mark Pizzato
Moscow Theatres for Young People by Manon van de Water
Absence and Memory in Colonial American Theatre by Odai Johnson
Performance and Femininity in Eighteenth-Century German Women's Writing by Wendy Arons

Performance and Femininity in Eighteenth-Century German Women's Writing

The Impossible Act

Wendy Arons

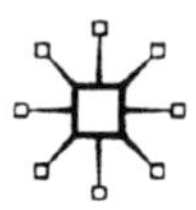

PERFORMANCE AND FEMININITY IN EIGHTEENTH-CENTURY GERMAN WOMEN'S WRITING

First published in 2006 by
PALGRAVE MACMILLAN™
175 Fifth Avenue, New York, N.Y. 10010 and
Houndmills, Basingstoke, Hampshire, England RG21 6XS
Companies and representatives throughout the world.

PALGRAVE MACMILLAN is the global academic imprint of the Palgrave Macmillan division of St. Martin's Press, LLC and of Palgrave Macmillan Ltd. Macmillan® is a registered trademark in the United States, United Kingdom and other countries. Palgrave is a registered trademark in the European Union and other countries.

ISBN-13: 978–1–4039–7329–0
ISBN-10: 1–4039–7329–6

Library of Congress Cataloging-in-Publication Data

Arons, Wendy.
Performance and femininity in eighteenth-century German women's writing : the impossible act / by Wendy Arons.
p. cm.—(Palgrave studies in theatre and performance history)
Includes bibliographical references and index.
ISBN 1–4039–7329–6 (alk. paper)
1. Women authors, German—18th century. 2. German literature—Women authors—History and criticism. 3. German literature—18th century—History and criticism. 4. Performance in literature. 5. Femininity in literature. I. Title. II. Series.

PT167.A75 2006
830.9′928709033—dc22 2005056606

A catalogue record for this book is available from the British Library.

Design by Newgen Imaging Systems (P) Ltd., Chennai, India.

First edition: October 2006

10 9 8 7 6 5 4 3 2 1

Printed in the United States of America.

For Roy, Toby, Mike, Avalon, and Leda

Contents

Acknowledgments

It is a pleasure, after these many years of working on this book, to be able to thank publicly the institutions, colleagues, and friends who have provided invaluable assistance to me along the way. For support for this project in its earliest stages, I am grateful to the University of California at San Diego for a dissertation-year fellowship that freed me from the burdens of teaching writing so that I could write myself. As a faculty member at the University of Notre Dame, I have been fortunate to receive several grants from the Institute for Scholarship in the Liberal Arts, College of Arts in Letters in support of this project; in addition, the University provided me with a sabbatical leave, and the Department of Film, Television, and Theatre arranged for a course reduction during a critical year of writing. Final, crucial archival work for this manuscript was made possible by a Merian Fellowship from the Erfurt Transatlantic Research Program, which gave me the opportunity to work with the handwritten memoirs of Karoline Schulze-Kummerfeld at the Thüringisches Hauptstaatsarchiv Weimar and conduct research into eighteenth-century theater at the Schloßbibliothek Gotha. For the assistance of the staff at these archives as well as at the Anna-Amalie-Bibliothek and the Staatsbibliothek Berlin, I am forever grateful. This book would also not have been possible without the heroic and cheerful assistance of Ken Kinslow and the Interlibrary Loan staff at the University of Notre Dame, who tracked down the endless lists of secondary literature I submitted online and helped extend loan periods when I needed more time with material. Margaret Porter and Robert Kusmer spared me a trip to Germany by obtaining a microfiche copy of Schulze-Kummerfeld's "Hamburg Manuscript," which is now part of the collection at the Hesburgh Library at Notre Dame; my gratitude to them both.

Many colleagues have either read and commented on my work or provided timely advice about the project. Todd Kontje and Katherine Shevelow introduced me to the field of eighteenth-century women's writing, encouraged me to follow what started out as a fanciful idea, and helped shape and guide this project in its earliest phase. Judith Halberstam, James Carmody, and Winifred Woodhull helped me to see a broader argument in my work and to articulate its historical significance. Several members of Women in German have not only served as mentors in the field but have also read and given feedback on this project at various stages, in particular Jeanine Blackwell, Cindy Brewer, Susan Cocalis, Marjorie Gelus, Marjanne Goozé, Nancy Kaiser, Susanne Kord, Ursula Mahlendorf, Katrin Sieg, Liliane Weissberg, and Susanne Zantop. For generously taking the time to read and comment on my manuscript I am grateful to my colleagues Don Crafton, Julia Douthwaite, Peter Holland, Robert Norton, and Pam Wojcik. I also owe thanks to people who shared their expertise along the way: Ruth Dawson, Lesley Walker, and Denise Della Rossa all responded to requests for assistance in locating primary texts; and Mary Frandzen unhesitatingly transcribed several pages of Schulze-Kummerfeld's manuscript for me, in the process also teaching me how to read what I had taken to be indecipherable scribbles. Unless otherwise noted, all the translations from the German in this book are mine; I was greatly assisted in that effort by a circle of colleagues who stepped in to help me with difficult passages or confirm my rendition of a phrase. For their quick and thorough responses, I thank Cindy Brewer, Jan Hagens, and especially Kirsten Christensen. Any errors in the translations are, of course, my own. Robert Goulding, Sara Maurer, Margaret Meserve, and Emily Osborn not only helped shape the final draft of each chapter through their incisive comments, but also provided emotional and psychological support: through their eyes I finally saw myself as the author of a book. Finally, this book would not be what it is today without the meticulous editorial guidance of Lisa Harteker, who asked the tough questions that needed to be asked and refused to accept lazy answers. I also thank Don Wilmeth for encouraging me to submit this book to his series, and Melissa Nosal, Emily Leithauser, and Julia Cohen at Palgrave for shepherding me through the publication process.

My greatest pillars of support have been my family, and this book is dedicated to them. To my parents, Toby and Roy Arons, who first taught me to love learning and then helped me take advantage of every opportunity to continue learning, I owe the deepest gratitude. My partner, Michael Perdriel, has encouraged me at every step and patiently helped me weather the ups and downs of writing in both tangible and intangible ways, taking care of children and household on the many weekends I needed to hole up in the office, and nourishing me both emotionally and physically. And finally, I thank my daughters, Avalon and Leda, who have waited their entire lives for me to finish this book, and who perform their own reinventions of femininity daily to my delight and astonishment.

Introduction

This book examines a series of texts by eighteenth-century German women that feature a heroine who engages with theater and performance. These heroines—La Roche's Sophie Sternheim, Ehrmann's Amalie, Unger's Melanie, Bürger's Aglaja, Mereau's Marie and unnamed "I," and Karoline Schulze-Kummerfeld's autobiographical self—lead lives with a public dimension and, in all but one case, work as professional actresses. At a time when women were (theoretically in any case) supposed to be confined to the domestic sphere, these heroines, much like their authors, perform in the public sphere.

These works thus prompt a reconsideration of how the eighteenth-century discourse of "separate spheres" affected women's understanding of their own subjectivity. Until fairly recently, much eighteenth-century scholarship has assumed that the discourse that divided the "male" public sphere from the "female" private one effectively excluded women from most public-sphere activity and, in addition, served as an explanatory device for the subject content of their writings. But given that women were often active in the public sphere, this "separate spheres" approach does not provide an adequate or accurate description of real women's experience of life in the late eighteenth century. Indeed, the mere fact of writing put women into the public sphere, and women's texts generally evince a strong consciousness of writing as a public activity that entails the risk of sanction. One of the ways this consciousness manifests itself is in women's use of the categories of theater and performance—another kind of public activity available to eighteenth-century women—to explore and engage with the implications and consequences of female activity in the public sphere. This book examines that engagement, and seeks to illuminate how eighteenth-century German women writers use the theater (as a space) and performance (as both an activity and an abstract idea) to investigate female subjectivity and intervene in the dominant discourse about ideal femininity.

In order to capture that discourse in all its rich complexity and tease out how these authors articulated their responses, I have taken an interdisciplinary approach that draws from the fields of literary criticism, cultural studies, theater history, and performance studies. Among other things, such an approach allows me to account for the aesthetic choices made by the authors under consideration; the cultural construction of categories like subjective sincerity and ideal femininity in late eighteenth-century Germany; the specific historical form of theater that these writers refer to in their texts; the range of attitudes and stereotypes held by the contemporary public about the theater and its practitioners; and these texts' engagement with the notion that performance is not only effective but also at times efficacious. Such an approach not only allows me to map out the conversation in which these writers were participating (and were to some extent trapped), but also lets me uncover certain aspects of their work that go beyond the bounds of eighteenth-century discourse and are only discernible when seen through the lens of current debates on gender and performance.

* * *

Eighteenth-century literary works in general—and, in particular, the eighteenth-century epistolary novel and autobiography—present human subjectivity in ways that are all too familiar to present-day readers: as transparent, interiorized, antitheatrical, and readable. In our daily interactions with others, most of us assume the kind of homology between inner and outer self that came to be formulated as a moral standard during the late eighteenth century. We are, on the whole, uncomfortable with (if not repelled by) the idea that a given person might not be presenting himself or herself to us honestly and sincerely. It is true that as a society we encourage a certain kind of polite suppression of true feelings in limited circumstances (i.e., "if you haven't something nice to say, don't say it"). Yet, on the whole, we put high cultural value on honesty and directness and expect (or at the very least hope) to be able to "read" each other's true motives and feelings in much the same way that an eighteenth-century reader might have read the motives and feelings of the "letter-writers" of the sentimental epistolary novel; and, like them, we are quick to condemn those "rakes" who seem to put on a new face for different company or in different settings. As Lionel Trilling notes in *Sincerity and Authenticity*, even though modern literature has fundamentally challenged the notion of subjective "authenticity," it would be absurd to imagine a similar repudiation in everyday interactions (41–42, 66).

Moreover, most of us, if and when we think about these issues, imagine that we simply "are" who we "are," and do not think of our interpersonal interactions with others as a "performance" unless we are facing the unusual pressures of something like a first date, a job interview, or a class presentation.[1] Even then we generally can distinguish those moments that feel like "performance" from those interactions in which, so to speak, we are "really ourselves," and, as a society, we privilege the openness and intimacy that mark the latter. In other words, in the realm of everyday experience, there remains, even in the face of theories that position the performance of self as a liberating phenomenon, a queasiness about performance, and a lingering suspicion that those who deliberately perform themselves in a nontheatrical setting are liars, hypocrites, or worse (i.e., politicians).[2]

In eighteenth-century literature, the anxiety about performance often manifests itself in narratives that feature a young naive girl victimized by an aristocratic deceiver. In the German context, this kind of deception is called *Verstellung*, a word weighted with several meanings that have rich connotations for the era under discussion. To begin with, *Verstellung* is quite specifically the aristocratic courtier's art of simulation and dissimulation. The term is used neutrally or even positively in the manuals of prudent behavior *(Klugheitslehre)* that proliferate in the seventeenth and early eighteenth centuries, but, by the late eighteenth century, it takes on a negative connotation as a description of forms of behavior antithetical to bourgeois values.[3] In addition, *Verstellung* is the term used to describe the art of the actor on stage: contextualized within the theater, it is the neutral word for "play-acting." Outside the theater, however, the word has a more sinister and dangerous connotation: it also means disguise, make-believe, and pretence, and it is the cardinal sign of the villain in a host of novels and plays. The term *Verstellung* thus carries a constellation of meanings that specifically evoke modes of performance pertinent to the eighteenth century.

Verstellung is not exactly the same as performance, but the eighteenth-century definition of proper subjectivity as the opposite of *Verstellung* is directly related to our own conception of human "beingness." For it is precisely in the late eighteenth century that the "performance" of self becomes an issue of both morality and identity (in ways that are recognizably modern) *because* of the shift to a conception of the self as "natural" and "essential," and therefore not consciously or deliberately performed. As a result, I use the terms *Verstellung* and performance interchangeably in this study, partly for the sake of readability, but also because the use of the modern terms "performance" and "performativity" call attention to the fact that, when theorists like Erwin Goffman and Judith Butler investigate the performativity of identity in the (post)modern context, they are to a certain extent still rehearsing many of the same dilemmas.

Because we continue to have a stake in both the eighteenth-century attitude toward performance and its definitions of gendered identity, I think it is important to look at the consequences of the shift toward what I term an *antitheatrical subjectivity* in its formative stages, particularly for women, on whom the ideology of transparent subjectivity laid both a discursive and a real burden. Toward the middle of the eighteenth century, interest in the morality of performance took on a particular urgency, fueled by the desire of those who identified with bourgeois culture to distinguish themselves from aristocratic modes of being. Eighteenth-century bourgeois theorists and philosophers wrote extensively about questions of subjectivity and were keenly interested in questions related to the homology between one's "inner" self and one's "outer" display of that self. For many eighteenth-century moralists and philosophers, a key characteristic of the proper mode of being was transparency: the virtuous bourgeois subject was expected to be true to himself or herself and to act honestly, consistently, and forthrightly in his or her dealings with others. Such interpersonal openness stood in marked opposition to aristocratic forms of social intercourse of the early modern and baroque periods, in which the performance of social role as a role was expected if not encouraged.[4] At the same time, eighteenth-century theoretical writings on subjectivity and identity increasingly tended to fix gender roles and to cement in place the bipolar gender system of the modern era, thus making what was supposed to be a sincere presentation of self at one and the same time an acquiescence to, and acceptance of, culturally defined roles.[5]

In writing about eighteenth-century subjectivity in terms of the extent to which it was not conceived of as "performed," I draw on Judith Butler's understanding of gendered subjectivity as constituted by and through performative "acts." Butler argues that "gender is in no way a stable identity or locus of agency from which various acts proceed; rather, it is an identity tenuously constituted in time—an identity instituted through a *stylized repetition of acts*," ("Performative Acts" 270) and that furthermore,

> As performance which is performative, gender is an "act," broadly construed, which constructs the social fiction of its own psychological interiority. . . . I am suggesting that this self is not only irretrievably "outside," constituted in social discourse, but that the ascription of interiority is itself a publically regulated and sanctioned form of essence fabrication. (279)

This "ascription of interiority," and the naturalizing of gendered identity as something that proceeds organically from a pregiven, biologically determined fixed interiority is, in my view, the project of eighteenth-century bourgeois discursive productions of the "proper mode of being."

Butler's theoretical framework thus helps me ask questions about how women writers of the era engaged with the notion of gender and identity as "performed" or "performable" during a time in which social pressures *against* the performance of self were highly visible in bourgeois attempts to delineate its culture, mores, values, and modes of being in opposition to the highly spectacularized and theatricalized self-performances put on display by the aristocracy. Consequently, I read the production of female subjectivity in these works in terms of their negotiation with the contradictory pressures resulting from an alignment with, and internalization of, bourgeois expectations (which entailed a rejection of the "false" self-performances of the aristocratic sphere), coupled with a resistance to the compulsion to "do" gender in proscribed, limiting ways.

My reading of these texts is also informed by Joan Riviere's notion of femininity as masquerade. In her 1929 essay "Womanliness as Masquerade," Riviere describes the case of an intellectual woman who compensated for her transgression of traditional gender roles by producing an excess of femininity. Such a masquerading of womanliness serves a double function: it deflects criticism, and it reveals the emptiness of categories of sexual difference. Riviere notes,

> Womanliness therefore could be assumed and worn as a mask, both to hide the possession of masculinity and to avert the reprisals expected if she was found to possess it. . . . The reader may now ask how I define womanliness or where I draw the line between genuine womanliness and the "masquerade". . . they are the same thing. (306)

The concept of masquerade is useful for my analysis in two important ways. First, women writers of the eighteenth century had to grapple with the pressures of maintaining their own status as "proper women" while engaging in an activity (writing) that represented an assumption of masculine prerogatives. In their writings, these women often produce and/or reproduce dominant cultural assumptions and normative prescriptions of "ideal womanhood," and, as a result, masquerade an idealized femininity that, at times, was at odds with their own lives, behaviors, and attitudes.[6] So, for example, Sophie von La Roche's sophistication and self-awareness dismayed her reader and fan Caroline Flachsland, who had expected the author to embody the *naiveté* and idealized femininity of her novel's heroine.[7] In such cases, the text's representation of femininity constitutes the compensatory masquerade, while the lived life itself negotiates subjectivity on different terms. The fact that readers wished to impose a transparent referentiality between author and work speaks to the difficulty, for women who published or who otherwise stepped outside the boundaries of the feminine, of maintaining the delicate balancing act between their own aspirations as artists and subjects, and social pressures to conform to circulating images of ideal womanhood.

Second—and this gets to the heart of my project—in their constructions of femininity it is possible to trace an acknowledgment of the essentially performed nature of womanhood—that is, its lack of essence and its status as masquerade—even as such works simultaneously participate in the reigning discourse of authenticity and transparency that served to naturalize sexual difference. Joan Riviere's observation that "genuine womanliness and masquerade . . . are the same thing" is borne out by a close reading of these texts, which undermine essentialized, naturalized constructions of womanhood even as they ostensibly work to establish them or shore them up. The opposition between performance and authenticity in the eighteenth century becomes highly unstable when women try to write about female experience within this discourse. Their attempts to reconcile women's dreams, desires, and experiences collide with the concepts and images of gendered subjectivity culturally available to them.

* * *

This book joins a number of recent works that have looked back at the late eighteenth century and examined the use of performative strategies in the age of sincerity. Much of this work has come out of the field of English literature—for example, the studies of British women writers and theatricality by Pascoe, Burroughs, and Donkin.[8] In the field of theater history, Wanko, Wikander, and Freeman have unpacked the eighteenth century's complex and often contradictory ideas about sincerity and authenticity as they related to the theater, and Davis has looked back at the coining of the term "theatricality" in the eighteenth century to argue for its utility in grounding civil social relations.[9] In German studies, Kord has employed twentieth-century notions of gender as a performative act to explore the question of why eighteenth-century women writers published anonymously, and Krimmer has examined the performative trope of cross-dressing in works by both men and women of the eighteenth century to expose differences in the ways male and female writers understood gendered subjectivity.[10]

Like many of these works, the present study seeks to historicize current debates about subjectivity—which center on questions about the extent to which our identity is determined by biological sex, culturally defined gender roles, and the social scripts we have been given—through an investigation of a culture and era that was heavily invested in both defining proper, virtuous being in terms of a transparency of self and naturalizing (socially defined) gender roles. Where my approach differs is in its focus on the ways that eighteenth-century theories of acting inflected and informed women's figuration of female subjectivity in their writing. That is, I investigate the mobilization of theater and performance in these texts not only through the lens of current performance theory, but also via historically specific notions of how a self is performed, what constitutes good or bad performance, and how observers and/or audience members differentiate between a sincere presentation of self and a feigned one. Indeed, perhaps the most crucial question such an approach allows me to investigate is precisely the issue of the relationship between audience expectation and the production of subjectivity: knowing what people defined *as* performance in the eighteenth century, where they expected to encounter it, and how they expected to read it affords greater insight into how women writers played with the terms of the debate.

Methodologically speaking, then, this book offers a different way of looking at a familiar set of issues. A number of recent essays have addressed the problems raised by what is often referred to as the "separate spheres" approach to eighteenth-century literature and culture. The idea that the late eighteenth century marked the beginning of the division between the public "male" sphere and the private "female" one no longer seems to be an adequate analytical device in the face of historical evidence revealing that women did indeed have "public dimensions to their lives" and that "engaging in those public practices involved a consciousness that they were behaving publicly and that their behavior implied its own sanction" (Klein 102).[11] In addition, many have also taken issue with Karin Hausen's claim that it was only in the late eighteenth century that gender role became both central to identity and cemented to biological sex and the "nature" of the sexes (Hausen maintains that, previous to the late eighteenth century, identity was tied to class rather than gender). Critics of Hausen's theory see both evidence of the bipolar gender system before the late eighteenth century (Olenhusen, Rang), and remnants of the importance of class on identity formation in the modern period (Kuhn); in addition, they also offer alternative models of how and why gender roles and stereotypes changed and/or developed at the turn of the century (Olenhusen, Kuhn, Frevert). At the same time, most historians agree that, at the end of the late eighteenth century, ideas about gender and identity shifted in a profound way, cementing in place the bipolar gender system of the modern era. As Ute Frevert observes, "during this period there seemed to be a *particular* need to reify and legitimate the bipolar gender system, and to modify it to fit the time" (Frevert, "Bürgerliche Meisterdenker" 43).

Focusing on the discursive shift toward a demand for antitheatricality in the late eighteenth century helps to account for that "particular" need to emphasize gender as a natural attribute of biological sex, because the antitheatrical subject is theoretically predicated on a "natural" being that, when gendered, expresses itself with a kind of mystical immediacy as public activity for men and private domesticity for women. But the ideology of authenticity promulgated in the late eighteenth century also contained the germ of its own unravelling by dint of the fact that a direct, unmediated knowledge of another is impossible. It is difficult to imagine what it might mean for a person to "be" in the absence of any public, performative dimension. Eighteenth-century theorists were not unaware of this paradox. As Habermas notes, "subjectivity, as the innermost core of the private, was always already oriented to an audience (*Publikum*)" (49). But, nonetheless, many moralists continued to insist upon—and discursively circulate—ideas about idealized femininity predicated upon the notion that proper womanhood eschewed all forms of performance and publicity. Hence the category of performance helps us get at a more precise account of gender in relation to publicity and privacy because it speaks to the very issue of how eighteenth-century women might have imagined "selfhood" in terms of both the private and public dimension.

My analysis thus offers a new category through which we can map the breadth and boundaries of female experience in the eighteenth century. While this study does not completely jettison the public/private opposition that in many ways structured eighteenth-century conceptions of gender, by shifting emphasis to an exploration of the demands placed on eighteenth-century women by the appeal to antitheatricality, my approach necessitates an acknowledgment that there is a public dimension to all subjectivity, since the only way a person can make themselves "knowable" to the world (even as authentic, direct, and natural) is through exterior signs made visible on the body and face, in gestures and in speech. Thus I pay particular attention to the ways in which these women writers imagine the public as a social audience (the German word for audience, *das Publikum*, incorporates both meanings) that not only both figuratively and literally represents the pressures of dominant discourse, but also functions to police and constrain female self-expression.

* * *

The selection of primary works for this study reflects my interest in investigating how and why women writers of the era used the theater and performance in their writing about female subjectivity, given the social and cultural constructions of ideal femininity that made the theater a dangerous site for women, and the deployment of performance a particularly risky strategy. Consequently, I have chosen to focus primarily on works written by women that describe the life of an actress. This study includes, to the best of my knowledge, all of the texts from the period under consideration that fit that criterion.[12] The texts range across several genres, including novels (La Roche, *Sternheim*; Ehrmann, *Amalie*; and Unger, *Melanie*), short stories (Bürger, "Aglaja"; Mereau, "Marie" and "Flight to the City"), and a memoir (Schulze-Kummerfeld). In considering these different types of texts I am less interested in what they might have to tell us about the "truth" of female experience in the eighteenth century—since such truth is always already mediated by the text itself—than in what they can reveal about how women thought about the relationship between female subjectivity and performance. Thus I read each of these texts, including the memoir, as a textual construction of subjectivity that might have served several, perhaps at times contradictory, purposes for both its author and its readership.

Given the theater mania of the late eighteenth century, it is a bit surprising that the number of works written by women about actresses is so small; but this dearth of female-authored stories about actresses can be partially attributed to the generally low social standing of the profession in general and actresses in particular—an association that might have mitigated against putting a fictional heroine into the profession. While the number of works covered in this study is thus by necessity small, it has the advantage of allowing me to provide deep readings of these works, an endeavor that is further warranted by the fact that their engagement with issues of femininity, theater, and performance is often complex and contradictory. In addition, my in-depth analyses of these works also participates in the ongoing project of calling attention to noncanonical writing that helps shape our understanding of the latter part of the eighteenth century. Many of these works are not very well known: only two have been translated into English (*Sternheim* and "Flight to the City"), and, of the rest, three are still only available in complete form on either microfiche or in archives ("Aglaja," *Melanie*, and Schulze-Kummerfeld's *Memoirs*).[13] But the obscurity of these works does not signal their negligibility. On the contrary, taken as a group they provide important insights into both how women were imagining femininity during the period in which gender was being more firmly cemented to biological sex, and the ways in which women writers might have resisted that process.

My inclusion of Sophie von La Roche's *History of Lady von Sternheim* in this study deserves a word of explanation, as it is the only text considered that does *not* describe the life of a professional actress. Ideas about performance and theatricality pervade the work, however, and, as the first domestic novel in German, *Sternheim* established many of the themes and concerns that later authors take up and respond to. In particular, La Roche's novel displays a deep concern about the ethics of performance and the dangers of dissimulation, and seems to reproduce the era's ideology of sincerity and authenticity. As such, it maps out some of the territory explored by subsequent authors. At the same time, La Roche's novel also engages in its own deployment of performance and provides rich material for exploring the paradoxical position women occupied vis-à-vis the discourse of sincerity.

I have also chosen to limit works chosen for this study to texts that appeared during a fairly short period, from 1771 (the date of publication of *Sternheim*) to just after the turn of the century. I have focused on this period because I wanted to explore women's engagement with ideas about theater and performance as it played out against two interrelated historical processes. The first is the discourse of sincerity, which began proliferating around mid-century and continued to the end of the century before being taken up and modified by Romantic writers. The second is the development of the theater as a cultural institution in eighteenth-century Germany, which also involved a turn toward antitheatricality as the theater took on the task of promulgating bourgeois mores and values through a more realistic and less theatricalized and stylized aesthetic. The mid-eighteenth century saw the first production of Lessing's *Miss Sara Sampson*, a work widely regarded as one of the first attempts to achieve a more naturalistic representation on the stage; just after the turn of the century, however, many critics, most notably Goethe, began to question the aesthetics of stage naturalism and promote a theatrical practice that was once again highly stylized. Thus my cutoff point for this study was determined by the fact that ideas about both "natural subjectivity" and the aesthetics of theater began to move in different directions after 1800.

The first chapter of this book traces out in more detail the interconnections between the discourse of sincerity and the development of the theater in the late eighteenth century. I then turn to a discussion of primary works and investigate their engagement with the categories of theater and performance. In order to be able to trace out how these authors might have picked up on each other's ideas and themes, modifying them, satirizing them, et cetera, I have addressed these works in roughly chronological order. The risk of such a structure is that it might give a false sense that there is a teleological progression in women's writing from 1771 to the end of the century—that is, the impression that Sophie Mereau, writing some twenty years after (her grandmother-in-law) Sophie von La Roche, was, merely by dint of being later in history, more sophisticated or advanced in her figuration of the relationship between female identity and performance. While there certainly are differences to be noted as the century progresses, it is not my intention to present the story of these works in terms of a linear progression through time. The authors of these texts are, after all, writing from the perspective of different life experiences, class positions, and political viewpoints; they had different reasons for writing these texts, and their activities as writers played out against the backdrop of different historical events. Consequently, although my reading of these texts looks backwards to note where each author might have been reacting to insights or provocations from earlier works, I deliberately avoid presenting a master narrative that frames these works in terms of a linear progression.

In using theater and performance as a means of intervening in the debate about what constitutes ideal femininity, these texts call attention to the difficulties that the eighteenth-century conception of the self as sincere and antitheatrical presented for women. For each of these writers, theater and performance function as loopholes in the discourse of antitheatricality. These loopholes provide the writers with the opportunity to question, challenge, confront, and subvert received images of ideal femininity, even as their texts ostensibly reproduce those images. By reading these texts through the lens of their use of performance and the theater, we can not only understand women's experience of their lives in a more fruitful way, but also recognize how savvy they were about how contemporary discourse positioned women. In particular, such a reading reveals their sophisticated understanding of the fact that the definition of femininity in terms of natural naiveté paradoxically coerced a performance of self. Each of the texts considered in this book highlights the fact that the social audience that functions to determine a woman's image and reputation in the public sphere is almost always a fickle and untrustworthy "reader" of female subjectivity, in particular in the absence of a woman's proactive management of the public's perception of her—that is, in the absence of her performance of self. As such, these texts expose the utterly untenable position into which the discourse of sincerity placed women, as it paradoxically required them to perform the very naiveté that was, by definition, not supposed to be performable at all—making ideal femininity an impossible act indeed.

1. "Sophie" and the "Theater"

The works treated in this book have two things in common: they all explore and challenge the notion of ideal femininity as defined in late eighteenth-century Germany, and they each depict an encounter between that ideal femininity and the theater. More precisely, each of these works mobilizes the theater and performance as a means of articulating its challenge to dominant notions of "natural" gender identity, particularly as they applied to women. Because these works are situated within, and draw upon, particular historical configurations of both ideal femininity and notions of performance, in this chapter I provide context for my discussion by mapping out those configurations.

While it is accurate to describe each of the works I discuss as depicting an encounter between the Ideal Woman—"Sophie"—and the "Theater," in fact what all of them engage with is the pervasive *antitheatricality* of late eighteenth-century discourse, as it applied both to discursive constructions of the Ideal Woman and, somewhat paradoxically, to the "Theater" itself. When I speak of a pervasive antitheatricality in late eighteenth-century discourse, I am referring to the era's hostility to performance, spectacle, and deception on both the social and the cultural levels.[1] On the social level, this hostility played out as a demand for sincerity and authenticity in human relations. Toward the end of the eighteenth century, bourgeois moralists increasingly promoted a mode of being based on honesty and forthrightness: an "antitheatrical subjectivity" intended to replace the politic self-performance characteristic of courtly culture.[2] This insistence on an antitheatrical subjectivity had particular implications for women, for whom being "natural" and sincere was bound up with domesticity, a linkage that, as I will argue below, made fulfilling the conditions of ideal femininity an exercise in contradiction and paradox.

On the cultural level, antitheatricality manifested itself in two ways. First, it appeared in the form of a generalized stereotype of the theater as a place of danger, debauchery, and, above all, deceit: a site populated by immoral, licentious, thieving actors; the antithesis of virtually everything bourgeois culture sought to valorize, and, theoretically, one of the last places a virtuous woman would want to be. Second, in yet another paradox, antitheatricality manifested itself on the cultural level in an emphasis on aesthetic transparency: art, writing, and performance—as theorized by Lessing, Condillac, Home, and others—were expected to shed artifice, become "realistic," and foster the readers' or viewers' absorption into the scene of the work of art, making them "forget" that what they were reading or seeing was, in fact, a fiction.

Antitheatrical subjectivity and aesthetic transparency were interrelated, as the latter was recognized as a powerful way to interpellate readers and spectators into their proper and "natural" roles in bourgeois culture.[3] Illusionistic representation served in particular to proliferate images of ideal femininity and reinforce, in the cultural imaginary, the tautologous cementing of woman's "nature" to a sincere and unmediated expression of those characteristics that had, in fact, been culturally assigned to women. As an important locus for the illusionistic representation of proper, and properly gendered, human beingness, the theater was fully imbricated in this ideological project. But at the same time it was also fertile territory for the exploration of alternatives to dominant constructions of identity. As a result, the theater remained a site where the paradoxical nature of identity—as both antitheatrical and fundamentally audience-oriented—was investigated and explored.

All of these categories are important to understanding what the writers I discuss were engaging with when they put "Sophie" into contact with the "Theater." For in wrangling with questions about how the discourse of sincerity and antitheatricality affected, shaped, and pressured female subjectivity, many of these works also begin more generally to interrogate the eighteenth-century project of sincerity. In several of these texts there is an implicit critique of the aesthetics of transparency on the work's formal level, either through an adoption of those aesthetics, which is then undermined by the work's content (La Roche and Schulze-Kummerfeld), or through an outright rejection of illusionism (Bürger, Unger, and Mereau). But, in every case, there is an implicit or explicit comment about the work's own status as an object of performance, a move at odds with the aesthetics of transparency, but utterly logical: it makes perfect sense that women writing an alternative to the dominant construction of proper femininity would choose to employ writerly strategies that likewise challenged the prevailing aesthetics.

The discourse of antitheatricality was in many ways a pan-European phenomenon, an expression of rich cross-fertilizations of theory and philosophy between France, England, and Germany. While the focus of this book is on German women's writing of the late eighteenth century, because so much of German thought was influenced by, and responding to, ideas from other parts of Europe, in what follows I map both the broader pan-European discourse and the more local German manifestations of that discourse.

* * *

"SOPHIE"

The ideal imagined woman of the late eighteenth-century has been the subject of a great deal of feminist scholarship in the past half century, and her characteristics have been well established: she was expected to be modest, chaste, honest, loyal, subordinate to her husband, a good mother, patient, kind, generous, self-sacrificing, demure, fragile . . . the list goes on, in predictable fashion, and has been well documented elsewhere.[4] In fact, as Hausen and Frevert note, many of the qualities that continued to be associated with femininity well into the twentieth century were cemented onto women's "nature," and imagined to be intrinsic to the female sex, by late eighteenth-century discourse, hence the predictability and familiarity of the list.[5] In that sense, the era is, as others have noted, a "mirror image" of our own: it was pivotal in establishing precisely the concept of a "natural" gendered being that twentieth-century gender theory has destabilized as both socially constructed, and, following Butler, performed (cf. Krimmer, *In the Company of Men* 2). Thus, the important discursive move around 1800 was not merely to establish *which* characteristics were essentially feminine but rather to reify those characteristics *as* essential and natural, effectively grounding ideal femininity in an antitheatrical subjectivity. That is to say, an opposition between "Sophie" and the "Theater" was embedded into the very definition of "Sophie."

In invoking the name "Sophie" I am, of course, conjuring one of the earliest and most influential models for Ideal Womanhood: the "Sophie" Rousseau imagined into existence as complement and wife to his "Émile." It is perhaps no accident that, in late eighteenth-century Germany, Sophie was a popular name among both real women and fictional characters, for Rousseau was widely read, interpreted, filtered, and disseminated throughout German culture and letters in the late eighteenth century. For example, Sophie von La Roche's use of the name for her eponymous heroine can be read as both self-referential and as an *homage* to Rousseau, whose ideas of what constituted a proper—and properly educated—girl La Roche adopts and revises in *The History of Lady von Sternheim (Geschichte des Fräuleins von Sternheim*, 1771), a work that, in turn, was influential in establishing a model of ideal femininity for late eighteenth-century Germany.[6] Thus my use of "Sophie" here is intended less to refer specifically to the original model than to the notions of imagined femininity that derived from that model. And among those notions of imagined femininity, my own investigation focuses on one specific—and key—aspect of ideal femininity: the expectation that the virtuous woman would be natural, and that she would be "naturally" sincere, authentic, and naive.

In both *Émile* and the *Letter to M. D'Alembert on the Theatre*, Rousseau produced an image of Ideal Womanhood that cemented gendered characteristics onto woman's nature, fixing her as "naturally" passive, receptive, timid, modest, weak, and destined for subjugation and domination by her husband. Woman, according to Rousseau, is completely bound up by biology: "The male is only a male at times;

the female is a female all her life and can never forget her sex" (*Émile* 132). Among the defining natural qualities of woman is *pudeur*, a decent shame or bashfulness in erotic manners. A woman without *pudeur* is "guilty and depraved, because she tramples on a sentiment natural to her sex," Rousseau claims in the *Letter*. He continues:

> Is it not nature which adorns young women with those features so sweet and which a little shame renders even more touching? Is it not nature which puts that timid and tender glance in their eyes which is resisted with such difficulty? Is it not nature which gives their complexion more lustre and their skin more delicacy so that a modest blush can be better perceived? Is it not nature which renders them apprehensive so that they flee, and feeble so that they succumb? To what end are they given a heart more sensitive to pity, in running less speed, a body less robust, a shorter stature, more delicate muscles, if nature had not destined them to let themselves be vanquished? (85–86)

For Rousseau, the natural qualities of the Ideal Woman all seem to convene in her *pudeur*—it is both the sign and symptom of her "natural" weakness, vanquishability, subordination, sensitivity, et cetera. But, more importantly, the "modest blush" that Rousseau imagines blooming on the chaste, natural woman's face links *pudeur* to woman's antitheatrical nature. As an involuntary gesture virtually impossible to feign, the blush suggests total subjective transparency, an immediate—and "natural"—translation of thought and feeling onto the body, where it becomes both proof of the authenticity of a woman's "self" and the quintessential emblem of her virtue and naiveté.

Naiveté was a concept that underwent substantial redefinition in the mid-eighteenth century. Within the aristocratic culture that defined social relations for the early part of the century, naiveté, the open and honest expression of one's true motives, was the mark of the socially inept: to be naive was to misapprehend fundamentally the rules of the courtly game and utterly fail at the socio-political level. But the mid-eighteenth century saw a recuperation and valorization of naiveté as a cardinal virtue of bourgeois subjectivity: the naive person was no longer socially inept, but innocent, pure, and uncontaminated by society.[7] Naiveté was closely associated with "naturalness," with an immediate, unreflected expression of self, and as such—by definition—the naive person was one who was not only unaware of his or her own performance of self, but also ideally blind to the possibility that the self might be performed at all. Naiveté, as reconceived in mid-century, was that which could be *observed* in the naive but which could not be the object of *self-observation*—once the naive reflected on their own naiveté, they were obviously no longer (quite so) naive. Thus naiveté came to be considered the mark of a perfect antitheatricality in self-presentation.

Such naiveté was, for the most part, an ideal—an abstract virtue. It demanded an absolute innocence about public and political life that would have been unworkable and unsustainable in everyday social intercourse, and, consequently, impossible for men, whose "natural" call to active participation in the public sphere demanded a certain amount of politesse and self-reflexivity.[8] Indeed, although the discourse of antitheatricality applied to men as well as women, treatises aimed at shaping male behavior presented authenticity as something that must be cultivated and learned, and not at all "natural" to men. While the "natural" state of man was something that Rousseau hearkened back to as an ideal, he also clearly recognized the impossibility of "natural" man in civilized society.[9] The goal of Rousseau's pedagogical novel *Émile* is to produce a properly socialized, authentic subjectivity: because man is no longer in a state of nature, Émile must be taught to be the authentic, transparent subject demanded by the republican ideal. Rousseau's novel is an extended deliberation on the means by which such authenticity might be inculcated in a young man.

In the German context, the most influential of such treatises was Adolph Freiherr von Knigge's *On Social Intercourse* (*Über den Umgang mit Menschen*), published in 1788. Knigge's book is a detailed set of instructions to the bourgeois young man (and he is specific about the gender of his reader)[10] on how to behave himself in the public arena, in order to both make a good impression on others and be effective as a social (public) person. His first command to his reader is to "show yourself with a certain modest sense of your inner worth, and above all, with a sense, which radiates from your brow, of truth and sincerity!" (35–36). Later, he advises, "Be, what you are, always wholly, and always the same!" (44). Like Rousseau, who links a cultivated antitheatrical subjectivity to a social organization in which men would see themselves as members of community rather than as political players in a game of perpetually competing individual interests, Knigge believes that, in order to have a harmonious and workable society, men must cultivate a strong sense of inner self and commit to displaying that self in an honest and consistent manner.[11]

There were thus two key differences between "Sophie" and "Émile." The first was that "Sophie's" antitheatricality was figured as bound up with her "natural" virtue, whereas masculine authenticity was cultivated. The second was the public dimension considered "natural" to men's lives. For while treatises concerned with male subjectivity insisted on a sincerity, transparency, and authenticity of the self, they also recognized that that self must be presented and monitored in public.[12] We see this concern in Knigge's advice to his reader to reflect on and continuously temper his behavior: "Show reason and knowledge, where you have cause to! But not so much, as to excite envy and usher in challenges, not so little, as to be overlooked and cried down! Make yourself scarce, without leaving cause for others to think you an odd character, or shy, or arrogant!" (36).[13] Likewise, Kant recognizes that "the more civilized men are, the more they are actors," and draws an important ethical distinction between the monitored self-presentation necessary for social *politesse* (what he refers to as a "beneficial" illusion) and the immorality of self-deception or fundamental dishonesty (*Anthropology* §14: "On the Admissible Moral Perception"). Clearly, while men were expected to maintain their inner integrity, present themselves honestly and sincerely, and shun deception, they also had to observe themselves and reflect on their actions so as to successfully negotiate the public sphere. They needed to cultivate antitheatricality: they could not afford to be naive.

The discursive burden of fully embodying naiveté was instead laid on the shoulders of "Sophie," who was imagined as ideally so transparently "naive" that she was oblivious not only of its presence in herself but even that it could be observed in her by others. She was expected to embody the kind of sincere naiveté invoked by the poet and moralist Christian Furchtegott Gellert who, in his *Moral Lectures (Moralische Vorlesungen)* of 1770, imagined no more heavenly sight than

> a beautiful woman on her knees in the hour of prayer, believing herself unobserved, upon whose brow are united the modesty and innocence of a pious soul. (153)

In proposing that the virtuous woman was unreflectively, transparently, antitheatrically naive, discursive constructions of ideal femininity thus necessitated woman's distancing from culture and society, indeed, from nearly all public activity. For not only did the maintenance of her essential naiveté depend upon such distancing, but also, in turn, her exclusion from society functioned as guarantee that she was, in fact, naive. And in a mutually reinforcing circle, her naiveté then signaled her exclusion from culture and, hence, her essential, "natural" femininity (cf. Geitner, *Die Sprache der Verstellung* 293).

Naiveté and *pudeur* thus functioned together as both explanation and justification for fixing "Sophie's" place in the private realm. The reasoning went like this: because the Ideal Woman is "naturally" modest and naive, her display of herself in the public sphere is logically "unnatural." Rousseau makes the link between woman's natural *pudeur* and her natural place (the home) through a sneaky tautological move (what Mary Trouille labels "bad faith" (62–64)). He begins by establishing woman's nature in the passage from the *Letter* cited above and using woman's natural *pudeur* to condemn the public woman as unnatural. Then, in response to an imagined critical objection that *pudeur* might be a societal convention rather than a natural quality, he hypothetically grants the validity of the protest and proceeds to yoke the social convention of *pudeur* to the "fact" that woman's "natural" place is in the domestic realm, and—even more important—to "society's" interest in keeping her there:

> Even if it could be denied that a special sentiment of chasteness (*pudeur*) was natural to women, would it be any the less true that in society their lot ought to be a domestic and retired life, and that they ought to be

> raised in principles appropriate to it? *If the timidity, chasteness, and modesty which are proper to them are social inventions, it is in society's interest that women acquire these qualities*; . . . Is there a sight in the world so touching, so respectable, as that of a mother surrounded by her children, directing the work of her domestics, procuring a happy life for her husband and prudently governing the home? It is here that she shows herself in all the dignity of a decent woman; it is here that she really commands respect, and beauty shares with honor the homages rendered to virtue. (*Letter* 87–88, emphasis added)

The tautological definition that results here—*pudeur* is a natural quality that makes the domestic the woman's natural sphere; and because the domestic is the woman's natural sphere, she ought to cultivate *pudeur*—serves to naturalize the relationship between gender and social role and equate woman's "being" with the mutually determining qualities of her modesty/naiveté and her domesticity. Later in the century, Friedrich Hardenberg would employ a similar logic, arguing that because women "are connected to the state, church, public, and so on only through their husbands," they live "in an actual condition of nature" (III: 568).

Many German theorists shared Rousseau's belief that feminine virtue was constituted in and by woman's lack of distance from herself, and her immediacy to a "natural state." In his 1783 manual, *On the Education of Middle Class Daughters (Über die Erziehung der Töchter des Mittelstandes)*, Konrad Friedrich Uden sees woman as a creature of greater natural immediacy than man:

> Nature has done more for women than for men. . . . The way to sadness or to joy is more open for them than for men. They are so constituted in all these things . . . that only the present moment works upon them, they don't keep ruminating on the past, in order to breed anxious cares about the future. . . . As a result, they experience things livelier and more strongly, but also more correctly than we do . . . they perceive impressions as they are, pure and good . . . . (65)

Likewise, in *Levana, or Doctrine of Education* (*Levana oder Erziehungslehre*, 1807) Jean Paul equates women and children on the grounds of their shared closeness to nature and the transparency of their feelings. He notes (as "flattery") that both have

> the same indivisible unity of nature—the same full view and comprehension of the present—the same quickness of wit—the sharp observation—the impetuousness and calm—the sensitive agility—the goodnatured quick transition from inward to outward concerns and vice versa . . . . (683)[14]

And, like Rousseau, German theorists saw a connection between woman's closeness to "nature" and her necessary *separation* from culture and society. For example, in his *Attempt at a Characterization of the Female Sex* (*Versuch einer Charakteristik des weiblichen Geschlechts*, 1797–1802), Carl Friedrich Pockels describes the woman with whom a man could "live happily" as follows:

> The character of her sex (*Geschlechtscharakter*) must have been preserved in all its naturalness; that is, the character of mildness, of patience, and of a striving to please in an *unaffected* and noble manner. Her feelings must be *pure and genuine*; she must *above all only enjoy simple and quiet pleasures*. Her moral sense must be tender and correct. Her heart must race at the charms of nature; she must *immediately sympathize* with everything noble and beautiful . . . . (II: 328, emphasis added)

Here, woman's subjective "authenticity" is linked to qualities that suit her ideally to confinement in the private sphere—the perfect wife in all her "naturalness" is unaffected, pure, genuine, and "above all only" wants "simple and quiet" (read: domestic) pleasures. The linking of woman's nature and virtue to her "natural" and proper place in the private sphere was a powerful and widespread ideological move that discursively rendered impossible the virtuous public woman.

In fact, the production of the image of the Ideal Woman as naturally chaste and domestic was specifically conceived in opposition to the debased and immoral theatricality of women who ventured into the public sphere. Where a man's conduct in the public arena served to confirm his authenticity, a woman could only authentically be a woman in the private realm—any public display was an affront to nature. For example, Rousseau writes in the *Letter to M. d'Alembert*:

> [A] woman outside of her home loses her greatest luster, and despoiled of her real ornaments, she displays herself indecently. If she has a husband,

> what is she seeking among men? If she does not, how can she expose herself to putting off, by an immodest bearing, he who might be tempted to become her husband? Whatever she may do, one feels that in public she is not in her place . . . . (88)

The worst offenders were, of course, actresses, whose exposure of themselves in public constituted the greatest societal indecency. Rousseau is quick to make the link between the actress and the prostitute, noting "how unlikely it is that she who sets herself for sale in performance would not soon do the same in person and never let herself be tempted to satisfy desires that she takes so much effort to excite" (90). Such an association of the actress with the prostitute was commonplace in the late eighteenth century, and it was a stereotype that was not entirely unjustified. Many actresses enjoyed a sexual freedom that both earned them the disdain of "good" society and cast a shadow on those female colleagues who lived chaster lives. But sexual availability was not the sole reason actresses were censured: even those actresses who *did* keep their sexuality in check were anathematized simply because they were public women who practiced deceit as their profession and put themselves regularly and boldly on display.[15] The actress was, in every respect, the antithesis of "Sophie": immodest, shameless, and self-aware; a brazen, audience-oriented, professional deceiver.

"Sophie," on the other hand, was expected to eschew performance of any kind, and simply "be" her natural, naive self. Yet the discourse that produced this image was riddled with contradictions and employed a slippery logic that made that particular subject position fairly elusive to pin down. For lurking beneath the eighteenth-century insistence that woman does not belong in the public sphere is a suspicion of woman's propensity toward a theatrical display of herself that must be forestalled. That is, the discursive pressure on women to simply "be" their natural, naive, antitheatrical selves is—quite illogically—at one and the same time a response to a conception of women as excessively inclined to put on appearances and show. As Michael Fried argues in *Absorption and Theatricality*, underlying the discourse of sincerity is the assumption that "women, in particular beautiful women, traditionally regarded as objects of beholding par excellence, are especially prone to give themselves up to the tainted and debasing pleasures of self-exhibition" (168). Likewise, Joan Landes observes that

> Rousseau draws a direct comparison between women and the theatre: they are two marks of a peculiarly modern aberration, a narcissistic over-investment in the image. . . . [I]t is modern public women—especially speaking women, the actresses of the stage, the salon-going women of the capital cities, and the illicit women of the court—who in their person and their speech best symbolize the evils of an excessively spectacular existence. (71–72)

Rousseau's relegation of woman to the domestic realm is thus part of a broader project of reimagining and reforming society as a republican community of the virtuous that abjures the spectacularity and theatricality of the "unnaturally feminine" absolutist public sphere, and that, in order to form properly, requires redefining human nature along antitheatrical lines.

Paradoxically, then, at the same time that Rousseau asserts the naturalness of woman's modesty and naiveté and fixes her as quintessentially antitheatrical, he also associates the world of appearances with a debasing and dangerous femininity and posits theatricality—gendered female—as a threat to man's virility, identity, and social stability. For Rousseau, the theatrical subject is a feminized, "unnatural" subject: any disruption of the homology between inner and outer persona threatens to catapult the subject into the feminized realm of appearances.[16] Hence antitheatricality became an important constitutive element in the formation of gendered identity through its establishment of yet another set of opposites (theatrical = feminine/antitheatrical = masculine) to shore up the bipolar gender system. The contradiction that emerges from such a formulation, moreover, is clear: woman, as imagined by discourse, is "naturally" both naively antitheatrical *and* quintessentially theatrical.

As irreconcilable as this contradiction seems, it has an important ideological function in late eighteenth-century discourse. For what is particularly worrisome about the theatrical woman is that she threatens to disrupt the natural patriarchal hierarchy: the woman who controls her own representation of herself denies man's privilege to produce her as an object of desire. As Friedrich Kittler argues, in the "discourse network" of 1800,

> nature keeps strict watch over women and any possibility that they might distort their domesticity by authorship. If an author is defined simply by naming certain discourses his own, women by contrast are defined by being the author's "able housewives," those who do not name anything their own any more than they "inspire" a husband to do "creative work." (126)

The chaste and naive woman anchors the bipolar gender system by taking her natural place as the blank slate on and against which masculine subjectivity writes and reads its own desire.

In other words—and here is the crux of the paradox, in particular for the writers considered in this study—the production of woman as a quintessentially antitheatrical subject (i.e., as modest and naive) also places her squarely in the realm of representation, as the imagined object that seems to have been crucial to the formation of bourgeois capitalist culture, dependent as that culture is upon a gendered division of both labor and the private/public sphere.[17] The imagined Ideal Woman's function as guarantor of bourgeois order is inextricably linked with her domestication. As Bovenschen notes,

> where the man dreams, fantasizes, imagines, poeticizes, the feminine is implemented as the medium of his idea of a happier world, as set in opposition to the constraints of bourgeois routine—Werther's Lotte surrounded by playing children, a picture of happiness and peace! (180–81)

The "discourse network" of 1800 not only excluded women from the public sphere but also projected an imagined femininity as an object of cultic reverence, a representation with divine status (cf. Kittler 125). This status, in turn, depended heavily on woman's ability to maintain and mobilize a representation of herself as "virtuous" and "naive." Thus while a woman's maintenance of her self as a representation of naiveté and modesty was necessary for the naturalization of the bipolar gender system, it also put her under suspicion of the very theatricality that was (no longer) supposed to be part of her "nature." The paradox here becomes obvious: naiveté—the state of being that could not be performed—was at one and the same time the characteristic that functioned as the sign of virtuous femininity. In other words, it was that which the virtuous woman could not perform and yet—not not perform.

The possibility that a woman's naiveté might be performed is a source of profound anxiety for male writers of the late eighteenth century. Schiller locates the power of the female sex in the conflation of woman's desire to appear naive and her natural naiveté: "It is to the opposite sex that nature has assigned the naive character in its highest perfection. Woman's desire to please manifests itself nowhere so much as in seeking the *appearance* of naiveté; proof enough, even if one had no other, that the greatest power of the sex depends upon this characteristic" (97–98). That a woman's naiveté might merely be show raised the threat of a host of social ills, most of which have already been alluded to in this chapter. Yet it is important to recognize that, to a certain extent, whether a woman's naiveté was genuine or merely performed was rather immaterial: it was, after all, the only "script" she was given to play, and her naiveté served the same societal function whether it was feigned or not. "Sophie," in other words, had to "be" good, or, failing that, a very good actress.

* * *

"THEATER"

As paradoxical as that last assertion might seem in light of the definition of the Ideal Woman as "naturally naive," it is in fact a central issue in each of the works I discuss in this book. Each challenges the dominant definition of ideal femininity as antitheatrical by revealing the difficulties and challenges that being in the public sphere posed for women. That most do so by putting a "Sophie" in contact with the "Theater" is unsurprising in light of the fact that acting was one of the few professions available to women in the eighteenth century, and certainly the one that most prominently placed women in a clear and visible relationship to the public sphere. In addition, many of the authors I write about—Schulze-Kummerfeld, Ehrmann, Bürger, and Unger—worked professionally in the theater, as actresses, playwrights, or both, and that experience clearly offered rich source material for their fictive constructions of femininity and its engagement with the public sphere. In fact, the dilemma of the actress writes large the dilemma of the public woman. As Rüppel observes of Elise Bürger,

> She was supposed to follow the masculine ideal of unspoiled feminine naturalness and be "all nature," yet as actress she simultaneously confirmed the prejudice that all women were "hypocritical masks." (229)

But even more importantly, the challenge to received notions of ideal femininity as essentially antitheatrical in each of these works is inflected and informed by important changes in both theatrical practice and the way people thought about performance and the theater around 1800, changes that both helped to shore up the dominant discursive definition of ideal femininity and opened loopholes for its destabilization.

The theater was an important cultural institution in late eighteenth-century Germany. Indeed, in the minds of many theorists, by the end of the century it had come to represent the privileged site for the dissemination of cultural mores and values. Theater played a pivotal role in the formation of the great German literary tradition begun in the mid-eighteenth century; the great actors of the German stage—Ackermann, Eckhof, Schröder, Iffland—were honored and esteemed for their contributions to culture and society; and by the end of the century the theater aspired to function as a "night school for moral citizens" (Haider-Pregler).

But the theater was, at the same time, not an "institution" at all, given that theatrical troupes were loosely organized, continually in flux, and perpetually on the road, and that public financing for the theater was both unpredictable and meager. As important as the theater might have been to the cultural imaginary, most who earned their living by it gained little material or social benefit from its elevated cultural status, as they continued to be relegated to the margins of "good" society. Even though actors and managers made a concerted effort to cleanse the theater of its traditional association with debauchery and vice, the theater and its practitioners remained objects of suspicion to bourgeois culture, not only because of the immoral behaviors associated with the theatrical lifestyle, but also—and more importantly—because theater in general, and acting in particular, were practices that depended upon performance and deception, two of the behaviors most reviled by bourgeois moralists.

This opposition—between the increasing institutionalization and legitimization of the theater as a moral/educational institution, and its continued status as the site of precisely those practices most in opposition to bourgeois mores and values—encapsulates the two ends of the spectrum of meanings the "Theater" took on around 1800. As such, the "Theater," as I discuss it in this section, is not an individual entity, but rather an intersecting and often contradictory set of historical changes, practices, theories, attitudes, and ideas about performance, literature, aesthetics, and ontology.

The late eighteenth century was an antitheatrical era in many ways, and it was also the era of the first great blossoming of the German theater. As paradoxical as this may seem, the two were in fact linked: the legitimation of the theater went hand in hand with its participation in the eighteenth-century project of sincerity, a project that involved wholesale transformations in both how people understood human beingness and, crucially, how they represented it to themselves. The expectation, mapped out in the previous section of this chapter, that the Ideal Woman would be natural, naive, and antitheatrical was part of this larger project of sincerity, which took as a moral imperative the notion that humans are naturally sincere and honest, and that the moral person should eschew performance. On the level of representation, the project of sincerity involved an analogous shift away from theatricality and toward an emphasis on aesthetic transparency. This shift is perhaps best exemplified by the epistolary novel, with its pretense of presenting "authentic" letters from "real" people as a strategy of fostering the reader's absorption into the "reality" of the story.[18] Such a trend toward aesthetic transparency cut across the genres of art and literature. We find it not only in the epistolary novels of writers like Richardson and Rousseau, but also in what Michael Fried describes as the "antitheatrical" paintings of the period, in the bourgeois drama, and in the development of a more realistic, antitheatrical theater practice.

In contrast to the theater of the late eighteenth century, the theater of the absolutist public sphere of the late seventeenth and early eighteenth centuries called attention to its own theatricality and spectacularity. There was little attempt on the part of theatrical practitioners of the baroque era to create, in the audience's mind, an illusion that what was happening in front of their eyes was "real." On the contrary, as Richard Alewyn notes,

> The baroque illusion is . . . always deliberate and studied, it does not aim at seducing the soul or even at deceiving the mind, rather it always only aims at the senses. . . . For just this reason it never leads to the depths of deception, but rather always stops at its edge, always ready to spring over the border and negate the deception, and of course always equally as ready to double it. (81)

The display of theatricality in theatrical entertainment reflected the baroque world's understanding of real life and real social relations as a series of theatricalized mobilizations of public appearances.[19] Theater in the absolutist public sphere did not attempt to give spectators access to "reality" but rather tried to highlight the baroque notion that all life was "theater." In this context, the proper relation of spectators to theatrical illusion was analogous to the proper relation of theatricalized subjects to their social roles: they needed to maintain a conscious distance from the illusion on stage. Alewyn remarks:

> If the reality of the spectator is itself only a theatre, as the comparison of the "World Theatre" will have it, then the theatre in reality is already a theatre within a theatre. Then the spectator, for his part, is already standing on the stage and playing in a play, whether he knows it or not. But he who wants to be a good actor will not allow himself to be deceived. He knows, that the most sumptuous decoration is just for show, and that the most splendid costume is only borrowed. But he will still play his role as well as he can. (89–90)

Thus when Rousseau criticized the theater as an institution in his *Letter to M. d'Alembert*, he objected not only to its pernicious moral effects, but also, and even more importantly, to the inherent *theatricality* and *spectacularity* of the theatrical event—to its function as a means of distancing the spectator and thereby foregrounding the very performativity he wished to see disappear from social life. He complained that theater could "present virtue to us as a theatrical game" and viewed the display of the performance (and performability) of both virtuous and vicious social relations as ideologically threatening to the republican state (26). Rousseau specifically disapproved of that aspect of theater that made visible, mocked, and thereby threatened to overturn the "natural" social order:

> See how [Moliére], for the sake of multiplying his jokes, shakes the whole order of society; how scandalously he overturns all the most sacred relations on which it is founded; how ridiculous he makes the respectable rights of fathers over their children, of husbands over their wives, of masters over their slaves! (35)

But more generally, Rousseau saw theatricality as in and of itself threatening to the "natural" social order because it called attention to its own artificiality and thereby made visible the constructedness and "unnaturalness" of the social relations it depicted. Theatricality was incompatible with the naturalization of power because it challenged the state's ability to render its ideology invisible. The aesthetics of illusionism, on the other hand, served an ideological state apparatus that functioned by naturalizing bourgeois mores and values and projecting them directly onto the absorbed spectator's internal mental screen.[20]

Like Rousseau, the theatrical reformers in eighteenth-century Germany who gave the theater the pedagogical mission of educating the citizenry and inculcating bourgeois mores and values in its audience adopted the aesthetics of illusionism as the means by which theater could most effectively fulfill that mission. In response to theoretical demands for a stage representation that more closely mirrored bourgeois social relations, theater practitioners attempted to strip theater of its "theatricality" and make it more transparently illusionistic. For example, Voltaire's banishing of the audience from the stage dates from this era, as does Diderot's invention of the idea of a "fourth wall" separating the actors from the audience. Indeed, there were a number of innovations in the late eighteenth century that attempted to make attending a performance at the theater mimic the reader's absorption into the world of a novel: costumes and sets became more realistic; the audience space gradually darkened, and patrons were given fixed seats to occupy (both of which served to focus the spectators' attention on the stage rather than on each other); and the style of playing became less declamatory and more naturalistic.[21] Many of the famous actors of the period built their considerable reputations and fame on their commitment to and skill at creating a level of believability and authenticity in performance that astonished and captivated their audiences.

Captivation is a key word here. It was, in fact, the stated goal of the theorists and artists who formed and fostered the bourgeois preference for illusion. The theater artists who participated in the project of aesthetic transparency believed that to have its most potent effect, the theater had to reduce the distance between the audience and the action on stage and draw audience members into a hallucinatory dream world in which they forgot they were attending a theatrical spectacle at all. So, for example, in his mid-century *Essay on Tragedies (Abhandlung vom Trauerspiele)* Friedrich Nicolai insisted that he wanted "to feel the effects of the play, not the artistry of the playwright" (42) and Klopstock wrote in 1755 that "the final and highest effects of works of genius are that they move the entire soul" (117); they "bring us with instant force to such a state that we call out, express our joy, are dumbstruck . . . or become pale, tremble, cry" (119). Or, as the Abbé Valdastri maintained in 1794, in the theater "the spectators must become so caught up in the illusion that they can place themselves completely into the position of the characters" (103).

For such theorists, immediacy and transparency were necessary preconditions for theater's effectiveness as both an aesthetic experience and a cultural institution in the business of universalizing bourgeois cultural values. So, for example, in 1793 Adolph Freiherr von Knigge, who was not only the author of *On Social Intercourse*, the conduct book for men, but also a leading theorist of the bourgeois drama in Germany, represented the views of many contemporary theorists when he imagined the stage as a place from which bourgeois mores and values could be promulgated through illusionistic representation:

> I stand by this conviction: that we must bring to our stages scenes and actions out of bourgeois life with the greatest possible illusion and truthfulness, and with the purpose of spreading, through examples from the real world and under cloak of pleasant entertainment, moral principles and general enlightenment among all classes of people. (Knigge, "Schriftstellern" 210)

Such scenes resonated powerfully with audiences, as evident from Johann Schink's enthusiastic response in 1790 to Iffland's play *The Hunters*:

> Here we are in a world that we all know, here unfolds a humanity with which we are all familiar, which is taken directly from our realm of experience and in which we find ourselves again. It is wholly natural, that its representation lies close to our hearts and interests. Its people are just like our brothers, friends and relatives, so we interest ourselves that much more intimately in their fates, their sufferings, their joys. These Father-, Spouse-, Child-, and Friend-relationships are the daily stories of our lives, we certainly recognize ourselves in one of these relationships. It seems to us as if we belonged to the family that is being represented, it is as if what was happening to them is happening to us; and so we cry and rejoice at their sorrows and joys as if they were our own . . . as if we ourselves were the father, son, daughter, and friend in this family. (Schink *Dramaturgische Monate* 223–24)

What we see in such critical theories and responses are some of the earliest and most pointed articulations of the ideological function of illusionism and the identificatory process it fosters. The eighteenth-century project of aesthetic transparency aimed with clear purpose and intent at hailing individuals into "familiar" roles, roles that in turn became familiar—and that demonstrated to spectators how to be proper members of both the social and private family—through illusionistic representation.[22]

The project of aesthetic transparency was instrumental in naturalizing and fixing gender roles, proliferating images of patriarchal fathers; obedient, domesticized wives; and innocent, naive daughters who put themselves in danger the moment they step out of the private sphere. But the practice of using a more realistic, transparent aesthetic in the theater to promote sincerity and authenticity in human relations illuminated a paradox that did not escape the notice of its proponents. For as actors became more adept at artificially producing the illusion of being "real people," their ability to feign "sincere being" threatened to undermine the division that eighteenth-century theorists strove to establish and maintain between the "authentic" and the "feigned" person.

The ironies and dilemmas posed by the use of the theater to model bourgeois sincerity—and, in particular, antitheatrical Ideal Womanhood—are perhaps nowhere better illustrated than in the example of G. E. Lessing's play *Miss Sara Sampson (Miß Sara Sampson*, 1755).[23] This early canonical work is worth exploring at some length, not only because it highlights the paradoxical relationship between performance and ontology in the late eighteenth century, but also because, in its configuration of performance and theatricality as both the antithesis of and a threat to female virtue, it establishes many of the touchpoints upon which the works I discuss draw in their own discursive configurations of "Sophie" and the "Theater." The plot of the play, which tells the story of Sara's elopement with her lover Mellefont and her death at the hands of his vengeful ex-lover Lady Marwood, hinges on Lady Marwood's successful deployment of a series of performances to get close to and eventually murder the innocent and naive Sara. One of Germany's first naturalistic plays, *Miss Sara Sampson* helped introduce realistic theater practices to the German stage and was thus an early example of antitheatrical theater in practice.[24]

Thematically, the play also revolves around antitheatricality in its exploration of the highly fraught and tenuous nature of the opposition between the naive and the theatrical. The virtuous, naive, and sincere Sara is a model of bourgeois femininity; her nemesis, the villainous dissimulator Lady Marwood, represents the debased theatricality of the aristocratic court. When Sara's father worriedly hopes upon discovering Sara at the inn that "in such a short remove from virtue she cannot yet have learned the art of dissimulation (*Verstellung*)" (III: i), he aligns his era's expectations of the virtuous woman along the axis of antitheatricality and, at the same time, establishes what is "natural" and what is not: dissimulation is learned, it involves a distancing from the natural state of virtue, which is naive and knows nothing of it.

But this stable taxonomy of values is disrupted and disturbed by the fact that, on the stage, *both* figures are represented by actresses. The opposition between Sara's naiveté and Marwood's *Verstellung* is partially cancelled through their mutual performability. With *Miss Sara Sampson*, German audiences were exposed for the first time to an acting style so naturalistic that they found it difficult to detect the "art" of acting in it. Thus one of most remarkable things about *Miss Sara Sampson* is that it aims simultaneously at erasing the signs of performance and putting those signs on display. In the persons of William Sampson, Sara, and Waitwell, Lessing's play has actors illusionistically represent models of antitheatrical, authentic subjectivity: characters who not only are completely sincere in their "being" of themselves, but who also are so vested in that notion of authenticity and virtue—Sara's father confidently tells Waitwell that he "will read [Sara's] entire soul in her face" (III. i)—that Marwood's performance easily dupes them. In Marwood, on the other hand, Lessing demands a double illusion: the actress playing Marwood must realistically and illusionistically portray a woman who "realistically and illusionistically" performs the part of an honest, sincere, and virtuous woman for the other characters in the play.

At no time, of course, is the *theater's* audience expected to be deceived by Marwood's ruse. Indeed, it could be argued that because Marwood's *Verstellung* is so prominently foregrounded by both the plot of the play and by the play's realistic performance mode, the play enables its audience to hold on to their illusions about the *difference* between world and stage, and that the visibility of Marwood's performance offers a comforting reassurance that the "penetrating glance of the virtuous" (i.e., the theater's audience) will always be able to detect such deception (Gellert 160).[25] Nonetheless—and this is key—the audience's absorption in the illusion depends on the skill of *both* the actress playing Marwood and the actress playing Sara to create the illusion of virtuous womanhood (of naiveté, honesty, innocence, etc.) and yet it is *only* in Marwood's performance within the diegesis that the audience is expected to recognize the craft and effort involved in producing that performance of virtue: for the play to have its proper hallucinatory effect, the audience should ideally "forget" that the actress playing Sara is acting at all.

In light of the eighteenth-century definition of female virtue as nonperformable, the fact that the realistic performability of ideal femininity is thus revealed (i.e., in Marwood's performance) is remarkable; indeed, the "performability" of both roles implicitly serves as a critique of the discursive definition of femininity in terms of absolute authenticity and transparency. But what is clearly problematized here is the (lack of) *difference* between acting and being. The mode of naturalistic acting used by *both* actresses, but only made visible by *one*, calls attention to the impossibility of knowing and determining what is "real" and what is "performed," especially in the face of a mode of performance that aims at and depends upon erasing all signs of its performativity. Consequently, the play radically undermines any guarantee of distinguishing the inauthentic from the authentic by putting naturalistic, illusionistic acting on display.

At the same time, however, *Miss Sara Sampson* establishes a hierarchy of values that places a premium on transparency (in both the aesthetic realm and the social realm) and equates it with virtue. Although at the beginning of the play Sara has compromised her virtue by eloping with Mellefont, her father is hopeful that "in such a short remove from virtue she can not yet have learned the art of dissimulation, to whose masks only deep-rooted vice takes its refuge" (III. i). *Verstellung*—which, in the world of the play, represents the refuge of deep-rooted vice, and which Sara's father assumes he would be able to readily recognize in his fallen daughter—is proven to be both a powerful and elusive enemy within the play's narrative, and an important aesthetic and pedagogical means of modeling, on the stage, the authentic, antitheatrical subjectivity that is its opposite. Lessing thus paradoxically uses a theory of acting both to support and complicate a theory of being: the actor who can successfully induce the signs by which, as he notes in his *Hamburg Dramaturgy*, "we believe we can dependably infer a person's inner feelings" becomes both a model for authentic subjectivity and a reminder that such authenticity may always already be dissembled (*Hamburgische Dramaturgie* 15–16).

Although I have focused on the ways in which one play, *Miss Sara Sampson*, foregrounds the problem of decoding *Verstellung* and distinguishing the real from the feigned in human behavior, even the most cursory glance at eighteenth-century literature reveals that this was a common and recurrent theme in fictional writing of the era. Samuel Richardson's *Clarissa* (1747–48) is perhaps the most prominent example of a novel that opposes the villainous use of deception and performance to a virtuous and authentic antitheatrical mode of being. Such literary and dramatic representations of the challenges presented by the societal dissembler were reflections of a larger philosophical and quasi-scientific debate about the means by which the virtuous could detect and identify the vicious. Throughout the era under consideration critics and philosophers sought to establish dependable means by which the dissembler could be unmasked. Many of these methods hearkened back to the idea that there is a "natural" correspondence between the soul and the body, and that the presence of deception could be detected by the lack of such a correspondence. Wolff and Gottsched proposed that the deceiver would lack a certain "freedom" in expression and gesture that corresponds to truth, and that the dissembler's actions would therefore always appear forced.[26] Gellert, like Sara's father, believed that the entire character of the mind and heart was displayed in the face and body: "truth in facial expression," he wrote in his *Moral Lectures* "is as easily read as the truth of a true and nakedly shimmering beautiful thought" (VI: 152–53).

Such confidence that the art of acting would be obvious to the virtuous eye was in many ways a holdover from an earlier era of both acting and being, in which actors put their craft on display and in which people were also self-conscious performers on the stage of life. As a result, critics who had faith in the self-evidence of the natural connection between authenticity and an authentic-seeming performance continuously found themselves confronting the same problem Lessing used the stage to thematize so brilliantly: the fact that the "freedom" of expression that was the sign of naturalness was eminently imitatable and performable by a practiced actor. The Lovelaces and Marwoods of eighteenth-century literature thus represented a working out in fiction of one of the most vexing ontological problems of the era. The relationship between performance and everyday "being" is also a central concern in each of the works I consider in this book, as each grapples with both the ways in which subjective authenticity succeeds or fails at effecting its own performance, and the difficulties audiences have in discerning the "authentic" from the "dissembled."

In fact, the question of performance and its relationship to subjectivity both on and off the stage was a philosophical concern that busied the minds and pens of writers from a wide variety of disciplines.[27] It is important to recall here that at the end of the eighteenth century there was as yet no concept of the split between the conscious and the unconscious; human behavior could not yet be explained in terms of a psychology of unconscious drives, desires, or motives. Indeed, it was often through the investigation of the art of the actor that eighteenth-century theorists could delve most deeply into the question of where human subjectivity was located, and also into the question of the relationship between mind and body, thought and action. Whether or not actors needed to emotionally engage themselves in their roles was completely bound up with the question of the relationship between the interior and the exterior self—with both the *means* by which our bodies signal our inner state to the outside world and with the *reliability* of those means. For bourgeois theorists interested in promoting the notion that moral people should simply "be" honestly, sincerely, and authentically themselves at all times, it was important to understand how someone might dissimulate their thoughts and emotions and, perhaps even more crucially, how such dissimulation could be detected in another.

Many studies of the art of acting found reassuring evidence that sincerity could *not*, in fact, be successfully feigned, particularly in their investigation of the difficult problem (for the actor, at least) of manifesting, as a readable sign on the body, those physical reactions to emotion that are not under a person's voluntary control—reactions like blushing in shame, having one's hair stand on end from fear, or paling in horror. Such reactions were thought to be sure signs of sincere emotion in a person—recall Rousseau's invocation of the blush as guarantor of a woman's "natural" *pudeur*. The fact that such reactions were impossible to fake pointed toward the existence of something unknown deep inside the self that could not be consciously performed and that made people constitutionally inclined to sincerity. Thus, for example, Henry Home concludes in his 1761 *Elements of Criticism*:

> The external signs of passion are a strong indication that man, by his very constitution, is framed to be open and sincere . . . even when men learn to dissemble their sentiments, and when behaviour degenerates into art, there still remain checks that keep dissimulation within bounds, and prevent a great part of its mischievous effects . . . luckily, the involuntary signs cannot, by any effort, be suppressed, nor even dissembled. An absolute hypocrisy, by which the character is concealed, and a fictitious one assumed, is made impracticable; and Nature has thereby prevented much harm to society. We may pronounce, therefore, that Nature, herself, sincere and candid, intends that mankind should preserve the same character, by cultivating simplicity and truth, and banishing every sort of dissimulation that tends to mischief. (197)

Thus, oddly enough, the study of the art of acting led critics like Home to conclude precisely the opposite of what we might expect—that effective dissimulation is impossible, and that people are naturally sincere—and to use such conclusions to argue that the bourgeois cultural imperative of sincerity was in fact the imperative of "Nature" herself, and that dissimulation was inherently and essentially "unnatural."

At the same time, however, theatergoers of the era *were* in fact captivated by more realistic representations of character on stage and frequently reported having been swept into the illusion of a theatrical scene, Home's confident assertions to the contrary notwithstanding. The fact that professional actors frequently *did* fool their audiences into believing that they were actually feeling emotions that they were merely professing suggests that, as Lessing's play anticipated, the manifestation of illusionistic acting on stage posed a serious challenge to bourgeois confidence in the ideological project of sincerity. Consequently, it was vitally important to theorists of aesthetic transparency to justify and legitimize the use of the actor—the dissembler, the dissimulator—to represent bourgeois morality.

There were two chief dimensions to this effort. First of all, as I previously noted, there were concerted attempts to rehabilitate the reputation of the theater in general, and actors in particular. Such rehabilitation was linked to the establishment of the theater as a site of moral education for its audiences and as a respectable venue for entertainment and enlightenment: in order for theater to gain legitimacy as a moral institution, it needed to practice what it preached. The prologue that actress Sophie Ackermann read at the opening of a new theater in Göttingen in 1764 reveals how conscious theater artists were of the relationship between their moral reputation and the mandate of the project of sincerity. Styled as a teleological history of the German stage, Ackermann's poem ends with a rumination on the actor's place in society that aligns the elevation of the actor's status with both the theater's mission as a moral institution and the project of sincerity's emphasis on judging a person by their interior being rather than exterior status:

> Unbridled jesting fled from our stages,
> The orderliness of good taste gushed into our hearts
> Actors now learned to honor through their actions
> The high moral philosophy that they proclaimed.
> They clearly saw that one who gives rules to others
> Is worthy of contempt, if he does not practice them himself
> The true fame of a person, the true shame of a person
> Lies always in his heart and never in his social station. (Litzmann 232)

Theatrical reformers sought to elevate the status of both the theater and actors mainly through the establishment of standing theaters, a development that would eliminate the need for constant travel and open to theater workers the possibility of remaining in one city and gaining citizenship there. At the same time, they also sought to raise the social standing of actors through an internal policing of their behavior, often via a restructuring of troupes along the lines of a family, headed by a manager who not only embodied the moral principles valued by bourgeois culture but who also wielded strict paternal authority over the members of his company. Konrad Ackermann, who was pivotal in the founding of the Hamburg National Theater, exemplified this type of manager, as did the actor-managers Friedrich Ludwig Schröder, Konrad Eckhof, and Johann Schönemann.[28] Theatrical reformers also elevated the theater by establishing guidelines for theater and acting through manuals, pamphlets, and schools, which had the effect of improving, in mutually reinforcing ways, both the actor's craft and reputation. For example, Eckhof's founding of an Academy for Actors in Schwerin in 1753 was considered by his contemporaries to have played a critical role in raising actors to the level of artists and conferring upon them the kind of moral legitimacy and respect enjoyed by writers and visual artists (H. Fetting 173; see also Kindermann).

The effectiveness of such attempts to rehabilitate the theater seems, however, to have been uneven at best. While some actors were granted social legitimacy—for example, Ackermann successfully negotiated his way to becoming a citizen of Hamburg when he moved there in 1764—most continued to inhabit the margins of bourgeois society. This was particularly true for actresses, for whom establishing and maintaining a good reputation was made doubly difficult by the continued stereotypical association of the actress with prostitution. Evidence of the prejudices and social outcasting actresses faced crops up in many of the works I investigate in this study, as do reflections on the kinds of reforms necessary for cleansing the theater, and commentaries on what makes both "good" and "bad" managers and companies. Indeed, as I argue in the subsequent chapters, most of these works can be understood as participating in the recuperation of the image of the actress, as they provide examples of women who remain virtuous in defiance of stereotype. As such, they are in themselves part and parcel of the generalized effort to rehabilitate actors as moral citizens.

The second dimension to the effort to justify the use of the actor to disseminate bourgeois mores and values had to do with theoretical writing on the art of acting itself. Most treatises on acting aimed at codifying the actor's craft for instructional purposes. But they also often had a second, crucial function: namely, to integrate acting, as an art, into the project of sincerity. That is, in order to make the case that what the actor did for a living was not hypocritically at odds with what he showed on stage, many writers twisted themselves into knots demonstrating that the actor's engagement in illusionistic dissimulation was, in fact, an honest and sincere endeavor. This took a number of forms, depending on where the author stood in the nascent debate—still current today—over the best way to create the illusion of a realistic character (i.e., from the inside out or outside in).[29] So, for example, in 1747 we see Sainte-Albine, one of the first to argue that actors needed to identify with their roles, equate acting with sincerity because actors "can never execute their parts with any degree of perfection, if they do not really feel in their own hearts, at least for that instant, all the tenderness, all the transports for one another, that the persons they represent are endowed with by the poet" (Sainte-Albine 104; translation from Hill 122). G. E. Lessing, on the other hand, takes the opposite approach: he believes that the best effect comes not from identification, but from studied imitation. However, Lessing notes, the repeated act of imitating the outward signs of an emotion invariably induce the emotion itself in the actor, and as a side effect, "bring forth some sign of the involuntary changes of the body, from whose presence alone we believe we can dependably infer a person's inner feelings" (Lessing, *Hamburgische Dramaturgie* 15–16, emphasis added). The imitation induces the feeling, and, paradoxically, once an actor is actually feeling the emotion he or she set out to feign, that performance becomes something of a "sincere" endeavor too.

The discursive maneuvering involved in claiming that the illusionistic representation of an "honest man" on stage was an honest endeavor is perhaps best illustrated in Friedrich Ludwig Schröder's gloss on Riccoboni's *Instructions on the Art of Acting* (*Vorschriften über die Schauspielkunst*), which was published posthumously in 1821. One of the leading illusionistic actors in late eighteenth-century Germany, Schröder was a proponent and practitioner of the "outside-in" approach to acting. But here Schröder explains that in his long career as an actor he discovered that the one type of character that eluded the mechanistic approach was that of the good and honest man. He confesses that in order to portray such a character

> *I struggled to be an honest man myself, and as I was in life, so I was on the stage*; the signs of representation of an honest expression were at my command without any learned skill: for they were given to me from inside, without my doing anything. (77, emphasis added)

He continues that he would advise young actors that they should never believe that one could seem noble, great, and sublime on the stage without being so in one's soul:

> [R]emember, you stand as an artist and as a work of art in the sight of a spectator who scrutinizes your soul, who penetrates your innermost, and who knows how to evaluate your worth as a human being through your acting. If you want to represent yourself truly and worthily . . . then let your own beautiful self be the mirror in which artistic and human worth transfigure themselves through the worship of wisdom. (78)

The homology Schröder makes here between his interior being and his exterior expression of self attests to the power of discursive constructions of authenticity in the late eighteenth century: even the professional deceiver seems convinced of the impossibility of feigning virtue. At the same time, Schröder's remarks may also be self-serving, as they can also be read backward to rescue the actor from the charge of deception: by claiming that only a moral person can successfully play a moral character, he implies that any actor who can convince an audience that he represents a moral character must *propter hoc* "be" moral. As the subsequent chapters reveal, a similar justification of performance on the grounds that it is always already an expression of a woman's innate morality and virtue is mobilized in several of the texts under consideration, as it opens a loophole in the discourse that precluded any performance of self on the part of a virtuous woman.

In addition, Schröder attributes to the theater audience the same scrutinizing, penetrating gaze that theorists from Wolff to Pernety believed could dependably unmask the deceiver—here, with the added talent of knowing how to "evaluate" the actor's worth as both human being *and* artist. But a persistent problem for eighteenth-century theorists—and also for the writers I discuss in the course of this study—is, in fact, the audience's gaze. The very presence of an audience at all destabilizes the project of sincerity by virtue of the fact that—as in the Heisenberg principle—the act of observation in and of itself changes the equation.

For both the theorists of the project of sincerity and the women writers discussed in this book, the problem that comes up revolves around the issue of one's "readability" to one's audience. This is a problem that remains essentially unresolved in the eighteenth century. At its core is the fact that the very act of observation has the potential to render the private, public, and to change what is being seen from a moment of antitheatrical "being" to a theatricalized performance—all depending upon the interpretive lens of the spectator. Recall for a moment Gellert's fantasy of the Ideal Woman "on her knees in the hour of prayer, believing herself unobserved, upon whose brow are united the modesty and innocence of a pious soul" (153). Gellert's confidence that such a woman would, indeed, be naive depends on his conviction that she would not realize she is being observed—that is, on the fiction of his absence. In a similar way, the project of aesthetic transparency also depended upon the fictional absence of an audience: in the theater, the realist convention of the "fourth wall" separating the audience from the stage was intended to promote the idea that what was happening on stage would be happening whether it was observed or not, just like the woman at prayer.

But, while the audience for the theatrical event could be certain that everyone in the theater, actors and spectators included, was only pretending that nobody was there to observe, Gellert could never in fact be confident that his fantasy woman was oblivious to his observation and not putting on an act for his benefit. In both cases, theatricality threatens to undermine the antitheatrical scene, as the suspicion that what is being observed might merely be show is always already present. For the antitheatrical theater this is clearly not much of an issue, depending as it does on the audience's complicity in creating the performance in the first place. But for Gellert's Ideal Woman it is. As long as Gellert is convinced that the woman at prayer has no idea he is there, he can confidently take her for the sincere, naive woman she appears to be. The moment he begins to suspect that she might be aware of his presence, however, the prospect that she might not be what she seems rears its ugly head. To complicate things further, in either case his reading may or may not be correct: in the first, she may be a "Marwood" who only appears sincere because of her posture and bearing in the present moment; in the second, the fact that she knows he is there may not change how she behaves or feels in the slightest. Indeed, in the latter case, her conscious awareness of the presence of an observer might elicit from her the kind of "sincere" performance described by Schröder, in which her conscious presentation of self could signal, at one and the same time, both a "truthful" expression of her "natural" authenticity and *naiveté*, and her lack of those qualities. The example is fanciful, but it calls attention to the complicated ways in which observation, self-observation, awareness of an audience, and awareness of self could affect how one person might be perceived by another.

There are two interrelated issues at hand: discerning the "truth" *of* another, and guaranteeing that one's own "truth" is correctly perceived *by* others. I have already addressed the first above: the question of determining whether or not a person was sincere engendered a large body of "enlightened *Kardiognostik*," writing devoted both to understanding and decoding human behavior and to defending a virtuous antitheatrical subjectivity against the seductions of performance.[30] The fact that such writing failed to resolve the problem of determining another's "sincerity" is attested to by the frequent use of the effectiveness of deception as a plot device in works such as *Clarissa*, *Miss Sara Sampson*, and *Sophie Sternheim*. Works like these can be read as both demonstrative of the evils and dangers of deception, and illustrative of the ways in which deception marks a social and moral distinction between aristocratic and bourgeois culture. The problem of "unmasking the deceiver" thus played a crucial role in the creation of the bourgeois imagined community, as the literary depiction of the difference between the authentic bourgeois subject and the dissembling aristocrat allowed the bourgeois "to visualize in a general way the existence of thousands and thousands like themselves through print language" (Anderson 74). At the same time, it is not coincidental that the victim of performative deception in such literature is almost always a woman, since (as both Frevert and Landes suggest) the "bourgeois class" seems to depend upon a naturalized gender hierarchy for its very existence.

Even more germane to the argument of this book, however, is the second issue: namely the problem of guaranteeing that others will correctly "read" one's own sincerity. This was less a concern for men, who had a "proper" public dimension to their lives through which they could legitimately make visible their honesty and authenticity, than it was for women, for whom being virtuous by definition precluded activity in the public sphere. The woman who was, for whatever reason, engaged in the public sphere was caught in an impossible double-bind: even if she *was* sincere, antitheatrical, honest, et cetera, her presence in public automatically put her under suspicion of performing herself, which in turn reduced the likelihood that she would be correctly "read" as the sincere being she really was. The only way to guarantee an audience's correct interpretation of her subjectivity was to police her image, and—in defiance of the definition of virtue—produce a performance of ideal femininity.

Each of the writers whose work I discuss in the course of this book had such a public dimension to their lives. As writers, actresses, playwrights, and *salonnieres*, they were women who, to varying degrees, had overstepped the boundaries of what had already been defined as ideal femininity in their own lives, and who recognized the impossibility of discursive definitions of virtuous femininity in terms of antitheatricality. As such, each was engaging not only intellectually with the eighteenth-century idea that "Sophie" and the "Theater" were mutually exclusive, but also materially, as they faced criticism and censure about their own morality and sincerity, and about the "properness" of their own embodiment of femininity. For each of these writers, the opposition between "Sophie" and the "Theater" proposed by dominant discourse invited an intervention, and they responded in individual ways. But in each of these works, ideal femininity comes to resemble an impossible act: that, which, by definition, the Ideal Woman could not perform, and yet, at the same time, which she could not "not perform."

2. Performance as Power

The History of Lady von Sternheim

With the publication in 1771 of *The History of Lady von Sternheim* (*Geschichte des Fräuleins von Sternheim*) Sophie von La Roche established herself in literary history as Germany's first female novelist. According to La Roche, her intention in the novel was to raise a "paper girl" once her own two daughters had moved out of her house (*Melusinens Sommerabende* 112). Her friend and editor Christoph Martin Wieland emphasized this intention in his introduction to the novel, in which he fictitiously positioned the book as the product of La Roche's leisure time—as a little project she undertook out of concern for Germany's daughters.[1] As a result of this positioning of the book, contemporary readers viewed it as a guide to proper womanhood, and literary historians have tended to interpret it in those terms.[2] Caroline Flachsland's reaction to *Sternheim* in a letter to Herder is evidence of the reception of La Roche's "paper girl":

> Meanwhile, I have also read the History of Lady Sternheim. My entire ideal of a woman! Soft, tender, beneficent, proud and virtuous and betrayed. I spent treasured, wonderful hours reading it. Oh, how far am I still from my own ideal of myself! What mountains stand towering before me! Oh! Oh, I will remain in the dust and ashes! (Schauer I: 238–39)

Flachsland's rapturous view of Sophie Sternheim is echoed by Merck in his famous characterization of the novel as "not just a book, but a soul" (*Frankfurter Gelehrte Anzeigen*, 85–86), an assessment that importantly points to the interrelationship between the transparency of the novel's form—that is, the epistolary novel as a window into a character's interiority—and the novel's construction of ideal femininity as quintessentially antitheatrical.[3]

But even though La Roche adopted and perpetuated the opposition between a moral antitheatricality and a debased theatricality, her depiction of the feminine ideal in terms of naiveté and transparency also reveals the contradictions inherent in that construction of womanhood for women of the eighteenth century. In this chapter, I look at La Roche's construction of the "soul" that came to represent ideal femininity to so many German readers and investigate the ways in which she mobilizes performance and theatricality to problematize the image of ideal femininity her novel ostensibly constructs. For La Roche's novel complicates its own discursive reproduction of the threat posed by theatricality by recognizing and exploring the power of performance, both as a social/political tool and as a means for self-transformation. Although at the beginning of the novel it is clear that Sophie not only has no place in a theatricalized world, but also must be wary of it, by the end she has skillfully appropriated performance as a means of defining and justifying purposeful female activity in the public sphere. As the novel progresses, theatricality is deployed in many different ways, and the concept of "acting" or the "performance of self" is radically revalued. As a result, the novel's engagement with performance at all levels—as theater, as courtly improvisation, and as a form of behavior modification—is in many ways at cross-purposes with its ideological positioning of Sophie Sternheim as a natural, naive, "authentic" model for Germany's female readers.

* * *

SOPHIE STERNHEIM AND THE "IDEAL" GERMAN WOMAN

The History of Lady von Sternheim offers the story of Sophie Sternheim's young-adult life through a series of letters written mainly by Sophie and her two English suitors to each of their respective confidantes. The daughter of a bourgeois intellectual (Colonel von Sternheim) and a baroness, Sophie represents an ideal combination of bourgeois values and aristocratic grace. After the death of her mother, she is raised by her father, and given an education that combines an Enlightenment focus on the development of the intellect with a Sentimental emphasis on the domestic skills proper to women. Thus she learns foreign languages, history, philosophy, and music; she also learns to dance, sing, play the lute, keep household records, and do needlework and other women's chores. Upon her father's death, Sophie is sent from her idyllic country home to live with her mother's embittered sister, the Countess von Löbau.

Unbeknownst to Sophie, her aunt has brought her to court with the express purpose of offering her to the prince as his mistress in order to gain the Löbaus an advantage in a lawsuit. Here Sophie also attracts the attention of two Englishmen, the virtuous and sincere Lord Seymour (to whom she ends up happily married at the end of the novel) and the despicable libertine Lord Derby. Uncomfortable and out of place at the court, Sophie tries to live according to her virtuous principles, secretly doing acts of charity for the poor, but she is no match for the intrigues of the court and unwittingly falls into the traps her aunt and uncle lay for her. When Sophie finally learns of the plot against her (from Lord Seymour, disguised at a masked ball) she turns to Lord Derby, who has in the meantime convinced her of his virtue by pretending to have been reformed by her virtuous example. Derby marries her in a sham ceremony, and they flee the court for a remote inn. But Sophie is a disappointing conquest for Derby, and after three weeks the libertine disdainfully informs her that their marriage is a false one.

Devastated by this loss of her reputation, Sophie changes her name to Madame Leidens ("Madame Suffering") and embarks on a life of "practicing virtue," dedicating herself to helping others. With the help of a rich local widow, Madame Hills, she sets up a school for indigent local girls and teaches them how to earn a living as servants, ladies' maids, and cooks. An elderly Englishwoman, Lady Summers, hears of her activities and invites her to England to continue the same. She accepts the invitation and goes to live as Lady Summers' companion, where she attracts the attention of a local bachelor, Lord Rich. When Lord Derby, who has in the meantime married Lady Summers' niece, discovers that Sophie is in residence with

Lady Summers, he has her abducted to the lead mines in Scotland, where she is held captive by a poor family and eventually left to die.

The fatally ill and repentant Lord Derby confesses what he has done to Sophie to Lord Rich and Lord Seymour—who, it is revealed, are half-brothers—and they travel to Scotland to bring back her body, only to discover that Sophie's death has been contrived by a local noblewoman, Lady Douglas, in order to protect her from Derby. Sophie marries Seymour and they retire to the idyllic peace of English country life. Rich becomes godfather and tutor to Sophie's children, and the novel ends with the depiction of what Barbara Becker-Cantarino calls a "feminine Utopia": Sophie happily married to the man she loves and leading a useful, productive, active life both inside and outside the home ("Nachwort" 415).

* * *

The History of Lady von Sternheim is by far the best known of the works I consider in this study—indeed, in the last twenty-five years it has achieved quasicanonical status as not only one of the first domestic novels in German, but also as a work that deeply influenced many writers, including Goethe, whose *Sorrows of Young Werther* (*Die Leiden des jungen Werthers*, 1774) has been interpreted as a response to *Sternheim*.[4] La Roche's novel was highly popular in its day and was translated almost immediately into both French and English. The English version, titled *The History of Lady Sophia Sternheim*, was reissued in 1991 and has helped contribute to La Roche's increased visibility in the canon of German literature. Because of its status and availability, *Sternheim* has been the subject of a large body of scholarship in both English and German.[5] Much of this criticism centers on situating La Roche within the cultural discourse of her time and, taking a cue from Wieland's preface, interprets the novel in terms of its construction of a model for female virtue, in many cases emphasizing La Roche's indebtedness to the epistolary tradition in England and France, in particular the writings of Richardson and Rousseau. But while La Roche does seem to have been heavily influenced by both of these writers—many of her ideas about what constitutes the ideal virtuous woman derive from

Rousseau, and the plot and form of the novel are reminiscent of Richardson's *Clarissa*—La Roche's image of the ideal woman also diverges from theirs in important ways.[6] Sophie Sternheim is a far better educated woman than her Rousseauian model, and, unlike her English sister Clarissa, she survives her narrative and goes on to thrive as a virtuous wife, mother, and active member of her community.

In fact, most recent feminist scholarship on *Sternheim* has emphasized that even though the image of ideal femininity produced in the novel is for the most part conservative, it is also rife with tension and contradiction.[7] Some scholars view the character of Sophie as a compromise between La Roche's desire to fashion an ideal "sentimental woman" à la Rousseau and yet at the same time not completely renounce Enlightenment ideas about women's intelligence and the need for educating women (Bovenschen 194; Winkle 89–91). The tension between these two competing ideas of proper femininity is evident not only within the novel, but also in the comparison between the author and her "paper girl": although eighteenth-century readers liked to imagine that Sophie Sternheim had her model in Sophie von La Roche, in fact La Roche was, according to her fan Caroline Flachsland, disappointingly urbane and coquettish (Bovenschen 193). Critics like Meise, Becker-Cantarino, and Nenon likewise attribute the contradictions in La Roche's novel to the discrepancy between the feminine ideal and La Roche's own life experience, in particular to her activity as a writer—an activity that was fundamentally incompatible with prescribed roles for women in the eighteenth century, notwithstanding Wieland's efforts in the editorial apparatus to contain her writing within the appropriate function of "motherhood" (Meise, "Frauenroman" 442). For Becker-Cantarino, the novel is not so much an attempt to imprint a restrictive ideal of femininity on its readers as it is La Roche's difficult negotiation between her acknowledgment of societal constraints on women and her experiential knowledge of a woman's potential to be intelligent and active in both the private and the public sphere (*Der Lange Weg* 296–97).

Nenon, who sees a stronger proto-feminist message in *Sternheim* than most critics, similarly reads La Roche's project as that of mirroring the tension between accommodation and independence that La Roche faced in her own life and claims that *Sternheim* teaches its readers how to negotiate a similar balancing act (99). Baldwin presents an argument that is closely related: although she is more interested in the novel's narrative strategies than in connecting La Roche's writing to her biography, she also interprets *Sternheim* in terms of its creation of a "new genre of character" and its "struggle to construct alternate scripts of female identity" and yet remain within the bounds of social norms (121–28, 140). A running theme in each of these works of criticism is that, like so many other female writers of the eighteenth century, La Roche trod a delicate line between "progressivism and accommodation" in both her life and her writing, and that she was less interested in changing social structures than in carving out space for women to "achieve the greatest independence and development within the given social structure" (Nenon 192; see also S. Schmid 60).

My reading of *Sternheim* also seeks to tease out the contradictions in this work, albeit from a different perspective. My emphasis is on the novel's paradoxical and at times contradictory engagement with the notion of antitheatricality, both as it is mobilized as an aesthetic and moral category, and as it is used to define ideal femininity. While on the one hand La Roche can be read as fully embracing the aesthetics of transparency—by adopting the epistolary form, and by having her protagonist wax philosophical about the "proper" form of art—on the other *Sternheim* problematizes the notion of aesthetic transparency by revealing how that aesthetic makes decoding dissimulation off the stage much more challenging. In addition, while the novel seems to be promoting a conservative image of the ideal woman, as natural, naive, and antitheatrically sincere, it also exposes the pitfalls of that subject position, and, in so doing, reveals ambivalence about its own condemnation of performance.

* * *

SOPHIE GOES TO THE THEATER

Shortly after her arrival at the court in D., young Sophie Sternheim goes to see her very first play—a comedy at the court theater.[8] She is not impressed. When asked how she likes the performance, she haughtily replies, "It perfectly matches the idea I had conceived of such spectacles" (*Geschichte des Fräuleins von Sternheim* (*GS)* 96–97/ *History of Lady Sophia Sternheim (HS)* 56).[9] Of course, the circumstances for enjoying a comedy are not the best: from the moment she enters the theater she is forced to hide behind her neighbor, Countess F., in order to avoid the unwanted attentions of the prince, and her viewing is repeatedly interrupted by people asking her what she thinks of the play. Yet she sees enough of the comedy to confirm her already formed prejudices against the theater. Her disdain for the theater is "an effect of the impression made on me by a description I once read in English of the ridiculousness and unnaturalness of a general singing on the battlefield, or of an enamoured heroine who ends her life with a trill" (*GS* 97/*HS* 56). Although she claims an appreciation for the "intelligence" with which the actress plays her role and the fact that the actress "enters entirely into the character that she represents," the performance leaves her cold, pleasing her only in purely aesthetic terms (*GS* 97/*HS* 56). She claims she feels nothing in the least for the hero and heroine, but admires "the combined efforts of so many different kinds of talent" (*GS* 94/*HS* 54). In the final analysis, she seems to have derived nothing from her visit to the theater but the satisfaction of having had her negative opinion of it confirmed: "On the whole, I am very satisfied at having seen a theater production, because the idea I had of them has been confirmed; but I will also be satisfied if I never see another" (*GS* 97–98/*HS* 56).

There is a contradictory demand of theater embedded in Sophie's critique of the comedy that both mirrors and critiques the aims of the antitheatrical, pedagogical theater. Sophie's displeasure with the theater derives from both the content and the function of the theatrical spectacle. On the one hand, she finds the content—the play itself and the production of it—"ridiculous" and "unnatural." The singing general on the battlefield earns Sophie's contempt because he falls outside the bounds of the real, the probable, the physically possible, and the socially admissible, and thus belongs to a mode of representation unsuitable to the project of sincerity. Like theatrical reformers of the eighteenth century, she wants representation to imitate nature and be faithful to the truth because such representation has a pedagogical function. Her assessment of the theater echoes that of the philosopher and critic Christian Freiherr von Wolff, who mused that if theatrical representation "does not appear similar to the truth . . . no one will be convinced that the events are happening and as a result the Comedies and Tragedies are more obstructive and destructive than they are useful" (*Vernünfftige Gedancken von dem Gesellschaftlichen Leben* 270–71). Along the same lines, Sophie's claim that the comedy did not affect her in the least, and her awareness of the theater's status as a performance event, are evidence that the performance failed to draw her into its illusion and provide her with a hallucinatory experience of its reality—one of the chief aims of the antitheatrical stage.

Where Sophie, in line with bourgeois theatrical reformers, demands that theater combine a depiction of reality with entertainment to serve the purposes of education, the court in *Sternheim* sees theater as a social event.[10] Sophie wants the performance to remain confined to the stage; the court understands itself to be a part of the spectacle. To a certain extent, even Sophie is aware of this: during her evening at the theater, she is thoroughly annoyed by the fact that *she* seems to be part of the entertainment for the evening; in fact, she hides behind the countess (thus blocking her own view of the play) in order not to be seen by the prince, who spends most of the evening looking at her and not the play. When the prince sends Count F. to ask his wife to move so that Sophie can see the play better, she answers that she can see fine where she is, and has the added pleasure of not being seen. The count's response makes clear that for at least some of the audience, the pleasure is not in the play: "But you rob so many of the pleasure of seeing you" (*GS* 94/*HS* 54). Sophie's first appearance at the theater *is* the theatrical event; *she* is the focus of attention and *her* performance is the one being most closely watched and critiqued.

La Roche's text thus describes a moment of historical transition in theatrical practice, from the "theatrical" theater of the baroque period, which mirrored the aristocratic social dynamic, and in which the play itself was less important than the interactions among audience members, to the "antitheatrical" theater demanded by bourgeois reformers (cf. Alewyn 119; Graf 283). At the same time, Sophie's critique of theatricality can be read as a promotion of the aesthetics of transparency that are at play in the text that represents her own story. That is, Sophie's comments discredit the very mode of representation that is also rejected by La Roche's novel. In contrast to the "bad" theater, which not only foregrounds its own spectacularity, but at which an audience member like Sophie would be excruciatingly aware of her physical presence as both observer and as object of another's gaze, *Sternheim* exemplifies an aesthetic that aims at both erasing its status as art and fostering the fiction of the reader's status as an unobserved observer.

Yet Sophie contradicts her wish for the natural and the real on stage in her praise of precisely the elements in the spectacle that render the representation "unnatural." What Sophie *likes* about the theater is what makes it artificial: the costuming, the dance, the music, et cetera. She writes to Emilia, "It is a pleasure to see the combination of so many arts working together for our eyes and ears" (*GS* 97/*HS* 56). Sophie's demand for both the representation of the "real" and the aesthetic pleasure of the spectacle reveals an ambivalence about antitheatricality that runs throughout La Roche's text. The problem for Sophie, as it was for eighteenth-century theorists concerned with detecting dissimulation, is that any representation that dupes its viewer into believing it is real risks no longer being read and framed as representation, especially if it happens to wander off the stage and into real life. The novel's ambivalence can be traced to the fact that the illusionistic, realistic acting that Sophie finds wanting on the stage is seen as necessary for the moral education of society through theater but as an immoral evil in society. *Verstellung*—the art of the actor—is socially acceptable only in the context of the theater, and only when it can be recognized as such. Thus, theatricality paradoxically serves an important purpose: it frames dissimulation *as* dissimulation—as the morally permissible, pedagogically necessary imitation or example—and thus renders it both visible and safe.

As a result, while the novel clearly aligns itself with the bourgeois cultural condemnation of performance and theatricality, at the same time it also reveals how problematic a commitment to antitheatricality can be. For what *Sternheim* makes clear is that it is precisely the bourgeois emphasis on the virtue of an antitheatrical subjectivity and its cultural use of the aesthetics of transparency that makes detecting dissimulation so difficult. Antitheatricality, as it played out in the cultural and social realms, rested on two fundamentally contradictory ideas about how dissimulation was read by an observer. On the one hand, it assumed that in the theater a spectator would enter so completely into the world created on stage that he or she would take the characters as real people. On the other, it took for granted that off the stage no dissimulation could be so perfect as to fool the penetrating glance of the virtuous. But La Roche's novel reveals that, in fact, the opposite is the case: for Sophie, the lack of a theatrical frame within the social context is what makes the performance of self on the part of the practiced dissimulators at court—in particular, Derby—unreadable. Like Home, who believed that dissimulation always appeared unnatural, Sophie feels confident accepting another's performance of self as real and sincere in the absence of clear signs of unnaturalness. But this commitment to reading all performances of self as "true" is highly dangerous, because it is virtually impossible to distinguish between the homologous expression of a "real self" on the part of a morally upright person and the dissimulation of a very good actor.

Thus, although Sophie is aware of the spectacle and theatricality of the court to the extent that it affects appearances (she notes that people flatter and put on masks, and she repeatedly complains to Emilia about her aunt's endless hours in front of the mirror), because those instances are transparently visible as performance, she sees them as isolated moments. She does not recognize the extent to which performance and dissimulation permeate every moment of court life, and, because of this, she lacks the contextualizing frame in which it would be possible to recognize dissimulation. Or perhaps Sophie's (confirmed) "*Vorstellung*" or idea about the theater (*Vorstellung*)—that it always contains "unnatural" and "ridiculous" acting (*Verstellung*)—renders her incapable of even conceiving of a *Verstellung* so perfect that she could mistake it for reality.[11] Sophie's complaint about the excessive theatricality of the theater is ironic precisely because it exposes the pitfalls of her commitment to antitheatricality and reveals how dangerous that commitment turns out to be for her.

In addition, despite its overt critique of theatricality—and despite its explicit embrace of sincerity and authenticity in both content and form—La Roche's novel repeatedly calls attention to how tenuous the distinction between fiction and reality can be. It does so, first and foremost, in its own self-positioning as both. From the outset, *Sternheim* presents a tension between its own artificiality and its claims to authenticity and aesthetic transparency. On the one hand, Wieland's preface foregrounds the novel's status as a fiction: he calls it a work of La Roche's "imagination . . . and heart, which has been written only for [her] own entertainment" (*GS* 9/*HS* 5). Such a positioning of the novel would have been important in preempting criticism of La Roche's audacity in penetrating the masculine sphere of writing, situating the novel instead as a private feminine diversion (cf. Baldwin 109 and Swanson). But on the other hand, the novel itself immediately adopts the convention used to authenticate the epistolary novel: it presents itself as a collection of real letters that provide access to the true history of the subjects who wrote them. The subtitle underscores this illusion: the full title translated reads *The History of Lady von Sternheim, by a friend of the same, drawn from Original-documents and other dependable sources*. La Roche maintains the illusion that the letters are real historical documents throughout her text, thus signalling her own adoption of the aesthetics of transparency. However, there is a countertext within the novel that simultaneously works against this illusion—Wieland's footnotes, which continually point to the novel's status as both fiction and history as they go back and forth between treating Sophie's letters as the product of her pen, and the product of La Roche's. Thus, for example, at one point Wieland seems to treat Sophie like a real person: "Few readers need to be reminded, that Miss von Sternheim's innocence and inexperience made it natural for her to take this purposeful artifice for an effect of coincidence" (*GS* 150/*HS* 82). At another, however, he notes that "Miss von Sternheim's bias toward the English nation" is a "blemish that I would have liked to remove from this excellent work" (*GS* 91/ *HS* 53), a comment that can only serve to remind the reader of the text's fictionality.

The novel's formal duplicity is mirrored in its content, for within the narrative itself the wall between representation and reality seems equally permeable. *Sternheim* is a history of deceptions and performances that blur the distinction between performance and reality. The novel moves from scenes of staged pleasure (the "peasant party," the visit to the comedy) to scenes of outright deception (the scheme to make Sophie the prince's mistress, Derby's fake marriage) to the use of theater as a pedagogical tool (Sophie's demonstration of a virtuous household to the G. Family), and it is often unclear where performance stops and reality begins. At times, performance determines reality (Derby's staging of the marriage, which has real consequences for Sophie), at others, the perception of a performance substitutes for reality (the imagined/perceived rendezvous between Sophie and the prince in the priest's garden house), and at still others, reality itself is wildly theatrical (Seymour and Rich's dramatic rescue of Sophie at the lead mines).

In thematizing the difficulty of distinguishing the fictional from the real in the face of a mode of dissimulation that aims at erasing its status as performance, La Roche fundamentally destabilizes the bourgeois valorization of sincerity. Sophie's inability to correctly decode dissimulation is shown to be less a flaw in her character than an essential paradox of eighteenth-century antitheatricality. Throughout the novel, La Roche calls attention to this paradox by highlighting the artfulness of artlessness and, in the process, underscores the potency of antitheatrical performance. The use of art to create the effect of artlessness in the novel ranges from the benign to the devastating. On the benign end of the spectrum, at the "peasant party" organized by the Löbaus as a means of bringing Sophie into closer contact with the prince, Sophie feels her costume lends her the "simplicity and unaffected virtue of a peasant" and seems enchanted by the realistic set design: "Simply constructed wooden benches had been placed between the trees, and two pleasing farmhouses had been built on either side of the walk, from which were served milk prepared in every different way, and other refreshments, in little porcelain bowls" (*GS* 147/*HS* 81). The artifice involved in creating an illusion of simplicity and innocence here is apparent even to Sophie, and her description of the event demonstrates a certain capacity for duplicitous knowing, that is, an ability to simultaneously acknowledge artifice and voluntarily suspend that knowledge in the spirit of fully entering into the illusion.

But, importantly, the peasant party is clearly framed as a fictional event; other instances of the art of artlessness in the novel are far more difficult to detect as such. In particular, Derby is shown to be a master of the art of performing artlessness—he succeeds in his goal of seducing Sophie precisely through his ability to perform innocence and sincerity. Derby's strategy involves both taking advantage of the lack of theatrical frame around his own performance and imitating those very behaviors that bourgeois moralists took as signals of antitheatrical sincerity. He enhances his chances of success by taking as his model the novel's own model for antitheatrical subjectivity: Sophie herself. So, for example, in order to convince her of his virtuous generosity and inherent goodness, he orchestrates a scene in which he lets Sophie catch him "unobserved" doing an act of charity, during which he signals his identity to her by muttering a phrase in English. This is, by his account, an ostentatious performance of virtue that directly mirrors Sophie's act of charity at the peasant party, at which she waited until she thought no one was watching before slipping out to give money to the parish priest (*GS* 148 /*HS* 82). Derby boasts about the cleverness of his strategy to his confidante in Paris: "It was an excellent idea on my part to mold myself according to her spirit of charity, and in the process *maintain the appearance that I wanted to hide what I was doing*" (*GS* 168/*HS* 93; emphasis added). Sophie's own version of the incident demonstrates that, for her, the performance is not ostentatious at all; on the contrary, Derby's manipulation of the signs of virtue convinces her that she had previously read his character wrong. She writes to Emilia: "He can't have known that I was there . . . or else he wouldn't have spoken English. I have often heard him express good sentiments in company, but I always took them for the hypocrisies of an artful, evil person; but this freely committed act, *done without the knowledge of any other*, cannot possibly be hypocrisy" (*GS* 161/*HS* 89; emphasis added).

This particular incident is noteworthy because it reveals La Roche's sophisticated understanding of the dynamic of observation and audience awareness that impacts the extent to which a person can be read as sincere or performing. Derby is successful in this scene precisely because he understands that he can make Sophie believe that she is seeing his "true self" by making her think that he does not know he is being watched. In revealing the mechanism by which Derby dissembles virtue, La Roche implicitly undermines bourgeois

Kardiognostikers like Gellert, Knigge, and Rousseau, who believed that the best way to judge a person was by observing them without their knowledge.[12] La Roche seems to have a much more nuanced understanding of how much control a perceptive and skillful actor has over his audience. Her insights into the ways a dissimulator could manipulate his audience's reading of his performance constitute a recognition of the power of the conventions of the antitheatrical theater. For, in a sense, Derby has simply exported the dynamic of the illusionistic theater (that Sophie theorized) into real life: he uses the skills of the illusionistic actor who, by playing his scene *as if unaware* of the presence of an audience, successfully convinces the audience of the authenticity of his actions.

If we look at *Sternheim* through the lens of eighteenth-century conceptions of theatricality and performance, it becomes clear that the novel is deeply concerned with interrogating how social audiences read and interpret being, a concern that serves—perhaps inadvertently, most certainly paradoxically—to expose being as performance, no matter how sincere it is. In other words, not only does the novel problematize the efficacy of the penetrating glance of the virtuous (in Sophie's failure to see through all of the performances around her) but it also destabilizes the assumption that sincerity is transparently readable. Sophie's virtuous and innocent behavior is continually misinterpreted by the members of the court, mainly due to her own lack of awareness that others are framing her "being" as performance.

From the moment Sophie arrives at the court in D., she is cast in a performance in which she does not know her role. Her aunt costumes her in the latest fashion and has her hair prepared for her *Erscheinung*—her "appearance" on the court stage. Unbeknownst to her, she has been cast as the prince's mistress, and her aunt and uncle repeatedly manipulate her appearance and behavior to create the illusion that she is playing her role. The first book of the novel catalogues a series of incidents in which the stage is set and Sophie is maneuvered into playing a role in which it appears that she has acquiesced to be the prince's mistress. To name but a few such incidents: her aunt has her serve sorbet to the prince at the peasant party to underscore the appearance that a rendezvous has just taken place (*GS* 136/*HS* 82); her aunt insists she publicly ask a favor of the prince (on behalf of her charity family), thus creating the impression that she is intimate with him (*GS* 156–58/*HS* 86); and the count literally stacks the deck so that she is forced to be the prince's partner at cards (*GS* 169/ *HS* 93).

Through their improvisation, the manipulative aunt, uncle, and Count F. create a context in which Sophie's conduct in real life meshes seamlessly into the scenario they are in the process of staging.[13] Even Seymour is deceived: when he sees her and the prince exit the garden house just moments apart (after Sophie has, in fact, given money to the priest; she has not seen the prince at all) he condemns her performance in both senses of the word. Derby describes Seymour's reaction:

> There was a most violent contempt in his remarks about her *dissembled virtue*; and her wretched sacrifice of the same; and about the impudence with which she *made herself into a spectacle* before all the nobility, and then wore such a pleased look. (*GS* 136/*HS* 74–75; emphasis added)

Seymour's response demonstrates once again the pitfalls of an antitheatrical attitude and yanks the rug out from under the notion that the antitheatrically sincere self is transparently readable. As a member of the court, Seymour has inside knowledge of the intrigue planned by the Löbaus, and because of this knowledge, the frame of theatricality surrounding Sophie is patently obvious to him—so obvious that he finds it "impossible that she could have been imposed upon" and thus assumes that she has not only surrendered her virtue, but also revealed herself to be as insincere as a professional actress he once fancied (*GS* 143, 145/*HS* 79).[14] Falsely believing that Sophie, too, is capable of "dissembling virtue," Seymour now reads all of her activities as a performance. But he is equally a victim of the court's play. Neither Seymour nor Sophie has enough knowledge of or experience with performance and deception to understand the complex way in which a "real life" could be incorporated into a collective performance: their faith in the readability of sincerity blinds them to the extent to which, for an audience at least, being is essentially an effect of performance.

Only Derby, the expert actor, understands immediately the way in which reality has enabled the performance and performance has determined reality. Court life, as the insider Derby describes it, is nothing but performance and dissimulation, and those who understand this have a decided advantage over those who do not. Ironically, Derby, the ultimate dissembler, is also the novel's best reader of Sophie's "true" self. While everyone else at the peasant party assumes that what they have seen—Sophie and the prince emerging from the same garden house—merits the conclusions that they have drawn (that they have had an assignation) Derby is less willing to take appearances for reality: "I thought, such a step was entirely too fresh and too stupid for her . . . I called my servant Will, and promised him a hundred guineas if he found out the truth of what had happened in the parish house between Sophie and the Prince" (*GS* 136/*HS* 75). Derby thus remains the only character in the novel who understands the truth of the situation, and he uses that knowledge to further ensnare Sophie in his own performance of sincerity—a performance aimed at robbing her of the virtue everyone else at court thinks she has already lost.

* * *

THE POWER OF PERFORMANCE

Derby's superior ability to read the truth of another's subjectivity points to another contradiction in *Sternheim*, namely, its mobilization of the opposition between virtuous antitheatricality and vicious deceptiveness. For although it appears that the novel's project is to model proper feminine sincerity and innocence while at the same time warning young female readers of the hazards of life's Derbys, the bigger lesson may in fact lie in the novel's ultimately ambivalent assessment of the value of naiveté and antitheatricality for women. As Derby's example indicates, there is an advantage to being more like a Derby and less like a Seymour or a Sophie, at least when it comes to the ability to distinguish between the real and the performed. But even more importantly, as Sophie progresses through the novel she comes to learn that the performance of self can be a useful survival skill, one that grants her the power to determine her own reputation and control her own representation in the greater world.

That the novel wants to valorize sincerity and vilify dissimulation is clear throughout. Even before Sophie is sent to the court, La Roche sets up an opposition between her own frank, sincere goodness and the vicious deceptions that await her. Sophie's father's dying letter to his friend the vicar begs him to "take care, that the nobleminded heart of this best of girls is not seduced by a *false virtue*. She comprehends the good in others with such eagerness, and overlooks their faults with such indulgence, that it is *only in this* that I fear for her" (*GS* 53/*HS* 30). He then goes on to express his misgivings about his sister-in-law, who is precisely the kind of dissembler he fears Sophie will not be able to see through: "The mildness and goodness that appear on this woman's exterior are *not in her heart*; the charming, pleasant wit, the fine, agreeable tone that she has gotten from the Court hide her many moral failings" (*GS* 54/*HS* 31).

The novel's opposition between sincerity and dissimulation depends, of course, on Sophie's embodiment of virtuous antitheatricality. She is repeatedly described as sincere, honest, and candid; the cardinal aspect of her character is her subjective transparency. Sophie herself emphasizes it—"You know, my Emilia, that my face always expresses the feelings of my soul" (*GS* 115/*HS* 67)—and other characters remark on it in their own letters. Even Derby admires her transparent readability. During the masked ball, he finds occasion to "note that the face . . . is really the expression of the soul. For unmasked my Sternheim was always the picture of modest beauty, insofar as the nobility and the purity of her soul seemed to shine forth from her face and looks" (*GS* 186/*HS* 103). Moreover, Wieland, in his preface to the novel, directs our reading so as to emphasize the praiseworthiness of this aspect of Sophie's character:

> I thought to myself in a hundred places: may my daughters learn to think and behave as Sophie Sternheim does! May heaven grant me the happiness of seeing expressed in my lovely creatures the same unadorned sincerity of soul . . . the same tender feeling for truth and beauty . . . the same unfeigned piety . . . . (*GS* 11/*HS* 6)

For Wieland, Sophie's subjective transparency is a positive attribute of her character, and one worth emulating by the daughters of good bourgeois fathers like himself.

As Wieland's remarks underscore, Sophie's sincere virtue is specifically linked to her embodiment of natural femininity. This is nowhere more evident than in a scene in which, echoing Rousseau's use of the blush to define the Ideal Woman, La Roche has Derby find himself momentarily smitten by Sophie's antitheatrical expression of self:

> The charming Miss Sternheim lifted her glance to a certain area [of the landscape]; a delicate red came over her face and breast, which seemed to take on a quickening movement from her feeling of pleasure. Yearning was diffused across her face, and a moment later tears sprung to her eyes. All of the charms that I have ever seen in others of her sex were nothing compared with the captivating expression of sentiment that poured over her whole person. I could hardly withstand the fervid desire to take her in my arms. (*GS* 121/*HS* 70)

It is, in fact, Sophie's embodiment of female perfection that makes Derby so determined to seduce her—her absolute virtue, signalled here as elsewhere by her transparent readability (and readable by Derby at every moment in the novel), makes her a challenging and worthy target of Derby's seduction plot.

Indeed, all of the good characters in the novel conceive of themselves and other good people as transparently readable, and they condemn the vicious characters for engaging in dissimulation and performance. Thus, Seymour's virtue is similarly signalled in the novel by his inability to dissemble: he writes that he can "seldom hide" his emotions (*GS* 105/*HS* 62), and that he has nothing but the sharpest criticism for those who have used deceit against Sophie (*GS* 207–10/*HS* 110–15). Sophie's disdain for artifice is also clearly and repeatedly expressed, and extends even to the "artificiality and unnaturalness I see in ideas, feelings, pleasures and virtues" at court (*GS* 179/*HS* 209). Derby's use of deception to seduce Sophie earns him the utmost contempt—by the novel's end, he is labeled a "villain" and "hypocrite" (*GS* 265/*HS* 151) and punished by a crippling and fatal disease.

But while La Roche seems to want to clearly oppose "good" sincerity to "bad" performance, there is also a strain in the novel that complicates that simple value judgment. It is plain, for example, that Sophie's naiveté is a liability for her, a fact that Wieland highlights in two of his footnotes (*GS* 119, 150/*HS* 69, 82) and that is made most manifest by Derby's exploitation of her inability to distinguish reality from performance. Less obvious is the novel's implication that Sophie would be better off if she were less committed to the notion that her actions speak for themselves and more aware of the necessity to police her reputation and perform the virtuous self she knows herself to really be. The novel calls attention to such performance as an alternative strategy precisely at the moment in which her reputation is lost, albeit doing so in a way that once again reproduces the prejudice against performance. At the ball, after Sophie has discovered the Löbaus' plans, she makes a scene and accuses her aunt and uncle of having destroyed her reputation. While this protest is sincere on her part, members of the court take it as an ostentatious display, whispering among themselves,

> One can be virtuous, without making a big noise about it; . . . there is a softer and more noble way to defend one's honor, without calling the whole world to be witness to it.*
>
> Others took it for a nice little comedy, and were curious to see how far she would play her part.
>
> ———
>
> *And those who spoke this way were not entirely incorrect. E. [Wieland] (*GS* 189/*HS* 104–05)

The irony of this moment is striking—the courtiers censure her for what they see as a performance of virtue, when in fact it was her failure to perform and make her actual virtue visible that led to her fall. The scene, in effect, raises the question of why Sophie has not been more proactive in defining herself all along and then answers it in Wieland's rather catty editorial comment, which succinctly encapsulates the social pressure on women to eschew performance and ostentation of any kind—and particularly the performance of virtue. Yet interestingly, the reader's knowledge that Sophie does not, in fact, protest too much here undercuts Wieland's censure of her, and as a result the scene implicitly undermines the logic that equates ideal femininity with pure antitheatricality by showing that she is damned if she performs virtue, and equally damned if she does not.

The lesson that might be best taken from this self-proclaimed didactic novel, then, seems to be that, given an audience that will read everything as performance anyway, it is prudent to produce a performance of one's self that matches one's idea of one's true self, rather than trusting matters to the audience's interpretation. It is a lesson that Derby has mastered before the action of the novel begins, and one that Sophie learns in the course of the narrative. For although performance and theatricality are framed as unequivocally bad in the first book of the novel, the second book contains a substantial reevaluation of what performing one's self might mean for the virtuous woman and begins to point to the positive potentialities of performance and theatricality.

In Book Two, Sophie puts the lessons she has learned at court (the ultimate acting school) to good use, deploying performance as both a means of self-discipline and in the service of bourgeois pedagogy: she disciplines her inner self through a performance of the self she wants to be, and, through her performance, she (paradoxically) teaches others how to be natural women, an activity that culminates in her becoming the very representation of the bourgeois ideal of virtue captured within the book's pages. Almost immediately after Sophie realizes she has been victimized by Derby's deception, she begins to put on her own act: she hides her "true" identity behind a pseudonym, she changes her mode of dress, and she pretends to be of a class (bourgeois) with which she has philosophical affinities but to which she does not properly belong. With this shift, the novel takes a radical departure from its negative portrayal of *Verstellung* and begins to problematize the bourgeois disdain for performance in complex and interesting ways. In the first place, Sophie's adoption of a false identity is presented as a logical and reasonable response to her altered circumstances. Rosina matter-of-factly explains: "[S]he didn't want anything known of her. She took on a false name; she wanted to be called *Madam Leidens* [*Madame Suffering*] in allusion to her fate, and to live with us as a young officer's widow" (*GS* 234/*HS* 132–33).

The narrative attaches no moral opprobrium to this patent use of disguise and deception. Rather, it is framed as a necessary step for her survival. Indeed, the mobilization of performance here sets La Roche's novel apart from its closest model, *Clarissa*: what distinguishes Sophie from Clarissa is her ability to reinvent herself and take on a new persona after her violation at the hands of the rake. Performance enables Sophie to move on.

In order to allow Sophie to continue to stand as the virtuous and ideal girl, however, the novel must take a more nuanced approach to defining what constitutes a virtuous or vicious performance of self. Thus, although Sophie takes on a new outward identity, she remains true to her "inner self," as is evidenced in her self-reflexive letters. In other words, unlike Derby, she never misrepresents her inner desires and motives, even though she does take on a false persona. In addition, her use of dissimulation—as limited as it is—makes her feel remorseful and guilty, another sign that her mode of performance is different. She writes that she "deeply deplored the fact that I had to deceive [Lady Summers] with a false story" (*GS* 287/*HS* 164). Paradoxically, and further problematizing the ethics of performance, Sophie's "real" self is as readable through her new disguise as it ever was: later in the same letter, she notes that Lady Summers' "heart understood mine" in mutual recognition of virtuous principles (*GS* 287/*HS* 164). In other words, Sophie's particular deployment of performance calls into question the assumption that virtue and theatricality are by definition mutually exclusive.

This reconfiguration of performance has two important functions in the novel. First, it situates the morally corrupt form of dissimulation squarely in the world of the aristocracy, in which historically identity was manifested in the public performance and display of self, and where court life resembled a perpetual performance.[15] Sophie's performance as Madame Leidens, on the other hand, answers to bourgeois demands of self-accountability, self-reflexivity, and morally upright behavior. Thus there is a clear qualitative difference between the kinds of performance mobilized in the novel—the evil "misrepresentation" of one's self for personal gain and the benevolent re-presentation of one's self as the person one strives to be. Hence the second important function of this reconfiguration of performance is that, unlike the deceptions of the court, where the performance hid a person's true nature, Madame Leidens' performance *determines* who she becomes—it has a transformative effect. The more Sophie, as Madame Leidens, enacts her moral principles in a purposeful way—the phrase used repeatedly in the novel is "practicing virtue" (*übende Tugend*)—the more she comes to embody the ideal bourgeois woman.

Such a use of performance to discipline and develop the self can be read as an acute engagement with one of the more ambivalent aspects of the relationship between the performance of self and the expression of inner identity as articulated in the eighteenth century. The pretense of virtue on the part of an inherently bad person (like Derby) was unequivocally immoral, but, paradoxically, the performance of virtue was also thought to be able to influence the inner self to become good. So, for example, in his *Anthropology from a Pragmatic Point of View*, Kant assigned performance a moral dimension that derails the unmitigated condemnation of deception as necessarily immoral:

> Collectively, the more civilized men are, the more they are actors. They assume the appearance of attachment, of esteem for others, of modesty, and of disinterestedness, without ever deceiving anyone, because everyone understands that nothing sincere is meant. Persons are familiar with this, and it is even a good thing that this is so in this world, for *when men play these roles, virtues are gradually established, whose appearance had up until now only been affected. These virtues ultimately will become part of the actor's disposition.* (37 [§14]; emphasis added)

Arguments like these helped both to recuperate the actor as the modeler of virtuous human behavior and to resolve the ambiguities posed by the use of theater and performance as a tool for moral education. Without such arguments, the edifice of the theater as a moral institution would have crumbled under the weight of its own paradoxes, viz: "How could one who only plays moral uprightness really be morally upright? And weren't imitation and gesture, when rehearsed, merely dissimulation? Wasn't one who disguised himself still deceitful and deeply immoral?" (Laermann 150).

Sophie's performance as Madame Leidens is thus in line with the bourgeois reassessment of deception in light of its desire to establish the theater as a site of moral education. Her use of performance as behavior modification might well have taken its cue from Lessing:

> I believe, that when the actor knows how to imitate all the outward signs and attributes and all the modifications of the body which, as we have discovered through experience, can express certain things, then as a result of the impression made upon his senses by this imitation his soul will achieve, on its own accord, that state, which is proper to his movements, posture, and tone. ("Auszug" 152)

But where Lessing and Kant seem to have faith in the mystical power of performance to work its magical effects on the actor, *Sternheim* clearly demonstrates that imitating virtue cannot be transformational on its own—otherwise, Derby would not remain a rake after his own imitation of virtue. La Roche is less willing to trust in professional deceivers; she sees performance as powerful in the service of good only in the hands of morally principled and virtuous people. That is, for La Roche—as it will be for Schröder later in the century—before a person can be a good actor, he or she must first be good.

In addition, not only does Sophie-as-Madame-Leidens use the performance of virtue to change herself, she also creates her own micro-version of theater as a moral and pedagogical institution. In her capacity as consultant to Madame Hills, she learns of the plight of the G. Family, whose household has fallen into disarray and poverty due to the husband's pride and the mother's failure to properly fulfill her domestic duties. Rather than continuing to provide them with financial support, Sophie comes up with a plan to use pedagogical theater to demonstrate to them how to improve their lives. Her method is grounded in the same premises that were used to establish the efficacy of the antitheatrical theater—the notion that realistic performance would lead to an internalization of the values represented. In order to educate the G. Family, Sophie "performs" the various roles of a virtuous household for them:

> On the second day I played Mrs. G. and in her person I spoke with Miss Lehne about our longstanding love, and told her how happily I granted her the position that she was going to fill in my house, because I believed that she would use a good heart in fulfilling it. I told her what

> I expected of her (according to Mrs. G's wishes, with whom I had spoken in private beforehand); I recommended the girls to her care, and added that we would always consult with each other and work together. Then for two days I was Miss Lehne—and the following three I took the place of each of the three daughters. (*GS* 251/*HS* 143)

Sophie uses her own performance here to model natural and correct gender roles for the family's women (it is noteworthy that she does not use this method to help Mr. G.), putting herself into the role so wholly that her own performance seems completely natural. In the process she also completely draws her audience into the scene. Notably, in so doing Sophie creates precisely the kind of theater she wishes she had seen earlier in the novel. But although her improvisation here has the intention of transforming Mrs. G. and her daughters into proper, natural women through role-playing, the very fact that these roles can be played convincingly and naturally undermines their "naturalness." In other words, implicit in Sophie's performance of the various roles in the household is a confirmation of the fact that when the women take on the roles themselves, they too will merely be "performing" them—for it could be said that Mrs. G. and her daughters were only doing what came "naturally" to them *before* Sophie's performative intervention. Consequently, one of the things that La Roche's mobilization of performance in this novel subtly puts at issue is what properly constitutes "natural" womanhood.

Finally, the example of Madame Leidens' and the G. Family's transformation through performance is encapsulated in two texts that are representations—and, in their own right, performances—of "Sophie Sternheim's" life: Sophie's diaries and letters, which she hands to Lord Rich as a substitute for her self at the end of the novel, and *Sternheim* itself, which Wieland positions as an authentic model of virtuous femininity for Germany's daughters. While neither of these texts can give unmediated access to the heroine's true self, both claim to do so, and both stake claims to embody or manifest ideal female "nature." Rich explicitly regards Sophie's letters and diaries as her surrogate self:

> He kissed the pages of my journal, pressed them to his breast, and asked my forgiveness for having taken a copy of it, which he then put back in

> my hands, along with the original. "But allow me," he added, "to request of you this faithful transcript of your sentiments; allow me . . . to possess this draft of your soul . . ." (*GS* 341/*HS* 200)

Rich's willingness to accept a textual representation of Sophie *as* her, and *as* a natural expression of virtuous femininity, parallels his earlier willingness to accept her performance as Madame Leidens as a sincere and unmediated expression of self. In both cases, Sophie's illusionistic performance of natural femininity is a complete success. Rich, in turn, models the kind of audience reception Wieland imagines for the book itself. Wieland wants readers to do what Rich does: accept the naturalness of both the writing and the character as true, applaud the illusionistic performance of both, and recognize the efficacy of that illusionistic performance. Equating Sophie's "naturalness" with the "naturalness" of La Roche's writing in his preface, Wieland urges an erasure of the performative status of both (*GS* 14–15/*HS* 8). At the same time, he highlights how powerful that erasure makes the text as a pedagogical tool. He ends the preface with these words:

> The naive beauty of [Sophie's] mind, the purity, the unbounded goodness of her heart, the correctness of her taste, the truth of her judgments . . . in short, all of her talents and virtues guarantee that she will please; that she will please all who can thank heaven for a healthy mind and a feeling heart;—and who else would we want to please?—But the dearest wish of our heroine is not the desire of vanity; she wants to be useful; she *wants* to do good, and she *will* do good, and in so doing will justify the step I have taken in daring to introduce her to the world without the knowledge and permission of her dear creator. (*GS* 16–17/*HS* 9)

The good Sophie can do in the real world as a fictional character depends upon performance being taken for reality—precisely the aims of aesthetic transparency, and precisely what causes Sophie's downfall. Thus among the lessons *Sternheim* teaches is the danger and power of performance, as both a negative and as a positive force. To the same extent that Derby's deception has a negative impact on Sophie's life, Sophie's performance as Madame Leidens and the representation of her life as depicted in her diary and in the novel itself have a positive influence—on the characters within the novel (even, in the end, Derby himself) and on Germany's daughters.

What Sophie seems to learn on her journey from innocent country girl to wise country wife is a mastery of the theatrical: the ability to take control of her own representation of self. This lesson may have been one that was absorbed by her readership along with the ideology of antitheatricality: for while *The History of Lady von Sternheim* clearly valorizes authenticity and naiveté, it also contains important lessons for young women about the costs of ignoring the performative dimension of human subjectivity, and of being too confident that the illusionistic theater, once established, could be safely contained on the stage. Sophie's mastery of performance not only enables her to survive her trials and tribulations but also empowers her to be active and effective in the public sphere. By the end of the novel, she has carved out a niche for herself in which her continued activity in the public sphere even after marriage is warranted by the demands of continuing to "be" the self she has performatively "become." In thus revaluing performance as a potential site of self-development toward virtue for her heroine, La Roche makes it clear that the Theater has rich rewards for the Sophie who knows what to do with it.

3. The Performance of a Lifetime

Karoline Schulze-Kummerfeld

When Karoline Schulze-Kummerfeld sat down to pen her memoirs, she brought to her writing desk a profound awareness of her life as a performance, both on the stage and off. As a professional actress, she had occupied an "in-between" space in German society, straddling many of the boundaries separating the bourgeois middle class from the nobility, public life from private life, men from women, and rich from poor. Although for much of her life she enjoyed a freedom and mobility unusual for a woman of her era, she had a profound understanding of the extent to which that mobility could be perceived and interpreted as transgressive and threatening to the bourgeois public to which she yearned to belong, and she knew that as an actress she was always already under suspicion not only of "unchasteness" but also of the debased theatricality that was the opposite of bourgeois virtue. During her life, Schulze-Kummerfeld experienced both the extreme mobility and publicity of the actress's life and the stifling isolation and domesticity of bourgeois marriage. Her first-hand knowledge of these two very different modes of being ties her awareness of what it means to perform—both on and off the stage—to her understanding of her status as a woman in society. As a result, these memoirs provide insights into the cultural and social meanings of performance for women of the time and reveal many of the contradictions inherent in the demand for a virtuous, antitheatrical femininity. Paradoxically, although Schulze-Kummerfeld thought of herself in terms of authenticity, transparency, and naiveté—that is, as an antitheatrical subject—she was also aware of the extent to which, as a public person, she needed to defend her reputation and her image in the public sphere by mobilizing performances of herself that could ward off suspicion of her virtue. In many ways, her memoirs can be seen as both a chronicle of those performances and the performance of her lifetime—her final, definitive representation of her "self" to her public.

Recent studies of eighteenth-century women's autobiographies have pointed out that such texts frequently represent complex negotiations with dominant ideas about gendered subjectivity.[1] In addition, poststructuralist theory has led to a questioning of the historical and "truth" value of memoirs in general: the very act of representing one's life in words renders that life to some degree fictive, no matter how close the author approaches historical accuracy. One model of reading autobiographical texts sees the text as a conscious, half-conscious, or unconscious "performance" of identity produced and contoured in response to, or reaction against, social and discursive pressures toward a fixed and "natural" gendered identity.[2] This is, of course, a twentieth-century perspective: an eighteenth-century memoir writer like Karoline Schulze-Kummerfeld understood her subjectivity and her writing about that subjectivity quite differently. She claims to "know" herself and the "truth" of her life with a confidence that historical hindsight and current theory find at best quaint, and, at worst, suspect. Yet reading her text as a "performance"—against her specific intentions to have it stand as the "truth" of her life—is particularly compelling in the case of Karoline Schulze-Kummerfeld because it helps to illuminate the contradictory subject position into which women of the late eighteenth century were interpellated by contemporary discourse, which equated ideal femininity with antitheatricality.

* * *

SCHULZE-KUMMERFELD'S MEMOIRS: GENESIS AND SUMMARY

Karoline Schulze-Kummerfeld (1745–1815) spent more than half of her life working and living in the theater. Her autobiographical manuscripts, "The Whole History of my Life" ("Die Ganze Geschichte meines Lebens"), which was begun in Linz toward the end of 1782, and "True History of my Theatrical Life" ("Wahre Geschichte meines Theatralischen Lebens"), written in Weimar in 1793, cover her life from birth to 1785, the year she finally left the stage to start a sewing school for young girls.[3] The two manuscripts were written at two different phases in her life, and for very different purposes. She wrote the first ("Hamburg") manuscript—which is straightforwardly autobiographical, covering both her personal life and her career—during a period of crisis in her life: she had been widowed and in perilous financial circumstances for five years, had been unable to resuscitate her acting career, and was suffering from worsening health. The note she attached to the Hamburg manuscript over a decade later indicates that she believed that she was close to the end of her life when she wrote it: she advises any potential publisher to combine it with the later ("Weimar") manuscript, because "when I wrote this history I did not think I would live so long and I rushed" ("Hamburg Manuscript" 683; see also Niethammer 148). But this first manuscript does not seem to have been written with the intention of publication; indeed, her reasons for writing her autobiography at this point are difficult to decipher. She claims at the beginning of the manuscript to be writing it "not out of vanity nor from desire for profit" but because she "wanted to do it" ("Hamburg Manuscript" 1), and her chief aim with this manuscript seems to have been to capture in words a "true" history of her life as an honest and transparent woman.

Schulze-Kummerfeld's motivation for writing the second version of her memoirs—the Weimar manuscript—is much clearer. Her goal here was to write a history of her acting career in response to what she perceived as an unflattering biographical portrait by Reichard in his *Theater-Kalender*. At worst, Reichard's article reads as a lukewarm assessment of her career, but Schulze-Kummerfeld was outraged that she had been damned with such faint praise.[4] Thus she wrote her second memoir with the hope of having it published: her letter to the publisher Friedrich Nicolai frames her autobiography as a pointed effort to rescue her reputation from what she perceived as Reichard's calumny. At the same time, however, she also insists here that what she has written is a "true history": "I represent myself now publicly to the world and say: that is what I was, that is what I am still" ("Letter to Nicolai").[5] Clearly, the polemical purpose of her Weimar manuscript—that is, its implicit argument that she was a better person and actress than she felt her critics painted her to be—make her truth claims somewhat suspect. But, in reading her memoirs, I am less interested in whether or not her writing does indeed represent the truth of her subjectivity—an impossible task, at any rate—than in her strategies for performing that subjectivity in the first place, a strategy that included attempting to publish a memoir of her life that was the "whole truth" ("Letter to Nicolai").

Nicolai rejected her manuscript, however, and her memoirs were not published until a century after her death. In 1915, Emil Benezé edited the two manuscripts together under the title *Memoirs of the Actress Karoline Schulze-Kummerfeld* (*Lebenserinnerungen der Komödiantin Karoline Schulze-Kummerfeld*), and, in 1988, Inge Buck published another version of her manuscripts under the title *A Traveling Woman* (*Ein fahrendes Frauenzimmer*). Neither of the published versions completely reproduces the two manuscripts, but, of the two, Benezé's is more complete: for ease of cross-reference I cite from the Benezé edition in the following except where he has elided or glossed Kummerfeld's text, in which case I draw from the manuscripts themselves (henceforward citations from Benezé appear as *KSK*; citations from the manuscripts under "HM" or "WM" respectively).[6]

In general, these memoirs provide a fascinating and highly detailed description of a German actress's experience of life in the eighteenth century. In fact, what little scholarship exists on these memoirs tends to rely upon them as a means of accessing historical information about the state of the theater and the working conditions of actresses in eighteenth-century theater.[7] Recently, several critics have begun to read Schulze-Kummerfeld's memoirs more interpretively. For example, Emde's study of actresses' self-representation as a form of performance deals briefly with Schulze-Kummerfeld's memoirs, and Gutjahr provides an analysis of these memoirs that dovetails in some respects with my own, as she reads them in the context of actresses' desire for acceptance into bourgeois society.[8] In her introduction to her edition of the memoirs, Buck calls attention to the issues of representation raised by the text, and Niethammer's study of eighteenth-century German women's autobiographies includes a lengthy section on Schulze-Kummerfeld's memoirs that sees her writing as reflecting a shift away from Enlightenment models of equality between the sexes and toward an internalization of the bourgeois gender hierarchy (Niethammer 146–75). Niethammer's analysis also importantly foregrounds the problematic status of Schulze-Kummerfeld's memoirs as a text, given that they have been published only in incomplete form, and that there are also gaps in the manuscripts themselves.

To my knowledge, my own work on this text is the only sustained analysis in English to date. Because the biographical material is of historical interest—and has never been described in any detail in English—before I begin a closer analysis of the text, I want to offer a summary of Schulze-Kummerfeld's life history as she recounts it in her memoirs. I do so fully aware that summarizing autobiography is a necessarily hazardous endeavor, as in so doing it is hard to avoid (re)presenting the writer's text as historical truth. Thus, a caveat: this summary of Schulze-Kummerfeld's memoirs should be read as a representation of the text itself, and not her life. I present it in the same spirit in which I present the plot summaries of the other works I treat in this book. In fact, we know very little of Schulze-Kummerfeld's life outside of her own representation of it: aside from a few reviews of her appearances on stage and the short biographies to which she objected, there are no contemporary accounts of her life.[9]

Karoline Schulze-Kummerfeld was born in Vienna in 1745 to the actor Christian Schulze and his second wife, Augustina. Both of her parents, she tells her reader, were "driven" to the theater by economic and social necessity. Upon the death of his father, who had been providing him with financial support, Christian Schulze left university to pursue a career in theater. Schulze-Kummerfeld's mother's journey to the theater seems to have come straight out of contemporary romance novels: the daughter of a degenerating aristocratic family, Augustina fled her sister's home to escape her brother-in-law's amorous advances and the threat of marriage to an unbearable local nobleman. Although she intended to join the court of the Czaress of Russia, she was hindered by an uprising in Eastern Europe and took refuge with a traveling theater troupe in Stettin. She joined the troupe as an actress, and several years later met, then married, Christian Schulze.[10] The Schulzes spent the rest of their lives in the theater.

The first twenty-two years of Schulze-Kummerfeld's life were marked by an astonishing mobility. From her birth until she married Wilhelm Kummerfeld in 1767, she and her family lived and worked in over fifty-two cities, sometimes traveling to four or five cities in a single year. For the most part these years were also plagued by terrible financial insecurity compounded by a series of betrayals on the part of various theater directors. Until the family became engaged with the relatively stable (and honest) Ackermann troupe in 1758, they led a life of itinerancy and insecurity, constantly on the edge of poverty, and moving almost as frequently between troupes as they did between cities.

Schulze-Kummerfeld and her younger brother, Karl, both began performing at a very early age. Karl trained principally in dance and eventually had a long career as a dancer, dance teacher, and choreographer. Schulze-Kummerfeld trod the boards almost as soon as she could walk and talk: she played her first two roles, one of which required her to speak Latin, at the age of three.[11] By the age of eleven—with the aid of high-heeled shoes and tall wigs—she was playing ingenues and young widows. In 1757, her father died in an epidemic in Freiburg; by 1758, she was a full-time actress and, at age thirteen, the principal provider for her family. Her mother had suffered a nervous breakdown as a result of Schulze's death and was no longer able to perform, and so until their mother's death in 1766, the teenaged Karoline and Karl were the chief support for the family and had responsibility for negotiating contracts with theater troupes, making arrangements for travel and housing, and procuring medical care for their mother.

Schulze-Kummerfeld recalls that she was not only precocious in the roles she played, she also seems to have been an extremely mature child. She was so mature, in fact, that, at the age of twelve, she was the object of passionate love from an army officer by the name of Count Nostitz. She engaged in a lengthy and rather risqué correspondence and relationship with him and almost caved in to his desires to have her for a mistress. But her loyalty to her father kept her from her secret rendezvous with the count, and, shortly after this episode, her family moved to Freiburg, where her father died. The description of her "affair" with the count, discussed in greater detail below, is interesting not only because it gives insight into her maturity and character, but also because it is presented as telling counterevidence to the prevailing notion that actors and actresses had loose moral standards. In the Schulze family, at least (and according to Schulze-Kummerfeld, at least), moral standards were quite high, and she claims to have led an exceedingly chaste life.[12] Indeed, Schulze-Kummerfeld also includes a lengthy anecdote that demonstrates the strength of those principles: at the age of eighteen she fell in love with an aristocrat, the Major Herr Baron von Dalwig. But when it became clear that the most she could hope was to become his illegitimate mistress, she gave him up, despite the fact that he also loved her passionately. It is a decision that she later claims to have regretted: "[M]y ideas of virtue were too strict. As your beloved, even as your mistress I would have been happier than I became many years later . . . ." (*KSK* I: 159).

From 1758 to 1767, Schulze-Kummerfeld and her brother, Karl, were steadily engaged with the Ackermann troupe, and it was with this company that she seems to have enjoyed her maturation and growth as an actress. She worked with the famous actor Konrad Eckhof and also seems to have been nurtured by Madame Ackermann, the director's wife. Her relationship with the Ackermann troupe was not an easy one, however. Early on, she encountered jealousy and resentment from the other actresses, and the troupe was plagued by financial and political problems. The troupe wandered from city to city from 1758 until 1764, when it found a home in Hamburg. Schulze-Kummerfeld claims in her memoirs that she mistrusted Hamburg the moment she saw its towers—this may be hindsight speaking, because she lived some of the saddest and most difficult times of her life in Hamburg. Although business was good for Ackermann in Hamburg, and life stabilized financially for the troupe as a whole, for Schulze-Kummerfeld, Hamburg offered nothing but misery. She writes that she was alienated by the city's customs and manners and found the inhabitants rude and unforgiving. In addition, her mother died there in 1766, and shortly thereafter she found herself the object of a vitriolic attack on her acting, which was masterminded by her chief rival, the actress Sophie Hensel.[13] After several vain attempts to fight back through the press and on the stage, Schulze-Kummerfeld left Hamburg to join the troupe directed by Koch, in Leipzig.

Her two years in Leipzig were unquestionably the high point of her career—she was a triumphant success in nearly every role she played.[14] While in Hamburg, however, she had begun a friendship with Wilhelm Kummerfeld, a banker some twenty-three years her senior, and through correspondence this friendship became a romance and eventually led to a marriage proposal. Schulze-Kummerfeld made the decision to marry based not on her love for Kummerfeld but on one very practical consideration: her desire to have financial stability. Her letters to Kummerfeld negotiating the terms of their marriage (which she includes in her memoirs) attest to her concern about her social and financial standing: even though she was still quite young when she married, she was already thinking about the inevitable end of her acting career, and she negotiated the conditions under which she would marry as carefully as she negotiated her theatrical engagements.[15]

But, from the start, their marriage was a rocky one. Kummerfeld's family did not approve of his choice of an actress for a wife, and she keenly felt their animosity. Her new husband quickly revealed a tendency toward depression, and Schulze-Kummerfeld describes him as a cold and spiritless man. Her first year of marriage was miserable: although in letters to friends she described herself as happy, she did not like to sign her new name—"it was an anxious, sorrowful name, a great vast field (*Feld*) planted with sorrow (*Kummer*)" ("HM" 576). But despite her loneliness and isolation, the nine years of her marriage represent the only period in Schulze-Kummerfeld's life in which she had financial stability and a permanent home.

In the latter years of his life, Kummerfeld sank deeper into mental illness and, unbeknownst to Schulze-Kummerfeld, became incapable of managing his finances or his career. He accrued large debts and made several bad loans. In 1777 Kummerfeld died "of insanity," leaving his widow to do battle with his family over his inheritance and the responsibility for his debts.[16] After a complicated legal fight,

Schulze-Kummerfeld was left with virtually nothing but the duty to repay her husband's debts, and reluctantly re-engaged with the Ackermann/Schröder troupe in Hamburg. But her return to the stage was difficult, and after a year playing only minor roles in Hamburg, she took an engagement with a company in Gotha in 1779 that promised her a pension at retirement. However, the Gotha director's irresponsible management so alienated the local aristocracy that the entire company was disbanded shortly after she arrived, and, instead of the hoped-for pension, she was left with even greater debts. From Gotha she traveled to Mannheim (1779–80), and in the following three years she was engaged with various companies in Mannheim, Innsbruck, Augsburg, Munich, Innsbruck again, and Linz.

In 1783, Schulze-Kummerfeld tried to leave the stage for a second time and traveled to Frankfurt at the invitation of her brother, Karl, who was living there with his wife. But difficulties with her sister-in-law forced her to return to the stage again after only five months of "retirement." She then contracted with the Großmann troupe in Bonn; but there she failed to please the town's most important audience member: Caroline Großman complained to her husband that "the Prince absolutely does not want to see K[ummerfeld] . . . any more, and he is right."[17] She was dismissed in 1784, after merely a year with the troupe. Almost immediately, an opportunity arose to be engaged with a troupe in Weimar, and she leapt at the chance, despite the fact that the director Bellomo had a shady reputation among the more legitimate theater artists. After an unhappy year with Bellomo's troupe, friends convinced her that they would support her and send their daughters to her if she began a sewing school for young girls. In 1785, she left the theater for the third and final time, and, nine years later, as she put the finishing touches on her manuscript, she had eighty-five students.

Schulze-Kummerfeld lived for another thirty years in Weimar as a sewing teacher. In her collection of stories about Weimar, Helene Böhlau paints a lively portrait of Schulze-Kummerfeld as a quaint and quirky old lady lecturing her young charges on propriety and virtue as she takes them on a tour of Weimar's literary and cultural landmarks.[18] Schulze-Kummerfeld also invented and marketed an ointment that helped against freckles and spots, which she had produced by a local apothecary.[19] She neither remarried nor returned to work in the theater. Her final years of life were once again marked by financial insecurity: although she received some financial help from her old colleague Friedrich Ludwig Schröder, she died in impoverished circumstances on April 20, 1815, at the age of seventy-five.

* * *

THE PERFORMANCE OF A LIFETIME

The manuscripts that Karoline Schulze-Kummerfeld left to posterity immediately disclose her difficulty in defining the subject of her autobiography. On the one hand, Schulze-Kummerfeld seems to have wanted to paint a portrait of her "self" in terms of both her personal history and her inner life; on the other hand, she also felt the need to leave behind a defense of her acting talent in response to her critics, and a defense of herself as an actress who had led a virtuous life.[20] Toward the end of her memoirs, Schulze-Kummerfeld confirms the double purpose of her autobiographical project:

> I had to speak as one who knows art, because I could not make myself visible in my roles to posterity in the same way as other artists can in their works of art. Thus I have represented myself in this book, a representation that will last until the barbaric, angry tooth of time destroys it and the spice and cheese merchants rip it apart. It would be a shame for this, my first and only child, to which I am both father and mother. Haven't once lost sight of the rule that truth is the duty of the history writer and that when it is missing, the writing has no value. Here is truth! It is not missing from my child. And so I hope to be consoled that it will have some value. (*KSK* II: 57)

Her reference to these memoirs as both the "representation" of her self and as her "only child" attests to her consciousness of the role her writing would perform for her after her death. She envisions it as both a testimony of how she performed as an artist and lived as a person, and as a substitute for the biological offspring, whom she had been unable to produce, and who would have otherwise carried on her memory.

Moreover, her insistence here on the "truth" value of her recollections—and this is but one of a series of such statements sprinkled throughout the text—functions not only to (self-)authorize her representation of history, but also aims to persuade her reader that these memoirs provide direct and unmediated access to the "truth" of her subjectivity. Schulze-Kummerfeld presents her life as the journey of a coherent and above all consistent "self" whose inner and outer contours can be truthfully described, delineated, and contained on the written page. Her attempt to reconstruct her "self" in this manner corresponds with the ideological demand for a transparency of being. Such a move can be read as an attempt to fend off suspicions of a theatricalized presentation of self—suspicions that would all too easily attach to her, as a professional actress. Hence, her memoirs insist both upon their own transparency and honesty ("Here is truth!") and upon the consistency and integrity of the life they document.

At the same time, despite her claims to the "truthfulness" of her account, the act of writing her autobiography already implicates Schulze-Kummerfeld in a performance of identity.[21] In fact, the quotation above acknowledges that her text is a representation: she explicitly frames it as a substitute performance compelled into existence by the ephemeral nature of theatrical performance. Likewise (as discussed in greater detail below), her description in the memoirs of repeated attempts to manipulate how others perceived her raises the suspicion that she was involved in performing herself in her daily life to a greater extent than she seems willing to admit. In other words, both the truth claims of her memoirs and her own claims to subjective integrity and transparency are belied by the necessity to make those claims visible and knowable to her reader and public. That Schulze-Kummerfeld seems caught in the act of performing an identity she wishes to present as natural and "the truth" is not surprising in light of the fact that, as Nussbaum notes, "eighteenth-century women who represent their subjectivity were . . . caught in mimicking the dominant ideologies of themselves" (133). Molded by such pressures toward mimicry, Schulze-Kummerfeld's memoirs bear witness to her need to negotiate her status as an outsider within and against dominant ideology (and within and against its image of "the actress"). Nussbaum observes that, for women writing autobiography in the eighteenth century, "the key to real character is the construction of a secret interiority . . . .[I]t becomes increasingly important for women to produce a private subjectivity that corresponds to public perceptions of character . . . ." (152). But for Schulze-Kummerfeld, the problem seems to be reversed. She describes herself as compelled to produce and perform a *public* character that corresponds to what she claims is her "real" *private* interiority.

That interiority bears the key marks of the antitheatrical subject. Two characteristics are central to Schulze-Kummerfeld's construction of herself: her absolute honesty and the fact that she cannot do or feel anything halfway. Both of these "facts" about her self come up repeatedly throughout the memoirs as fixed and unchanging features of her identity. The first of these embraces both an inability to lie and an essential honesty in her presentation of self. Early on, she explains that, even as a child, "I hated nothing more than lies. And because of this, because I always told the truth and never committed a naughty act twice, I never received a blow from either father or mother" (*KSK* I: 7). In addition, despite the fact that she was a professional actress, she insists that she did not—indeed could not—represent herself falsely in real life. This comes up repeatedly in the course of her memoirs, often as a direct address to her reader:

> Show me the person of rank or the humble person who can say: I crawled before them or flattered them. If I liked a person, I told them, and if I couldn't stand a person—and in that case it was probably his fault—I would certainly say nothing to him, that might have flattered him. And where I could, I would certainly avoid him, in order not to have to lie a single false politeness to him. (*KSK* I: 134)

The second key feature of Schulze-Kummerfeld's "self" as she fashions it in her memoirs is closely related to the first: the fact that she does and feels everything in life *ganz* ("totally" or "wholly"). Benezé writes that Schulze-Kummerfeld

> had, from early childhood, perceived the events around her with the liveliest feeling, penetrated them with her whole soul and made them her own. . . . above all she let no one, neither her mother, nor husband, nor

> friends, discourage her from being wholly all that she was. No one was more hateful to her than a soulless, wooden, mechanical person. (*KSK* I: xiii)

Schulze-Kummerfeld depicts herself as a person who gave full reign to the expression of her inner passions. She threw herself wholly into her art and into life, and this was not only a trait that she was proud of possessing herself, but also one she looked for in others. Her highest praise for a person she admired was that they, too, were *ganz*.

Thus, in her characterization of herself, Schulze-Kummerfeld demonstrates how she conceived of human subjectivity in general: she sought in herself and in others a full, direct, and true expression of the inner being. Her description of her many close bourgeois friends reflects this expectation and reveals the extent to which she internalized the concept of an antitheatrical subjectivity. Her relationships with her friends are deeply intimate and involve honesty, forthrightness, and a great deal of sharing of the "inner self."[22] An illustrative example here is her close friendship with Friederike Günther-Fleischer. Schulze-Kummerfeld recalls a reunion with her friend after an eight-year separation, shortly after she had ended her relationship with Dalwig, her aristocratic lover. She claims:

> My friend's eye saw deep into my heart. Once when I was alone with her, the good soul said to me: "Child, when I see you dancing in the theater or playing a merry role, you are a completely different creature than you are when you are with me or in company. When you are with me I see you only as a Sara, Lindane, or Pamela; all your merriness is forced. Often I suffer greatly with you, when I see how much effort you put into keeping it from being noticed and affecting our happiness. (*KSK* I: 168)

Not only can Friederike see that her friend is putting on a mask of happiness in order to hide her "true feelings," but she also virtually hits the nail on the head by comparing her to romantic heroines like Sara and Pamela—she sees that her friend's suffering results from a doomed romance.[23] In response to Friederike's offer of help, Schulze-Kummerfeld reports, "I poured my heart completely into the loyal bosom of my friend. She shared my pain with her own; and I owed my peace to her tender solicitude and her assiduous efforts" (*KSK* I: 169)

While such a scene plainly depicts the transparent and open nature Schulze-Kummerfeld wishes to claim for herself in her memoirs, what is particularly remarkable about this incident is how rare it is. Despite her repeated claims about her own honesty, consistency, integrity, and openness, this is one of the very few places in her memoirs Schulze-Kummerfeld depicts herself as having unreservedly shared her inner self without regard to how she might be perceived by her audience. Honesty, transparency, and openness are here shown to be audience-dependent: she only really shares herself unreservedly with a close, trusted friend.

Thus, although it is clear from Schulze-Kummerfeld's memoirs that she conceives of her "self" in antitheatrical terms—she claims that she does not lie about her feelings or thoughts; she presents herself honestly to the world; and what she feels or thinks, she expresses wholly—she also seems continuously aware of the presence of the *Publikum*, both as observer of her life actions at the time they occurred and as reader of her memoirs.[24] This duality is vividly illustrated in her description of her introduction to Hamburg society:

> Then Herr Ackermann led some Hamburg citizens to me and wanted to introduce them to me. But they were all received very coldly by me; for I couldn't help myself, I couldn't lie about my feelings, and all of them had the fortune or misfortune, however they wanted to take it, to displease me to the bottom of my heart. (*KSK* I: 193)

What Schulze-Kummerfeld claims to have detested about Hamburg was the political nature of life there. She describes it as a city ruled by economic relations: wealthy people were respected whether they were good or not, and the poor were treated rudely regardless of their inner virtue. In her memoirs, the citizens of Hamburg emerge as quintessential hypocrites, forever suspecting *her* of dissimulation while practicing it themselves. Thus, on the one hand, her refusal to be politic with the citizens of Hamburg can be interpreted as an extreme manifestation of the bourgeois imperatives of honesty, sincerity, authenticity, and transparency: she refuses to "perform" politeness to people she finds hypocritical and rude. At the same time her coldness clearly signals—and is clearly intended to signal—her disdain. In other words, she is fully aware of the performative effects of her refusal to perform, of the extent to which her feelings—as manifested in her behavior—will be interpreted and read by the "audience" to whom it is directed (e.g., the citizens).

In the context of her memoirs, Schulze-Kummerfeld's cognizance of this performative dimension of her identity paradoxically calls attention to the constructedness of this "self" that she desires to present to her reader as "the truth." While on the one hand, Schulze-Kummerfeld is interested in "declaring a 'self' that matches hegemonic ideologies about the individual in culture," on the other hand, her memoirs reveal the impossibility of such a project, for the life she relates is one that, in her "honest" appraisal and recollection of it, had to be perpetually performed (Nussbaum 6). Schulze-Kummerfeld demonstrates repeatedly that she knew precisely how she wanted herself to be seen in the public eye at all times in her life and made every effort to ensure she succeeded. As a result, these memoirs destabilize the illusion that they present the "truth" of her subjectivity; at the same time, they serve as both record and instance of the contradictions she faced in "being" the woman she believed (or imagined) herself to be.

Schulze-Kummerfeld's alertness to the performative dimension of her "self," and her skill in manipulating it, derive in large part from the fact that she led an extraordinarily *public* existence for a woman of her day. As she recounts it, everything she does, every move she makes, every visit she receives is scrutinized and judged by her public, and she is constantly aware of and on guard against anything that might open her to criticism or taint her reputation. For example, she points to the particular challenges of visiting university towns (where there were a lot of single young men):

> Anyone who knows what it means to play at a university like the one in Göttingen, where there had been no theater for such a long time . . . will know that it demands intelligence and talent to play one's role both in the theater and as oneself, and rather suffer rebuke as an actress than as a good bourgeois woman *(Bürgerin)*. (*KSK* I: 183)

The passage goes on to describe the strategies she employed to maintain her reputation, including always walking in the company of her brother and refusing to accept visitors. Examples like this show that at times she felt quite keenly the necessity of consciously playing and policing her "self" as a means of countering popular expectations. Moreover, she also recognized that such policing risked sacrificing the acclaim due to her as an actress (the implication being that, by withholding her attention from her admirers, she risked alienating them from her on-stage performances).[25] In other words, Schulze-Kummerfeld found herself compelled to perform her "self" in such a way as to maintain a delicate balance between her "self" as commodity (as alluring stage presence) and the "self" she claimed as her interiority (as virtuous woman).

Unlike Rousseau's imagined Ideal Woman, who had no place in the public sphere, and hence no (morally justifiable) reason to put her virtue on theatrical display, Schulze-Kummerfeld's status as an actress put her in the awkward and difficult position of having to do precisely what the virtuous woman was not supposed to have to do: to perform the innocence and naiveté that was not supposed to be performable.[26] Negotiating the public sphere as an actress required keen self-observation and a savvy knowledge of how her behavior and actions in both the public and private realm might be interpreted by her "audience"—the very antithesis of the naiveté she wished to project. Reading Schulze-Kummerfeld's memoirs is thus something akin to entering a house of mirrors. On the one hand, her mobilization of performance comes across as a justifiable—and wholly sincere—attempt not to deceive her public, but to ensure that the image of herself proliferating in the public arena honestly matched who she felt she "was." Yet, on the other, it seems hard to escape the impression that she was having the last word in writing for herself the role she wanted to be perceived as playing, and that the honest, natural self was nothing more than a construction on her part. But if we look at the dilemma from Schulze-Kummerfeld's point of view—a position that is hard to avoid, given that these are her memoirs—the problem was not that she might produce a performance of subjectivity that did not match her inner feelings and motives, but rather that she was in constant danger of having her actions misread by a public eager to attribute to her all of the vices associated with the actress. As a result, one of the major objectives of these memoirs—the "performance of her lifetime"—is to recuperate the actress as a virtuous woman and to recast the public woman as one who struggles not to remain virtuous but rather to maintain her reputation as a virtuous woman without making visible the effort and craft this requires.[27] In other words, Schulze-Kummerfeld's memoirs document her ongoing effort—culminating in the memoirs themselves—to produce a performance of virtuous womanhood that erased all signs of its own performative dimension.

It is also clear from the text that a strong impetus behind the writing of these memoirs was Schulze-Kummerfeld's desire to retroactively control the public's image of her career as an actress and artist. We should recall here that her letter to Nicolai asking him to publish the memoirs is quite explicit about their purpose as a recuperation of her career. So, for example, in her memoirs she recalls the publishing of a highly flattering poem written by Daniel Schiebeler, which, because it set her on a pedestal as a "priestess of virtue," threatened to cast the taint of immodesty and vanity on her. What is striking is that, although Schulze-Kummerfeld attempted to have the poem suppressed at the time it was written, she copies it in full in her memoirs, along with several other poems written in praise of her during the same era. In other words, she takes full advantage of the opportunity these poems present to create the version of her "self" that she wants remembered after her death. It must be remembered that these memoirs were written at a time of her life when she was considered a has-been, and that one of her chief aims in putting pen to paper was to prove that she was, indeed, once highly acclaimed as an actress, even if that praise was damaging to her reputation at the time.

There are several other places in the memoirs where she very deliberately and consciously answers her contemporary critics and claims the fame she feels she deserves. For example, she describes how, when she first joined Ackermann's troupe, she was put in the awkward position of playing the role of Iphigenie, which she had never played or seen performed before. As a result, she made a very weak impression on the audience. But when she was finally allowed to play a role she knew, she was a smashing success:

> The applause, which rang out from every corner, was immense. And because I had achieved at my age what could only be demanded of the oldest and most experienced of actors, people said: "Yes, she played very well today; but that is because she has adopted our tone." . . . Actually I owe my theatrical development to no one but myself, my diligence, and the good principles of my father. Who could have taught me? . . . I do not believe that either before or after me there was ever an actress who suffered more persecution or who was more oppressed than I. And I myself admit that it is a miracle that I became what I was. (*KSK* I: 109)

Here, she not only offers "proof" that she had been a talented and beloved performer in her day, but she also creates an image of herself as a "self-made" woman, which resonates both with her own sense of independence and self-worth and with her knowledge of the extent to which she perpetually created her "self" in the public sphere.

* * *

ROMANTIC PUBLICITY: THE ACTRESS'S BENEFIT AND BURDEN

One of the most intriguing aspects of Schulze-Kummerfeld's memoirs is the way in which her (re)construction of her life is mediated by her consciousness of her position as an actress, with all of the associations the eighteenth century brought to bear on that profession. Her memoirs both undermine and exploit contemporary assumptions about actresses. The text is marked, on the one hand, by a powerful description of the hard work and sacrifices involved in her profession, and, on the other hand, by highly romanticized, perhaps even fictionalized, accounts of a glamorous, independent, and heady existence. Her self-representation hovers at the intersection of her desire to respond to publicly circulating images of the actress's life (as depicted in novels and newspapers), the "reality" of her life as she remembers it, her recollections of her own deliberate performance of that life, and the imperatives of the current performance—the memoirs themselves—to leave behind a positive (and perhaps nostalgically distorted) image of that life.

Schulze-Kummerfeld vividly depicts the extreme hardship of the life of an actress. Although she enjoyed a modicum of success in her youth, Schulze-Kummerfeld was never a star, and, in many ways, she was typical of an actress of her day. Her memoirs reveal a great deal about the conditions of life for women working in the theater. She worked incredibly hard for very low wages and was constantly on the edge of financial ruin. Audiences had a huge appetite for novelty, and, as a result, performers were required to learn an astonishing number of new roles each year. Schulze-Kummerfeld relates with a mixture of pride and complaint that in the year 1783 the Linz company put on two-hundred performances. "I appeared one hundred twenty times, not counting the ballet. I had 63 roles, 39 of which were newly learned" (*KSK* II: 121).[28] She was required not only to act, but also to sing and dance, and she describes several occasions in which she was forced to dance with an injury or perform while extremely ill (*KSK* I: 171, I: 210). Women with children faced additional difficulties in their careers: Schulze-Kummerfeld relates that her mother was required to perform the evening after her infant died and that another actress had to dance in the advanced stages of pregnancy (*KSK* I: 25, I: 208). In addition, she was constantly in transit, exposed not only to the dangers of the weather and the poor road conditions, but also to predatory men (*KSK* I: 91). The stress of constant work and travel and the lack of a stable home or finances took a toll on her physical and mental health, and her memoirs foreground the extent to which the labor of acting and the lifestyle associated with it were an exhausting drain on the spirit.[29]

From a very young age Schulze-Kummerfeld understood all too well both the stereotypes under which she labored as an actress and the pressures that threatened her virtue and reputation. The image of the promiscuous actress prevailed throughout the century, and audiences frequently made a connection between an actress's on-stage performance and her off-stage behavior, and vice versa.[30] There were, of course, enough actresses who filled the stereotype to lend it weight, and Schulze-Kummerfeld even gives anecdotal evidence of an actress in her own troupe whose illicit affair not only tainted the company's reputation but also engendered a boycott from their audience. Although like many other young actresses of her era (including Charlotte and Dorothea Ackermann), Schulze-Kummerfeld (claims she) adhered to very strict moral standards, she was empathetic to how hard it was for an actress to resist temptation because of her heavy exposure to passion and love on stage. She insists "that no woman in the world has more merit, when she remains completely virtuous, than a woman in the theater. Before she even knows a difference, that there is another sex besides hers, she is taught about love and hears sweet nothings prattled about" (*KSK* I: 60).

Because of such widely held prejudices against actresses, Schulze-Kummerfeld was extremely vulnerable to the public's view of her and had to be constantly on guard against even the faintest appearance of impropriety on her part. Not only did she have to take care to preserve her own virtue and morality, but she was also held responsible for that of her admirers. A recurring theme in her narrative is her need to forestall potential criticism against herself for the extreme and romantic behavior of male fans who fall in love with her. One young man ran away from home out of infatuation for her; two others attempted suicide. In all three cases, Schulze-Kummerfeld describes herself as hard pressed to defend *her* virtue, even though she (claims she) did nothing to encourage her fans in their obsession with her.

One of these cases is also noteworthy because of the way Schulze-Kummerfeld remembers responding to it, and it is worth spelling out at length (*KSK* I: 201–07). A friend of her brother in Hamburg, a man named Soltau, falls in love with her and makes public that he is planning to convert to Catholicism (her faith). Instantly understanding that the public will blame her for this and claim that she had "seduced" him, Schulze-Kummerfeld forbids Soltau entrance into her house. Soltau tries to drown himself, and Schulze-Kummerfeld is immediately the subject of scandal—rumor spreads that she had even been corresponding with Soltau in secret code. Instead of quietly allowing the scandal to run its course, however, Schulze-Kummerfeld writes a testimony that she has read aloud and archived in the city council. Her statement reads, in part,

> I am still capable of providing for myself in a difficult but virtuous manner. I am under no curses, I live out my days happily in myself. And

> I should want to forfeit this happiness for a young man? *I, who praise virtue and punish vice on the stage, I should believe otherwise than I wish to teach others? Cursed be the thought, that I could be the seductress of a young man!* (*KSK* I: 207, emphasis added)

Because she is an actress, and because she is daily on public display, the only way to "be" the moral woman that she claims she "is" is to publicize her morality and make visible and knowable to the public that she is a virtuous woman. That she has this statement recorded in the city hall marks the extent to which she felt her reputation threatened. But even more interesting here is the way that she calls upon her profession to defend her: in response to the public's stereotyping her as an immoral actress, she maintains that, as an actress, she considers it to be her moral duty to be what she portrays, to live up to the image which she projects on the stage. Schulze-Kummerfeld takes the moral mission the theatrical reformers staked out for the theater quite seriously and cherishes and perpetuates an image of herself as a teacher, practitioner, and preacher of virtue both on and off the stage.

This is even more vividly demonstrated by yet another incident involving one of her fans. A boy who is infatuated with her rebels against his father and tries to run away from home to become an actor. Schulze-Kummerfeld goes to the family's house and confronts the young man in the presence of his father and mother. She preaches to the boy, enumerating to him his duties to his parents, and then turns to his father, a pastor, and admonishes *him* for having prejudged *her*:

> Just think, if your son had attached himself to a frivolous girl! Happy are the parents whose child's first love lights upon a respectable object! You had probably already damned me in your hearts, cursed me, when you should have blessed me! . . . You see, one should never be hasty in judgment. Learn from this, good father, that every station has its upright, honorable people, that one must look not at the station, but at the person himself. (*KSK* I: 247)

Although on the one hand, her profession brings her under suspicion and makes her vulnerable to attack, on the other, it also enables her to counter her critics by allowing her to take on the moral authority of the theater's mission, which aimed at disseminating and reinforcing bourgeois values such as the idea that a person should be judged by who they are and not what they appear to be. She feels so empowered by her calling as an actress that she even dares to preach to a preacher—who, she then pointedly boasts, praised her little sermon as the best lesson he had heard in forty-five years of service to the church.

Ironically, however, publicizing her morality and virtue opened her to a very different challenge to her public reputation: the suspicion that she might think *too* highly of herself. For example, Schulze-Kummerfeld claims she tried to have the above-mentioned Schiebeler poem suppressed because "people might think I had a high opinion of myself, made myself vain or proud" (*KSK* I: 196). But, despite her wishes, the poem was eventually published, and, in retaliation for what they felt was exaggerated praise, her rivals mounted a vitriolic attack that eventually drove her out of Hamburg. In this case, Schulze-Kummerfeld demonstrates that, even as a young woman, she possessed a profound sensitivity to the myriad ways in which her conduct and being could be (mis)interpreted in the public arena, grasping instantly that praise could be as damaging to her public image as criticism, especially when the image she wanted to put forward was that of her essential modesty: "What help was my modesty, which, as true as God is God, was not affected? This ode provoked the most bitter trouble" (*KSK* I: 197). She rings a similar bell in her letter to Nicolai when she claims: "I did not belong among the swaggerers. The more I was praised, the more I was indispensable: the more I was humble. I always pulled myself back into my little house like a snail" ("Letter to Nicolai"). Despite—or perhaps because of—her commitment to bourgeois ideas of virtuous femininity, Schulze-Kummerfeld reveals here that she was anything but naive: she shows all too sophisticated a knowledge of how she appeared to others and how her appearance could be manipulated to create an impression contrary to how she wanted to be perceived.

The descriptions of her "troubles" with her fans also have another function within the memoirs: they create and confirm the image of the young Schulze-Kummerfeld as an attractive and alluring celebrity. Thus, while on the one hand her memoirs work to counter the stereotype of the actress by giving the lie to the image of carefree pleasure and loose morals among actors in fiction, on the other hand they also exploit those fictional stereotypes by calling attention to the many social and emotional benefits of the profession. Fictional accounts of actresses during the period tended to ignore the physical conditions of labor in favor of looking at the advantages that accrued to actresses: that is, their independence and freedom to lead a glamorous and exciting life off the stage. In his detailed comparison of Schulze-Kummerfeld's memoirs to Goethe's portrait of the actress in *Wilhelm Meister*, Walter Wetzels points out how starkly that fiction clashed with reality, in particular Goethe's glamorization of the work involved in performing on a daily basis. But even though Schulze-Kummerfeld found life as an actress extremely difficult and claimed that her "pet project" was "to lead a peaceful life, far from the stage," her memoirs also corroborate the image of the actress' life as a whirlwind of romance and adventure (*KSK* II: 121).

Schulze-Kummerfeld narrates a young adulthood filled with parties, love affairs, and encounters with the rich and famous. Because of her status as a performer, she was frequently on the guest lists to glittering all-night balls thrown by the local aristocracy, and she counts among her "friends" the Duchess of Weimar and the Margravine of Karlsruhe. On several occasions, she is literally the center of public attention. Her description of her last appearance on the Leipzig stage before her marriage strikingly evokes both the extreme publicity of her private life and the extent to which her profession connected her emotionally and psychologically with a public social sphere. For her finale, she danced a ballet with her brother, Karl. The house was packed.

> As my brother and I approached the end of the "Minor" in the Finale, I stood still and indicated through pantomime that I would now cease to dance with him. My brother expressed his loss through a melancholic stance. I stepped forward, bowed to the pit, the boxes, and the balcony. My look said what I was feeling, tears, which rushed violently from my eyes, said more, much more, than words ever could. . . . As I took my silent leave, my brother stood there as if beside himself, threw his arms around me, and kissed me. Everyone cried aloud, there wasn't a dry eye in the house. People called out, they clapped their hands and

> shouted: "Vivat, live well, be happy, thank you! Thank you!" A leavetaking such as this had probably never been experienced before. (*KSK* I: 281)

It is remarkable that what in many ways was a very private decision and private loss—her decision to give up the theater and get married—becomes the occasion for a public performance of emotion in which her authentic feelings of loss and regret, mediated through pantomime and dance, are read and interpreted by the audience, and intended to be read and interpreted by the reader of the memoirs, as an authentic, unmediated expression of her state of being. Although Schulze-Kummerfeld is describing a performance here, it is evident that that performance is meant to stand in for and transparently convey how she "really felt." Where in other places in her memoirs she intimates that she consciously performed her self for her public, here she presents the performance as having an involuntary, "natural" quality. And yet the melodrama in her description is inescapable: the romanticization of this event cannot help but raise the suspicion that what she has recast as a natural, organic upwelling of emotion in herself and in the audience might have its roots in the world of fiction.

Such a nostalgic revision of her life as an actress (if it is indeed a revision) may be attributable to the fact that she first began writing her memoirs shortly after her husband's death, and it is possible that, in (re)constructing her life, she attempted to recapture a heady existence that she felt she had sacrificed to the tedium of marriage. Yet, here and elsewhere in her autobiography, there seems to be a half-conscious fictional borrowing from literature and drama that performs an important function in her self-representation: namely, it serves the purpose of locating her "self" within a discursive production of ideal womanhood. We see this most vividly illustrated in her narration of the love affair she had when she was just a child of twelve. She claims that she had been pursued by a young soldier named Count Nostitz, who pleaded with her in secret love letters to run off with him. Although at the time she was too young to have any knowledge of sex or marriage, she nevertheless insisted that they be married. He finally agreed to marry her, but in secret, because he could not let the marriage become public until after his mother had died. Schulze-Kummerfeld writes that she was on the verge of joining him for the secret ceremony when, one night, tossing and turning in bed, it occurred to her that the ceremony could be a sham. She tells us what she imagined:

> Have you ever seen a wedding ceremony? No! You're going to be married by a Lutheran priest and not a Catholic one? Do you know how to identify them? . . . My God, what if it's a disguised servant, you don't know all the Count's people—then instead of being his wife, you'd be his mistress! (*KSK* I: 71)

This thought, she claims, jolted her into reality, and, the moment she arose the next morning she sent word to the count that she would not elope with him.

Two things are remarkable about this early affair. First, the scene she recalls having imagined to herself is virtually identical to the sham marriage depicted in *The History of Lady von Sternheim*, which appeared a decade before Schulze-Kummerfeld began writing her memoirs.[31] The similarity between the two scenes points to the ways in which Schulze-Kummerfeld's self-representation is mediated by popular fictional representations of female virtue under attack and raises the question of the extent to which, in this final performance, Schulze-Kummerfeld has retroactively cast herself as a Pamela or a Sophie. Such a move—whether conscious or not—would be consistent with her desire, evident throughout the memoirs, to align and identify herself with images of virtuous bourgeois womanhood and contradict the stereotype of the actress as a loose woman.[32] The depiction of such a glamorous, tormented relationship thus gestures to her internalization of, and accommodation to, bourgeois expectations of the virtuous woman, while at the same time highlighting the extreme and precarious circumstances under which she struggled to maintain her virtue.[33]

But second, and even more crucially, her narration of this romantic adventure demonstrates that, as an actress, her life and her understanding of herself were profoundly different from that of the imagined domestic bourgeois woman who was both subject and object of the sentimental fiction from which her memoirs seem to draw. What is truly remarkable is that Schulze-Kummerfeld claims to have been able to imagine to herself as a very young girl the act of *Verstellung* that the "sham marriage" would involve, and she claims that her ability to recognize that reality could be performed in such a way "saved" her. What sets her apart from the Sophies and Clarissas of the world of romance fiction is her astute awareness of performance both on and off the stage.

Putting aside the issue of whether or not Schulze-Kummerfeld actually *had* this epiphanic revelation about the marriage, what is relevant here is her depiction of herself as one who simultaneously embraced the idea of an antitheatrical subjectivity—in her understanding of herself as "honest" and "*ganz*"—and rejected it as a reliable means of ensuring the proper interpretation of that self by her own audience *and* as a means of decoding and reading the behavior of others.[34] In many ways, Schulze-Kummerfeld seems to occupy a complex and paradoxical position vis-à-vis the demands for an honest representation of self, and this position can be linked to her understanding of the art of acting. As an actress, Schulze-Kummerfeld belonged to a generation of players who practiced a highly stylized, aestheticized form of acting: she saw her task as a performer to put her artistry and skill on display. Such an attitude was at odds with later theatrical trends toward illusionism, which aimed to erase the signs of its artificiality. But Schulze-Kummerfeld conceived of performance—both on and off the stage—in terms of *image* and *effect*, and, in her off-stage performances, was perpetually concerned with creating a performance that most perfectly expressed her inner self. In her memoirs, she does not seem to conceive of the outward self as a naturally homologous outgrowth or expression of her inner life, but rather as an image that must be voluntarily produced.

Imagining her self in terms of an image that must be produced clearly stands in opposition to the ideological construction of ideal womanhood in terms of antitheatricality, naiveté, and transparent, "natural" virtuousness. But the imagined Ideal Woman was not only supposed to be naive, she was also expected to remain within the private sphere; in fact, according to theorists like Rousseau, woman undermined any claims to naiveté—which was her "natural state"—the moment she stepped into the public arena.[35] Schulze-Kummerfeld's status as a public woman, as an actress, catapults her into the middle of the contradiction such a demand posed for women. On the one hand, her memoirs document a deep inner subjectivity and a real concern for consistency and integrity of self along the antitheatrical model. Yet, on the other hand, she is obsessively concerned with managing and manipulating her appearance and reputation in public, because it is not sufficient for her, as a woman and as an actress, to merely *be* virtuous; she must also put her "self" on display and perform it in such a way that there can be no mistake about who she is. At the same time, the publicity of her life, and the fact that she practiced deception professionally, rendered her suspect to the very accusations of theatricality and performativity that she labored so strenuously to forestall.

* * *

MARRIAGE AS A "FIELD OF SORROW" ("KUMMERFELD")

Up to this point, I have focused on Schulze-Kummerfeld's (actual and textual) performance of her life as an actress, and her struggle to align herself with discursive productions of Ideal Womanhood from the position of a public woman. But a large section of her memoirs documents her experience of bourgeois domestic life from within, during the ten-year period of her marriage to Wilhelm Kummerfeld. Where as an actress Schulze-Kummerfeld represents herself as a confident woman who "knew" who she was, the language she uses to represent her marriage intimates that she experienced it as an annihilation of identity.[36] Although her marriage brought her the legitimacy and financial security she had yearned for all her life, the price she paid for these—her freedom, independence, mobility, and self-knowledge—appears steep. In sharp contrast to the "self" that emerges in the first part of her memoirs, the portrait of the married woman is marked primarily by an inability to define who she "was" as a bourgeois wife. The following discussion of Schulze-Kummerfeld's description of herself as a married woman will help to highlight the profound disjuncture between the discursive constructions of bourgeois feminine identity that Schulze-Kummerfeld seems to have taken as her model and her lived (or recollected) experience of trying to conform to that model.[37]

Even though Schulze-Kummerfeld categorically refuses to condemn or regret her decision to get married, the picture she paints of her life in matrimony makes clear that it was a grim and monotonous existence, in particular in comparison to her life as an actress. From the moment of her return to Hamburg Schulze-Kummerfeld is exposed to the dark side of bourgeois domesticity in the claustrophobic and tense atmosphere of the Kummerfeld family home. Although Kummerfeld's family is coolly polite toward her, they barely conceal their displeasure and resentment that he has chosen to marry an actress. The family's emotional distress manifests itself in several uncomfortable moments for Schulze-Kummerfeld, culminating in a fight at the dinner table that Schulze-Kummerfeld must quell: "It had almost reached the point where they called each other scoundrels and threw bottles and plates at each other's heads" ("HM" 536). While the tension seems to be occasioned by Kummerfeld's choice of an actress for a bride, in fact, as Schulze-Kummerfeld later learns, this supposedly proper bourgeois family conceals quite a bit of domestic violence behind its public face of harmony and contentment.

Schulze-Kummerfeld is not only made uncomfortable by the tense family atmosphere, she also chafes under the restrictions and rituals surrounding the wedding. Because of a delay in the arrival of her luggage, she is kept from venturing out in public for the first week and forced to stay in with Kummerfeld's family. When she finally is allowed to go out, it is under highly ritualized conditions that she finds extremely unpleasant:

> Meanwhile I do not deny that all the formal visits had become noxious to me. I knew no one closely. When I would be introduced with all imaginable ceremony into a new house, there would be two large armchairs at the head of the room. No old worthy matron or gentleman was allowed to sit there. No, those were for the bridal couple. How often did I murmur in Wilhelm's ear: "The devil's got another pair of those chairs again!" And when you think about it: Today you sit at the head, and the day after your wedding as the youngest woman you'll be at the bottom—that did not fit with my way of thinking. I, who would rather rise than

> fall, or even happily remain in a certain middle place, where you neither rise nor fall. (*KSK* II: 5)

Schulze-Kummerfeld indicates here that her imminent marriage to Kummerfeld entailed the loss of status as an individual in society that she had always held as an actress, however tenuously. Where in her former life she had been a quasi-public person with the freedom to form real friendships according to her likes and dislikes, with marriage she becomes constrained by sets of rituals that assure her place among bourgeois society as a representative of the family, and, instead of being placed according to her worth as a person (or according to her talent as an actress), she is placed according to a hierarchy of age and date of entrance into the family.[38]

For Schulze-Kummerfeld, the entrance into bourgeois domesticity seems to entail a profound cancellation of her identity: she recalls feeling as if she literally no longer knew who she was. On her wedding day, the Kummerfeld family is openly hostile toward her, and she sits alone at her own wedding reception while her new husband goes off to play cards. After the wedding party, as she rides silently home in the coach with Wilhelm, he asks her why she is so quiet. She replies, "What I am, I myself know not. Is it really so, or is it a mistake? Was I really married today or am I just playing in a comedy? God knows what's with me, I do not." Kummerfeld assures her, "No, it's no comedy, from today on you are my wife." She replies: "It doesn't seem so to me" (*KSK* II: 11). This is a remarkable moment in the text. Throughout her memoirs Schulze-Kummerfeld insists on the strength of her own sense of self, of knowing who she is and was and of having been wholly (*ganz*) what she was at all times. Shortly before her marriage to Kummerfeld, she repeats what is virtually her mantra: that she has always been "wholly daughter, wholly sister, wholly friend, wholly lover and must be able to be wholly wife" ("HM" 545). But her marriage clearly threw her into doubt about her identity, and, for the first time in these memoirs, she uses a theatrical metaphor to describe her "real life"—marriage makes her wonder if her life has just become nothing but a performance.

This is a telling indication of the extent to which her assumption of a new identity as a wife appeared to her as a role—as something apart and separate from herself, as something that she could never completely "be." Countering the notion that married bourgeois domesticity was the "natural" role for the eighteenth-century woman—and with it, the notion that women naturally belong and enjoy this role above all others, and would not experience it as a thing separate from "being" in general—Schulze-Kummerfeld shows us that, for a woman like herself, who possessed a sense of identity and independence, marriage was an institution that involved an erasure of one's "true self."[39] Even the process of signing her new name is traumatic: she writes that a year after her marriage she still had difficulty bringing herself to sign the name Kummerfeld to her letters because she could not imagine herself as anyone but Karoline Schulze ("HM" 574–76).

Her memoirs vividly convey the isolation and bewilderment she felt in her new existence. She depicts herself as completely dependent on her husband for praise, kindness, flattery—in short, for her sense of self-worth, and he changes almost overnight from an enchanted lover into a bored husband. He falls asleep when she reads love poems to him, he is irritated when she is attentive to his needs, he stops holding her coat and helping her into the coach, and he snaps at her for meeting him at the door. Baffled by his lack of esteem for her, she seems unable to find herself outside of his opinion:

> A girl, as I was, healthy, so extremely proper that it was an exaggeration, as my mother often called it. What is with him, what does he have against you? My youth, my warm blood! The feelings which nature gives us, they demand justice. How often I cried entire nights through! . . . Ask him? Complain? No, I couldn't do that. Is it really aversion, is it aversion? (*KSK* II: 14)

Interestingly, here again we see Schulze-Kummerfeld allude to a fictive representation of ideal femininity—yet in this instance it not only buttresses her own claims to bourgeois respectability but also at the same time complicates the relationship between dominant discursive productions of "femininity" and her own experience of her "proper role." Her reference above to "My youth, my warm blood!" is a direct and recognizable allusion to the penultimate scene of Lessing's *Emilia Galotti*, in which Emilia begs her father for death rather than be handed over to a man who will compromise her virtue.[40] In the play, Emilia's words, "I have blood, my father; blood that is as youthful and warm as anyone's," simultaneously point to her own sensuality—to the "natural" passions and desires that she must control and police in order to remain virtuous—and imply that such sensuality comprises woman's natural weakness. Emilia uses this "weakness" to justify her desire for death, arguing that she fears she will be unable to withstand the seductions of Grimaldi's "house of pleasures" (*Emilia Galotti* V: 7). Like Sara Sampson, Emilia is better off dead than compromised.

Schulze-Kummerfeld's allusion to this famous scene indicates her desire to identify herself with this bourgeois heroine, but the context in which she uses it—in which she implicitly mourns the *loss* of that natural, passionate nature that has disappeared with marriage—underscores both her previous sense of identity and the fact that she equates her sacrifice with that of Emilia. In other words, for Schulze-Kummerfeld, marriage itself seems to represent the death of her "self" and the loss of her identity. Gone from her writing is the vivacious, self-assured, assertive young woman of her acting days. Marriage turns her into a wretched recluse, driven to deception to keep up appearances. For the only time in her memoirs she admits to deceiving her friends: when she writes to them, she tells them how happy she is and secretly wipes up her tears with her handkerchief so that they do not stain the paper ("HM" 574). Tellingly, it is in her "natural role" as a wife that Schulze-Kummerfeld describes herself as driven to produce what she claims are her only false representations of self.

Concomitant with the erasure of her personal identity through her marriage into bourgeois domesticity comes the necessity for her to take on a role as representative of the family. Ironically, it is in the private domestic sphere (where Schulze-Kummerfeld—and her society—believed she should be most secure in her identity as a virtuous woman) that she feels she must deploy the most "false" representation of her "self." Schulze-Kummerfeld represents herself as shocked and dismayed by the hypocrisy she encounters in the behavior of the respectably bourgeois Kummerfeld family, and by their demands for her complicity in maintaining a facade to society. In short, the Kummerfeld family hides a very dirty secret: Wilhelm's brother-in-law, Abendroth, abuses his wife, Wilhelm's sister. Schulze-Kummerfeld discovers this in a most unpleasant manner. On her wedding night, she enters Wilhelm's bedroom expecting to consummate the marriage and finds him in tears, moaning that he is the unhappiest man in the world. She of course thinks that he has decided it was a mistake to marry her and is devastated for several dramatic minutes before he lets her in on the family scandal. Earlier, at the dinner table during the party, she had perceptively noted that

> Madame Abendroth was trying to hide the tears that filled her eyes. Nevertheless she slowly swallowed them into her stomach with a glass of wine mixed with water. Her husband looked at her a few times with a countenance that said a great deal, only nothing that would have been pleasant to hear aloud. She smiled at this, and it was a smile like that of a child who has been beaten bloody, and who is then commanded to kiss with a smile the rod which caused him so much pain. (*KSK* II: 10)

While this account of eighteenth-century domestic violence is of considerable historical interest—and would provide yet another reason why marriage might not have felt like the "right" or "natural" place for a woman—for the purposes of my argument what is most relevant here is the extent to which the family attempts to conceal what is clearly a scandalous situation behind a public mask of contentment and normality, even from their prospective daughter-in-law. Schulze-Kummerfeld is let in on the secret only after her marriage, and then also forced to collude in keeping it from becoming public. The situation is highly ironic. On one hand, Abendroth, the respectable bourgeois businessman, is welcomed heartily into the family circle, only to reveal his "true" abusive self—he is the kind of "actor" in the public sphere who is portrayed as so dangerous in novels and plays of the time, the *Versteller* who seduces and ruins young women. In this case, instead of compromising a single woman's virtue, he threatens an entire family's reputation. In response, the family rallies to protect both him and themselves by putting on a performance of happiness and peace in public that erupts into terrible fights in private. Thus the private family members are forced to violate their own personal integrity in order to maintain the integrity of the family as a public unit. On the other hand, Schulze-Kummerfeld, the actress, is received from the start with suspicion and resentment and never completely welcomed into the family, despite the fact that she is more concerned with preserving her personal integrity than any member of the family. The actress depicts herself as having internalized bourgeois values more fully and deeply than the bourgeois family she marries into, and, to a certain extent, her misery in her new station in life stems from her deep disillusionment with the reality of the outwardly bourgeois and their hypocrisy in judging people according to exterior behavior and at the expense of "who they are" as people on the "inside."

That Schulze-Kummerfeld experienced marriage as an erasure of her identity is also evidenced in the way in which her retrospective description of herself shifts when she describes moments of escape from the confines of bourgeois life. In her ten years of marriage, she managed precisely two journeys outside of Hamburg—a one-month trip to Weimar with her husband in 1773, and a short trip to Leipzig alone in the spring of 1776. Here again, the memoirs sharply foreground the contrast between her mobile and independent life as an actress and her seclusion and isolation as bourgeois wife: she must beg her husband to let her travel, and it becomes a rare event. In both instances she represents the journey out of Hamburg—and away from her restricted existence there—as a coming again to her old "self." On the trip to Weimar, she becomes suddenly quite active again in her own life, taking charge of the finances, itinerary, and routing of the trip, while the provincial Kummerfeld—who had never been further from Hamburg than Lübeck—seems to have merely come along for the ride. As evidence that traveling has revived the independent woman who knew "who she was," her old mantra suddenly reappears after being absent for several pages (and years) of narrative. When, just outside of Weimar, Wilhelm anxiously reproves her for being too excited about the imminent arrival of her brother, Schulze-Kummerfeld replies, "O leave me alone, darling! Let me be, what I am. Everything completely (*ganz*). What pitiful people are those in-betweeners, who can't feel anything!" (*KSK* II: 29).

Although Schulze-Kummerfeld finds such people pitiful, her constant referral to a loss of self—and the necessity to perform a false self—within her marriage gives the stark impression that as a domesticated bourgeois wife she, too, had become an "in-betweener, who can't feel anything." Remarkably, there are only two instances in her memoirs where she deploys theatrical metaphors to speak of her life, and these theatrical metaphors virtually bracket her narration of her marriage. The first instance has already been mentioned—on her wedding night she wonders if she is suddenly in a comedy. The second comes as she relates her discovery that her husband's insanity had led him to lend or give away his fortune. Had she known about his foolish lending, she claims, she would have played a different role as wife. She "would have played the role of Frau von Ehrlichsdorf in the comedy 'The Spendthrift' (*Der Verschwender*)" ("WM" 332–33). Although there is nothing unusual about the fact that Schulze-Kummerfeld wishes that she had acted differently during her marriage, the way in which she conceives it is noteworthy in the context of this study: had she "played" her marriage out of a comic script, it might not have had the tragic ending it did. The theatrical metaphors Schulze-Kummerfeld mobilizes only in the context of her married life suggest that, for at least one real woman of the eighteenth century, the privatized domesticity that was imagined to be the woman's "natural" state was not only nothing but a role to play, but the only role in which she was literally required to lose herself in order to succeed.

In these memoirs—the "performance of her lifetime"—Schulze-Kummerfeld brings into relief the contradictory subject position into which real women were interpellated by the ideology of a virtuous, naive, antitheatrical femininity imagined as "Sophie." As a public woman and an actress, Schulze-Kummerfeld reveals herself as always already suspect and demonstrates that she was constrained both to produce the naiveté and virtue that she claimed was her "real" inner state, and to police and manage the circulation and reception of the performances she produced in the public sphere. This puts her in the barely tenable position of having to perform the unperformable: to play the role of virtuous femininity that was, by definition, not a role that could be consciously or deliberately "played." Yet, paradoxically, it is in the context of her "natural" role as a privatized, domesticated bourgeois wife that Schulze-Kummerfeld's description of her life reveals the impossibility of her understanding of herself in terms of "let me be, what I am." She "is" nothing outside of her own self-fashioning, as her own sense of annihilation within the marriage so clearly reveals. Schulze-Kummerfeld's memoirs intimate, above all, the impossibility for the virtuous woman merely to "be." It is only in the public performance of her identity—on the street, on the stage, and, finally, in the pages of these memoirs—that Karoline Schulze-Kummerfeld can lay claim to and define what and who she "was."

4. Antitheatricality and the Public Woman

Marianne Ehrmann's *Amalie: A True Story in Letters*

Karoline Schulze-Kummerfeld's memoirs were never published in her lifetime. For a description of the life of an actress from the perspective of a woman who had worked as one, eighteenth-century readers of German had to turn to a fictional source. Marianne Ehrmann's *Amalie: A True Story in Letters* (*Amalie: eine wahre Geschichte in Briefen*, 1788) is a loosely autobiographical epistolary novel that portrays the trials and tribulations of a virtuous woman whose life circumstances catapult her out of the domestic sphere and into the public sphere—and, eventually, onto the stage—at a very young age. The novel's grounding in Ehrmann's own life trajectory might make the answer to the question of why she wrote about the theater and performance seem obvious: it contributes to the realism and veracity of her story. But, in fact, Ehrmann's engagement with the theater in this novel goes beyond simple verisimilitude, for it also opens up an opportunity for her to confront the discourse of antitheatricality that put public women like herself in an impossible position and to challenge the notion that virtuous women had no appropriate space or activity in the public sphere.

In *Amalie*, Ehrmann creates a model for ideal femininity that simultaneously embraces the association of ideal femininity with sincerity and antitheatricality and disconnects that sincerity from its discursive connection to female "nature" and "naiveté." *Amalie* proposes instead that the Ideal Woman is knowledgeable about both herself and the world, and that her proper behavior and activity stems from the kind of self-reflexivity and self-awareness that is generally precluded by true naiveté. At the same time, the novel reveals the impossibility of a woman simply "being" who she really "is" once she leaves the domestic sphere, as the mere fact of being in public puts her at the mercy of other people's interpretation of her. Like Schulze-Kummerfeld, Ehrmann shows that female subjectivity does not exist in a social vacuum: it must be correctly perceived by a social audience. The depiction of Amalie's difficulties in making her "true" self readable thus contradicts the novel's intention of presenting ideal femininity as an embodiment of sincere, antitheatrical being, as it—unwittingly, perhaps—also reveals ideal femininity as essentially a masquerade, as that which *must not* be performed and at the same time *cannot not* be performed.

* * *

MARIANNE EHRMANN AND THE "TRUE STORY" OF *AMALIE*

Marianne Ehrmann published her first novel, *Amalie*, in 1788, a few years after abandoning acting in favor of writing. The novel had been preceded by three other works: *Leisure Hours of a Gentlewoman* (*Müssige Stunden eines Frauenzimmers*, 1784), which contained eighteen letters that would later form the beginning of *Amalie*; *Philosophy of a Woman* (*Philosophie eines Weibs*, 1784), a highly successful, seventy-two-page booklet that engages with and offers a veiled critique of Rousseau's ideas about gender relations; and a play, *Frivolity and a Good Heart, or the Results of Education* (*Leichtsinn und Gutes Herz, oder die Folgen der Erziehung*, 1786).[1] In the year she published *Amalie*, Ehrmann also published two other novels and a short booklet entitled *Little Fragments for Women Thinkers* (*Kleine Fragmente für Denkerinnen*). She then moved into journal publishing, first as a contributor to her husband Theophil Ehrmann's *The Observer* (*Der Beobachter*), and then with her own women's periodical, which appeared first under the title *Amalie's Leisure Hours* (*Amaliens*

Erholungsstunden, 1790–92), and then, with a new publisher, as *The Woman Hermit from the Alps* (*Die Einsiedlerin aus den Alpen*, 1793–94).

Like many eighteenth-century women authors, Ehrmann published many of her works anonymously: her first text was published under an acronym for her stage name, "Nan. St**" (for "Sternheim"), and *Philosophy of a Woman* claims to have been written "by a female observer." But *Philosophy of a Woman* appears to have established her reputation as a writer, for several later works—including *Amalie*—are identified as penned "by the author of the *Philosophy of a Woman*." Helga Stipa Madland notes that Ehrmann seems to have "wanted connections made between her texts and her person," as she made a chain of references between each of her texts until, in the end, she abandoned anonymity altogether when she took on editor- and authorship of her periodicals (*Marianne Ehrmann* 26–27).

Amalie's popularity among eighteenth-century readers might be gauged by its republication, in 1795, under the title *Antonie von Warnstein*. Reviews of her novel in the eighteenth century were, however, mixed: where one critic praised its "subtlety of thought and ease of expression, unforced vitality, and jocular true emotion," another yearned for proof that it was "worth the effort to write down such common things" (reviews reprinted in Madland, *Marianne Ehrmann* 117–18). In her comprehensive study of the eighteenth-century women's novel, Christine Touaillon evidently agrees with the latter, dismissing Ehrmann's novel (which she identifies by the title of the reprint) as a work with "no literary significance" (228). Touaillon's assessment has some merit: the plot of *Amalie* is slow and uneven, the two main characters are hardly distinguishable from one another, and much of the novel (especially Fanny's responses to Amalie) consists of heavy moralizing. But while the novel is not particularly good literature, it does provide rich material for understanding how eighteenth-century women were engaging with prevalent ideas about gendered subjectivity, and, in particular, with the way in which theater and performance were used to frame, contain, and circumscribe femininity.

As its title indicates, *Amalie: a True Story in Letters* purports, like much epistolary fiction of the eighteenth century, to recount the "true" story of its protagonist. Amalie's life unfolds in a series of letters between herself and her best friend Fanny. The novel begins with the death of Amalie's mother, which has left her and her father and younger sister in a financially precarious situation. Amalie spends the first part of the novel fretting about her family's finances, traveling on business for her father, and relaying details of her minor romantic adventures and girlhood crushes to Fanny. Fanny's responses to Amalie's letters provide (usually moralizing) commentary on the events Amalie relates and also often predict their consequences. Thirty-nine letters into the novel, Amalie's father dies, leaving her to the care of a kindly uncle, a Catholic priest who has good will toward her but no means of supporting her himself. He sends her to work as housekeeper for another priest, who makes sexual advances toward her and generally creates misery for her; when this priest sends her away from his parish, her uncle boards her at a convent.

While there, she is courted by an officer she had met during a brief stay with a friend; she impetuously decides to marry him in order to be able to rescue her sister from being forced to take the veil by the greedy guardian who wants to take over her estate. But not only does the marriage fail to save the sister (who dies of fever brought on by despair before the officer can reach her), it is also disastrous for Amalie: in her haste, she has failed to protect herself financially in the marriage, and the officer turns out to be a gambler who loses everything at cards. He is also abusive and beats Amalie on several occasions, once even triggering a miscarriage.

Eventually, her uncle persuades her to separate from her husband; she once again boards at a convent for some time (where she starts an amateur theater among the female students), but, finding convent life intolerable, she embarks on a trip to Venice to visit relatives. After some time there, she learns that her husband has died and left her in debt. Returning to Germany, she tries to find work as a governess, but is repeatedly turned down, and so turns to the only other available option: the theater. She manages to get herself engaged with a theater troupe and spends the next several years working as an actress. Finally, after performing with several troupes in various cities, and after a couple of unlucky experiences with men, she meets the man of her dreams, and, at the end of the novel, she marries (although whether or not she remains an actress is left unstated).

The story told in *Amalie* coincides in much of its detail with Ehrmann's own biography: Ehrmann also was orphaned at a young age, lost her only sister shortly thereafter "at the cruel greedy hands of our guardian," worked briefly as a governess and housekeeper, married an officer who was abusive, alcoholic, and addicted to gambling, suffered a miscarriage (possibly as a result of her husband's abuse), was abandoned by him, tried to find work as a governess, and then turned to acting (Ehrmann, "Brief an Lavater" 525). She had a successful acting career (under the stage name "Mme. Sternheim") for several years (1779–ca. 1785), and, while still an actress, met and married Theophil Ehrmann, who—like Wilhelm, the man Amalie marries at the end of the novel—had to overcome his family's prejudices against actresses in order to marry her.[2] The strong link between Ehrmann's life history and the events she relates in the novel raises the methodological question of how to read and interpret the autobiographical strains within it. As Widmer points out, the novel does not so much tell us about Ehrmann's life as how she imagined female subjectivity: we should understand the use of biographical fact as a means by and through which Ehrmann creates an "image of woman that oscillates in suspension between the norm and individuality, between a feminine ideal and a mastery of life" (Widmer, "Amalie—eine wahre Geschichte?" 502).

At the same time, however, we cannot ignore the fact that the book's editorial apparatus encourages an autobiographical reading of the novel. In his prologue to the novel, Theophil Ehrmann insists that the novel presents "a fundamentally true history" (*Amalie* I: 5); in her epilogue, Ehrmann repeats the claim: "I can assure you of this much, my most valued friends: this little work of mine is a true story and not an idealized novel . . . It seems to me that one learns best how to study people, their hearts and their conduct from this completely comprehensible type of fate, and from similarly probable events, because they are not based on chimeras and ideals" (II: 246). While, on the one hand, such an insistence on the veracity of her story can be read as a common ploy of eighteenth-century fictions aspiring to realism, on the other, the fact that Ehrmann deliberately linked the novel to her autobiography through the title (her own nickname was Amalie, an identity she forged in print in *Leisure*

Hours of a Gentlewoman, her first work) begs for an acknowledgment that many of the events narrated in the novel did indeed happen (if not exactly in that form) to the novel's author.[3] Such a reading is important because, given the sympathy the novel engenders for the main character, the knowledge that the story presents experiences that were actually part of a woman's life—and in particular, that of the smart, thoughtful, and clearly virtuous author of *Philosophy of a Woman*, the work that established Ehrmann's reputation as an author—would have made the critique that it offers all the more potent and urgent to her contemporary readers.

Ehrmann's writings often present a contradictory mix of progressivism and accommodation. Across the board, her writings offer a steady, if not always consistent, critique of women's social position and of patriarchal double standards, and an equally steady and far more consistent argument for the importance of a proper education and upbringing for women. Nonetheless, as cultural critique, her writing displays an ambivalence typical of eighteenth-century women's writing. *Amalie* is no exception: it wavers between sharp and incisive condemnation of social inequities and a wholesale repetition of dominant ideas about "proper" class and gender roles.[4] Ruth Dawson identifies Ehrmann's work as protofeminist, a term signalling "the internal inconsistencies, gaps, and incompleteness of [her] feminist vision" (*The Contested Quill* 221). Eighteenth-century protofeminism, Dawson writes, "objected to oppression but not to subordination" and was characterized by a vacillation between submission and subversion, accommodation and critique (274).

What is particularly progressive about this novel is its insightful portrayal of the Catch-22 of women's lives: they are at the mercy of men (fathers, husbands, guardians, theater directors) whose deaths, financial errors, alcoholism, thievery, duplicity, et cetera can catapult them into poverty and destitution. In Amalie's story we see that even the most virtuous and chaste woman can find herself abandoned to her own resources in a world in which women's options for survival are limited to marriage, the convent, work as governess or actress, or prostitution—and Amalie is forced into each but the last. But because of her solid upbringing and her firm principles, Amalie remains virtuous throughout. As such, her story rebukes both those cultural commentators who insisted that female virtue and publicity were mutually exclusive and those who claimed that female virtue was innate, and only ruined by education.

At the same time, however, the novel replicates many dominant ideas about proper gender roles, chief among them that women's greatest happiness lay in marriage, and that it is a woman's duty to be obedient, patient, supportive, and subordinate to her husband. Such inconsistencies and contradictions can be frustrating to modern readers hoping for a more solidly feminist—or if nothing else, a more firmly occupied—position, but they stand as evidence of the complex subject position women writers occupied, and they speak to the difficulty of imagining oneself outside one's own discursive realm and social reality. Such inconsistencies are also evident when we read *Amalie* in light of Ehrmann's engagement with both the discourse of antitheatricality and her use of the theater as a site for engagement with prevailing ideas about women's place in the public sphere: accommodation, on the one hand; critique, on the other.

* * *

ANTITHEATRICALITY AND IDEAL FEMININITY IN *AMALIE*

At first glance, both Amalie and Fanny appear to be quintessentially virtuous, antitheatrical women. They condemn performance in others; they are honest, forthright, chaste, and obedient; and both want nothing more from life than a happy, peaceful domestic marriage. In conformity with late eighteenth-century notions of subjective transparency, the two women not only share their thoughts and feelings in full in their respective letters, but they also perceive themselves as so open and utterly knowable to each other that they could be the same person. Amalie writes to Fanny:

> Are we not one soul, one thought?—Does not my entire Being, with its most dreadful web of suffering, pour itself into the bosom you have opened for me? . . . let us continue to behave towards each other with

> the most openhearted honesty, even at our times of error, and the effect of this conduct will work more powerfully to improve our weak sinful natural tendencies than the thundering growls of a . . . priest in the confessional . . . . (I: 103)

"Openhearted honesty" is not only the basis of their friendship; it is also framed as key to self-improvement. Amalie puts forth the belief that the way to overcome one's "natural" tendency to sin is to establish an open and transparent relationship with a like-minded person. Thus, the trusting relationship modeled by Amalie and Fanny represents not just a friendship but also a social good: it is presented as having the potential to foster virtue more effectively than even the church. But, at the same time, as I discuss in more detail below, the description of their friendship reverses eighteenth-century assumptions about what is "natural" to women: where theorists like Rousseau believe women to be "naturally" open and naive, Amalie sees "openhearted honesty" as a form of conduct that must be cultivated and practiced.

In addition to valorizing subjective transparency, the novel also participates in the eighteenth-century positioning of deception as both immoral and dangerous. Early in the novel Amalie expresses her condemnation of *Verstellung*, recognizing its danger for both men and women:

> As far as I'm concerned coquetry means hiding one's feelings, and taking delight in torturing men. God protect me from such deception *(Verstellung)*!—I would defame my own heart and insult that dear Mother Nature who created us to feel! Woe to the man who fails to return my honest, upright feelings, and double woe to him, if the remembrance is painful, if I have to be ashamed of it when it is too late. (I: 59)

Like other eighteenth-century novels that take women's victimization at the hands of a deceiver as their theme, *Amalie* worries about the consequences of a woman's faith in the honest conduct of others. Amalie and Fanny continually fret over the possibility that one of the men Amalie meets might mislead or attempt to seduce her.

But Ehrmann's novel is also particularly concerned about the consequences—for both men and women—of *women*'s dishonesty.

"Coquetry" is a term that comes up repeatedly in the novel as a pejorative for women who put on an act to attract the attentions of men. In several letters, Amalie and Fanny lament the fact that there are so few honest and transparent women like themselves. Fanny writes:

> So few women know how to affect a charming liveliness in company without coquetry, openheartedness without affectation, propriety without prudishness, candidness without slavish fear. They sit there tied in knots, bound to vacuous etiquette, accustomed to devilish deception and politics, each false to the other, out of pride, stupidity, or jealousy. . . . If women would give more nourishment to their lives through natural, intelligent, social intercourse, both sexes would be happier, and defamation would have to cease if something more, and better, could be sought from a woman than the mere enjoyment of her body. (I: 107)

While coquettes are problematic for a number of reasons, Fanny and Amalie's main complaint against such women is that because they appeal to men's sensual desires rather than their emotions or intellect, they effectively make the world a more difficult and dangerous place for honest women like themselves. As Amalie puts it,

> If only these boring, useless creatures would learn to entertain men with something better than just their bodies. Excess and disdain would prevail less, if men didn't have to escort women out of either boredom or conviction—It is an eternal shame, that men can seek only pleasure from women, and that women don't know to give anything better. Men's violent maltreatment stems from this, because so few women understand the good tone of society. (I: 192)

What is interesting here is that although Ehrmann is, in effect, replicating the eighteenth century's condemnation of spectacular women as dangerous, her assessment of *why* and *how* they are dangerous reflects a sophisticated and worldly understanding of the relationship between the sexes. Where Schiller and Rousseau see the performing woman as a threat to masculine wholeness, Ehrmann astutely recognizes that such women pose relatively little danger to men (who, after all, possess all of the social power). Through its critique of coquetry, *Amalie* not only points to the disruptive and destructive effects of performance on gender relations but also importantly underscores the extent to which such performance reifies a social structure that puts women's fate in the hands of men.

Thus, at the end of the novel, when Amalie decides to play the coquette in order to get revenge on men in general for her poor treatment at the hands of her most recent suitor, she gets only a temporary and fleeting pleasure from the feeling of power such performance confers. Instead, the novel emphasizes the fact that such an act can only reinforce a woman's overall powerlessness, by playing into stereotype and thereby reconfirming social prejudices against women. Amalie realizes the danger of her little game when one of the men she has been flirting with insults her by dropping a bill of exchange in her lap:

> Only then did I begin to feel what insults my careless teasing had exposed me to. I felt the whole humiliation of this treatment; saw myself debased, degraded, and grievously injured! My heart, my sense of honor, my reason suddenly awoke in me . . . . (II: 222)

Ehrmann's realistic depiction of the consequences of Amalie's performance of femininity—she is treated as a whore by one of her suitors—offers a view of the coquette as weak and threatened rather than deceptive and manipulative, and reveals such a performance of femininity to be a larger social evil because of the way it conditions men to view women. As a result, the people who are truly threatened by the kind of performance of femininity that coquetry represents are those women who—like Amalie—*do* conform to social pressures toward honesty and authenticity but who are, because of their social station, assumed to be putting on the same "act" as the coquettes and treated with the same contempt.

The novel's insistence on antitheatricality as a component of ideal femininity is thus more progressive than it might appear at first glance. Rather than using the rhetoric of authenticity as a means of anchoring what are perceived as "natural" differences between the sexes, Ehrmann's novel continually calls attention to the social utility of antitheatrical conduct. Authenticity makes for better social relations, and, in particular, for better marriages. As Amalie's life trajectory makes all too clear, in a society in which the best survival option for a woman is marriage, and in which marriage means, for a woman, putting her fate in the hands of a husband who has complete power over her, her fortune, her children, et cetera, marriage can only work out for the woman if she can have complete trust and faith in her husband.

Authenticity is thus framed as a *practice* rather than a natural attribute. In other words, while Amalie and Fanny perceive themselves as honest, authentic, and transparent, it does not follow that they see themselves as *naturally* so. It is clear from the letter in which Amalie claims to be of "one Soul" with Fanny that she conceives of her honesty as a form of conduct that she has learned, and, moreover, one that could help her combat her "weak sinful natural tendencies" (I: 103). Ehrmann's construction of the antitheatrical female subject diverges on this point from the dominant definition of ideal femininity: as I noted in the first chapter of this book, women, because they were thought to be "naturally" naive and transparent, theoretically had no need to cultivate such openness. They needed merely to "be" who they were. While Ehrmann agrees that the Ideal Woman is subjectively transparent and open, where she disagrees with eighteenth-century ideas about gender is in the assumption that openness and naiveté are part of women's nature.

In fact, as several critics have noted, what distinguishes Ehrmann as a writer in the late eighteenth century—and what makes her work so progressive—is her insistence on seeing gender attributes as socially imposed and as an effect of patriarchal power.[5] All of her writing is marked by a concern about how female identity is impacted by a social system in which women can only guarantee their security by entering into a dependent relationship with a man. While Ehrmann agrees that marriage is the ideal situation for a woman, her advocacy of marriage is based on her acknowledgment of its practical necessity within a male-dominated society, rather than on any belief in women's "natural" proclivity to marriage. Thus, as Eva Kammler has pointed out, although Ehrmann seems to be in agreement with Rousseau's description of the proper relationship between men and women, the context in which she reproduces his argument puts a progressive spin on what he posits as the "natural" order of things (88–89).[6]

For example, in *Philosophy of a Woman*, Ehrmann's first work, she reframes Rousseau's infamous reification of the unequal relationship between men and women as an effect not of nature but of social power. She begins by rehearsing Rousseau for her reader (citing verbatim from *Émile*, albeit without quotes or attribution):

> Men and women are made for each other, but their mutual dependence differs in degree; man is dependent on woman through his desires; woman is dependent on man through her desires and also through her needs; he could do without her better than she can do without him. (35)[7]

But then Ehrmann undermines the implied agreement with Rousseau's philosophy a few pages later in her emphasis on the extent to which such inequality puts women at the mercy of men: "[E]xperience confirms that a woman puts much more at risk in marriage than a man. We give our happiness over to the stewardship of our spouse" (56). Where Rousseau sees the natural inequality between the sexes as the basis for a proper (and properly mutually dependent) relationship, Ehrmann not only recognizes the potential for women's victimization but also sees quite clearly that the reason the man "could do without her better than she can do without him" has less to do with nature than with a social system that affords few means of survival for an unattached woman.

So, in her short story "A Warning," Ehrmann tells the tale of a woman who, after having lost her virtue, was thrown out on her own by her parents and soon began to prostitute herself. She dares her readers to judge the girl:

> I don't want to hear anyone declaring: the girl could have worked! For what if, right when she was most severely driven by hunger, she found no work?—What if she perhaps had learned no skills with which she could feed herself?—What if she were too weak to be a servant, too clumsy to be a chambermaid, what then? (*Amaliens Erholungsstunden* I: 87)

Where her reader might attribute the girl's decidedly unvirtuous behavior to her lack of morals or character, Ehrmann shifts the blame onto society and calls attention to the paucity of alternatives available to women.

A related theme that runs throughout Ehrmann's work is a critique of the double standard that punishes women for behavior allowed to men. Ehrmann calls attention to that double standard explicitly to contest what her society defined as the "nature" of men and women. In *Philosophy* she writes:

> Nature does not permit you any more than us to misuse her drives, and yet you establish political principles that serve your comfort,—and yet you damn the excesses of a woman far more than your own? (11)

Ehrmann has Amalie voice her complaints about this double standard even more pointedly:

> Can there be anything less noticed in the world than a female creature, and is there anything more miserable, than when she is too well noticed? Are we not a true sacrificial animal to a certain prejudice, and is this prejudice not necessary to our upbringing in order to shock our vanity and make us victims of men's love of domination? This just takes the cake! What is imputed to us as vice, decorates their freedom, and though it brings them no great fame just the same, no one—least of all they themselves—punishes or scolds them for it . . . They call us weak, and yet in certain cases we are far stronger than they. (I: 16)

What is remarkable here is Ehrmann's clear-eyed understanding of the relationship between discourse ("prejudice"), education, gendered identity, and social power. In Ehrmann's view, "prejudice" about women's nature becomes justification for an upbringing guaranteed to put women at the mercy of men and to position them as blameworthy if they act outside the boundaries of their given role.

What follows from Ehrmann's understanding of gender as an effect of patriarchal discourse and power is a conviction that virtue and virtuous behavior are the result not of "nature," but of upbringing and education: "Everything depends on upbringing . . . we would then have women with intelligence and feeling instead of so many nameless monsters composed of nothing but weaknesses" (*Philosophy*, 33). For Ehrmann, virtue stems from reason; virtuous behavior, a result of acting according to principles. Like other eighteenth-century moralists, she valorizes innocence (*Unschuld*) and virtue (*Tugend*) as essential qualities of a woman; unlike others, she sees them not as innate but as primarily learned and socially conditioned. Her short story "The Consequences of the first Mistake, a True Story" begins with a statement of her belief in the necessity of a sound education for women:

> We women would not so easily sink into the lowest degree of destruction, if we were taught early enough to look out for ourselves better . . . The tragic story of Miss von Wall . . . will convince us, that even the best, most good hearted girl can sink to the most miserable outcast if she doesn't have the good fortune to gain the principles from her upbringing that can protect her from a fall. This story will prove to us, that neither birth nor reputation, neither nobility nor money can insure against the snares of seduction! (*Amaliens Erholungsstunden* I: 30)

What thus emerges from Ehrmann's writing—despite her commitment to antitheatrical subjectivity—is a conception of proper female subjectivity as an "act" that is divorced from both the woman's social role and from her given "nature." In stories like the one about Miss von Wall, she presents a woman whose fall is *not* attributable to any innate lack of virtue or an inability or refusal to occupy woman's proper social role, but rather to her lack of preparation to respond appropriately to the pressures women inevitably face in their encounters with men. Because Miss von Wall never learns how to act in the face of seduction, she is an easy victim. Amalie, on the other hand, stands as a model for ideal femininity even though for most of the novel she does not occupy a social role proper to a woman, because she knows precisely how she should act, and her conduct serves as a guarantee of her morality. In demonstrating that women must learn to conduct and defend themselves appropriately, Ehrmann undermines the eighteenth-century equation between the virtuous woman and naiveté.[8]

In fact, it is on the point of naiveté that Ehrmann's departure from eighteenth-century discourse on femininity is most visible and radical. In her *Little Fragments for Women Thinkers*, Ehrmann argues quite explicitly against the idea that women should be naive:

> Mothers, teach your daughters to know the world, its seductions, and themselves better; shame will then certainly only seldom visit you and

> yours. Inexperienced girls are always most easily seduced—neither feelings, nor experience, nor reason holds them back. People in the world maintain the false principle that inexperience will hold innocence fast, but this is precisely what brings so many girls to a fall. (57–58)

The rejection of naiveté is also prominent in *Amalie*. Even though Amalie is presented to the reader as an honest, forthright, transparent person, she is anything but naive in any sense of the word. Unlike the Clarissa Harlowes, Sara Sampsons, and Sophie Sternheims of the eighteenth-century fictional world, Amalie is not only deeply self-reflexive, but also fully aware of the ways in which her antitheatrical upbringing makes her vulnerable to seduction and deception.

In many ways, Amalie is a kind of anti–Sophie Sternheim: she knows all about seducers and their methods, she is constantly on guard against potential deception and attack, she is skeptical and cautious with suitors, and she even goes so far as to visit a brothel (disguised as a man) in order to become more informed about how the world operates. In short, Amalie is savvy from the beginning of the novel in a way that Sophie Sternheim only learns to be after much trial and tribulation. In *Amalie*, Ehrmann offers a model for a different kind of Ideal Woman: in place of naive nonperformers like Clarissa and Sophie, she presents a self-aware, cautious, purposefully "honest" character whose success is predicated on knowing, understanding, and learning to master the world she inhabits—a form of being in the world that conforms more closely to the deliberate, pragmatic antitheatricality advocated by Knigge in his conduct book for bourgeois men than to the ideal modeled by Rousseau's "Sophie." Ehrmann's progressivism and critique lie in her adoption of a masculine model for her female character, combating the notion that women are "naturally" naive through her depiction of a character who is simultaneously virtuous, antitheatrical, and fully aware. Where La Roche's novel presents its reader with an ideal maid whose naiveté is both part of her virtue and cause of her distress, Ehrmann's gives us a more realistic portrait of what a woman needs to be armed with in order to survive alone in the world.

At the same time, Ehrmann's engagement with the discourse of antitheatricality serves to reveal the paradoxical and impossible position such a demand placed on late eighteenth-century women, particularly for women who found themselves confronted with the necessity—for whatever reason—of maneuvering in the public world. For even though Amalie's admirable lack of naiveté prevents her from becoming a victim of the duplicity of others, she is not served well by her faith in her own authenticity and readability. Unlike Schulze-Kummerfeld, whose memoirs indicate a strong awareness of her public image, Amalie is presented as a character with an astonishing blindness to the various ways in which her thoroughly virtuous and upright conduct might be "read" by others. Ehrmann's plot depends, in fact, upon this blindness: it hinges on the pitfalls of *not* performing femininity. As a result, the novel undermines its own depiction of the ideal antitheatrical woman by exposing the dangers of not performing to others' expectations. For even though Amalie "is" an Ideal Woman, she is frequently shown to be the victim of other people's perception that she has failed to play her part correctly.

Ironically, virtually all of Amalie's misadventures stem from her stubborn insistence on adhering to her principles and being forthrightly and honestly who she *is*, and from others' misreading of that activity as exceeding the bounds of the properly feminine. Because she conceives of her "self" as something that has no need of being performed in the first place, she fails to understand the necessity of moderating and mediating her self-presentation in order to be perceived as the virtuous and upright woman that she truly is. So, for example, early in the novel she is baffled when her openness and honesty toward her cousin's husband elicits a jealous reaction from the cousin:

> My cousin, the fool, is jealous of me. . . . Certainly, my friend, I am innocent. I couldn't very well forcibly refuse her husband's little favors. Often I have felt myself break out in a sweat, when he would lie in wait for me and snatch at every opportunity to show me his zeal. (I: 33–34)

Fanny is equally perplexed: "Your cousin is jealous of you?—My God!—What nonsense!—A girl, who doesn't allow herself to be seen with the slightest trace of excess; how could anyone vex her with suspicion?" (I: 35). But the cause of the cousin's jealousy is patently clear: obviously, Amalie appears to be encouraging the husband's advances, and her behavior toward him is doing little to disabuse the cousin of her belief. Even though Ehrmann clearly wants to align her reader's sympathies with the two friends, the depiction of Amalie's ignorance of the effects of her behavior can be read as a critique of the notion that the virtuous woman's "virtue" is transparently self-evident to the world. And, in fact, even Fanny acknowledges that merely being virtuous is not always enough: although she agrees with Amalie that she should be above suspicion, in her letter she goes on to advise Amalie to parry the husband's advances more forcefully, actively, and—above all—diplomatically.

Ehrmann frequently employs this strategy of splitting the reader's sympathies between agreement and approval of Amalie's antitheatrical conduct and recognition of the fact that her conduct is not transparently readable to other characters in the novel. It is a strategy that functions to highlight the impossibility of a woman's "being" virtuous without consciously playing the expected part. In so doing, Ehrmann also calls attention to the power that the social audience has to determine what is, in fact, the proper act.

Moreover, by positioning the reader as an audience to both Amalie's "non-performance" of virtuous femininity (a transparency that *should* be readable to her audience) and the failure of other characters to read it properly, Ehrmann further problematizes and complicates the issue. On the one hand, we, as readers, are reassured of our own ability to see the truth of Amalie's subjectivity and recognize the misreadings of others—we are confirmed in our belief that we possess that "penetrating glance of the virtuous" that enables a proper perception of another's being. But our confidence in our own perceptive glance is simultaneously undermined by Ehrmann's demonstration that others' misreadings of Amalie's behavior are often not deliberate or malicious, but simply a consequence of the fact that audiences are subjective and unpredictable in their response. Ehrmann perceptively uncovers two of the factors that make antitheatrical subjectivity such an impossible act: the fundamental opacity of actors' thoughts and motivations, and the utter unreliability of audience reception.

Ehrmann also makes clear just how high the stakes can be for the woman who attempts such an impossible act. The most telling incident in this regard comes after Amalie's father's death, when her trustworthy uncle in K*** sends her to live with another cousin, a cleric who makes unseemly and inappropriate advances toward her. Amalie is successful in fending off his advances, but she is so repulsed by him, and by the narrow-mindedness of the chaplains who assist him with the parish, that she is haughty and scornful toward them. Amalie seems fully justified in her contempt for the priests: she describes them to Fanny as unenlightened, fearful, antisocial, surly bigots whose only concern seems to be collecting money for the parish. Thus, we are fully sympathetic when she complains with righteous indignation that they have reported to her cousin on her mockery of them "as if I stood, with all my liveliness, on the direct path to hell.—Amazing!—As if virtue could be found nowhere except in some uptight creature" (I: 113). But Amalie suffers heavy consequences for her refusal to play to the priests' expectations: her cousin kicks her out and leaves her to her own resources. The letter he sends to her telling her of his decision shows just how sorely her motives and character have been misread:

> Mademoiselle! Through your lack of peaceable disposition you have made yourself unworthy of staying here. When one is of modest means, one must be able to accommodate oneself to all people. Blame the consequences on yourself. . . . I wish that your little head might become more pliant, and more than that you can truly not demand of me. (I: 125)

While both Amalie and Fanny interpret the cousin's actions as yet another instance of attack on Amalie's virtue, the novel leaves open the possibility that in fact Amalie might indeed be at fault for having been *too* forthrightly virtuous. In other words, by providing the cousin's justification in his own words, Ehrmann reveals the gap between Amalie's (non)performance of self, which she sees as a cornerstone of her virtue, and the cousin's perception of that refusal to perform, which he frames as rudeness and ingratitude. What is telling about this incident is that it not only calls attention to the subjective opacity that thwarts her efforts to be "read" correctly, but it also suggests that a more proactive, audience-oriented performance of virtue might have been a better survival strategy for Amalie.

On this point, a comparison with the memoirs of Schulze-Kummerfeld is instructive: both texts engage with the vexing problem of the social "audience" for a woman's self-performance, albeit in different ways. Where Schulze-Kummerfeld presents herself as always sensitive to the ways in which her behavior in public might be (mis)interpreted, Ehrmann gives us a heroine whose faith in the self-evidence of her virtuous being blinds her to potential misreadings. Amalie does not seem to understand what it means to "be" in public. The problem for the virtuous woman, as Ehrmann presents it, is not in being virtuous (Amalie conforms in every way to the era's notion of ideal femininity) but in its performance and reception. In every case, Amalie would be better served with a more deliberate, audience-sensitive performance of femininity. Her lack of success "projecting" Ideal Womanhood by merely "being" the virtuous girl she "is" paradoxically reveals femininity's status as masquerade: that is, Ehrmann shows how the failure to properly masquerade femininity produces adverse responses. As a result, Ehrmann's novel presents us with a stark contradiction, depicting femininity as ideally "not performed" (in her virtuous main character) and, at the same time, revealing it as that which cannot not be performed.

This contradiction receives its fullest and most paradoxical articulation in Amalie's description of her adventures in Venice. She travels there to visit relatives, accompanied only by her maid. Shortly after her arrival, she is invited to visit St. Mark's square with her cousin. His wife urges her to wear a mask, because "it's necessary here, in order to avoid persecution from men" (II: 169). Amalie refuses to hide her face in such manner. To her, the mask can only signify viciousness and deception. Even though she is told that the mask is primarily a means of defense in Venice, she still interprets it as the refuge of the dissembler. Her observations seem to bear this out. As she wanders St. Mark's square, she notes all of the disreputable activities enabled by the mask: spying, gambling, whoring, hypocritical lying, cheating, and swindling. While it is unclear precisely how she identifies these activities, or the extent to which she is simply assuming that what she sees confirms her already held stereotypes, what is important here is Amalie's deeply held suspicion of masking and her association of it with the worst kind of vices. Amalie's distaste for the mask matches that of eighteenth-century critics of the masquerade, who, as Terry Castle has pointed out, feared and detested the way in which masking and masquerading led to an "unholy mixing of things meant to be kept apart" (79). Amalie sees the mask as dangerous and contemptible because it encourages women to indulge in and exploit their sexuality: it leads to a dangerously excessive performance of femininity.

But contrary to her assumptions, what is dangerous in St. Mark's square is not being masked, but being unmasked. No sooner is Amalie in the square than she is pushed, poked, and harassed by "Masks":

> The Masks here presume the most ill-mannered impudence towards a foreign unmasked woman.—A foreign woman has to disguise herself in men's clothing if she wants to walk the streets undisturbed.—At home this type of costuming gives a woman a bad reputation, and here it serves as defense. (II: 70)

Where Amalie sees the mask as a form of deception and as a means of hiding one's self, to the Masks in St. Mark's square, an unmasked woman is audacious. In a sense, Amalie's misunderstanding of the mask encapsulates her problem with publicity and audience: she goes through life as an "unmasked woman," and it does not serve her particularly well because the world wants to see the mask of proper womanhood, a mask she refuses to "put on" because she—in line with dominant discourse—believes it unnecessary. She thinks her embodiment of ideal femininity is self-evident, but, time and again, the novel reveals the inadequacy of merely "being" virtuous. As with her refusal to wear the mask in Venice, the fact that she does not proactively perform her self leaves her open to a multitude of misinterpretations. Consequently, Amalie's journey through the world as an unmasked woman raises—and leaves largely unresolved—the question of what ideal femininity is when it lacks a deliberately performed dimension.

Interestingly, Amalie proposes to avoid the performance of femininity that she thinks is inherent in masking by engaging in a performance of masculinity: she remarks that the best strategy for coping with the harassment she receives as an unmasked woman would be to disguise herself as a man. Cross-dressing is a fairly common trope in the eighteenth century, often mobilized by female authors as a means of giving a female character access to the power and privileges that eighteenth-century society reserved for men (Krimmer, *In the Company of Men* 31). This seems to be Amalie's purpose and plan in the novel, but on the two occasions when she *does* dress as a man, she is unable to pull it off. The first time she disguises herself as a man is to visit a brothel with her cousin (so that he can prove to her that they primarily cater to foreigners). The second is to allow her to travel back to Germany alone without fear of molestation. At the brothel, the woman sent to entertain them is not fooled for a moment by Amalie's cross-dressing, and, during her travel to Germany, Amalie's disguise is penetrated quickly by everyone except a lady "who must have been a great lover of German milksops" and who seems blinded by her own desire to trade sexual favors for financial reward (II: 111).

While Amalie's inability to perform masculinity successfully adds to the novel's realism by refusing to take the flight into fantasy that fully successful cross-dressing might require, this failed performance presents yet another instance of what appears to be Ehrmann's ambivalence about the performability of gender. Elisabeth Krimmer notes that texts that feature cross-dressed characters "seek to come to terms with the as yet undecided contest between two different models of the body: one that defines the body as a neutral surface whose gendered meaning derives from its clothing, and an authentic body whose gender truth shines forth through its apparel" (*In the Company of Men* 35). Ehrmann seems to occupy the latter camp: her refusal to allow her heroine success in impersonating a man can be read as evidence of her belief that gender has an essential dimension that firmly ties it to identity. For Ehrmann, Amalie cannot "be" anything other than a woman. In fact, what undermines Amalie's disguise is her lack of interiorization of her "role" as a man: she reacts to the advances of both the prostitute and the lady in the coach not with the interest of a young man but with the aversion of a virtuous woman.

Yet by including Amalie's failed attempts at cross-dressing, Ehrmann presents us with a paradox: when Amalie is simply "being" herself, she is repeatedly misread, but when she tries to masquerade as something she is not, her "true" subjectivity is patently obvious. While the latter situation speaks to Ehrmann's belief in an essentiality of gendered identity, the former reveals her lack of confidence in the efficacy of its reception. This is a contradiction and paradox that pervades the novel. Ehrmann seems unable to reconcile her embrace of the notion that the Ideal Woman is antitheatrical with her astute understanding of the fact that audiences need to be shown what they are supposed to perceive. As a result of these unresolved contradictions, Ehrmann's novel reads as an exploratory, and ultimately inconclusive, investigation of the question of the extent to which a woman's subjective interiority is readable in the absence of performance.

* * *

IDEAL FEMININITY IN/AND THE PUBLIC SPHERE

The main effect of Ehrmann's engagement with the discourse of antitheatricality is to demonstrate that the rules that govern women's private conduct are unworkable in the public sphere—but unlike Rousseau, Ehrmann uses this as an argument to critique and challenge the rules, rather than to exclude women from the public sphere. Above all, Amalie's story reveals how impossible it would be for a woman to conform to behavioral expectations of antitheatricality if—for reasons over which she had no control or choice—she found herself on her own and acting in the public sphere. In its realistic description of the difficulties and challenges virtuous women face in the public sphere, *Amalie* demonstrates how pernicious the ideology of authenticity was for such women. For simply by exposing themselves to public intercourse, they lost the guarantee of transparency and naiveté that came, by definition, with domesticity. Thus even though Ehrmann essentially agrees throughout her writing that antitheatricality and domesticity are a woman's true calling, she is also aware and critical of the extent to which that doctrine negatively impacted women whose fates took them out of the private sphere.

Consequently, Ehrmann's novel also confronts the discourse about "proper" femininity through its use of theater to combat the notion that virtuous bourgeois women have no appropriate space or activity in the public sphere. In the novel, theater functions not only as a physical space in which women participate in public sphere activities (as actor and spectator), but more crucially as a site in and around which women are imagined to engage in public discourse and influence public opinion. The novel shows this happening in a number of ways. First, Amalie and Fanny frequently share anecdotes and opinions about the actors Amalie encounters as she bounces from troupe to troupe. For example, at one point Amalie describes her reception by two other actresses at her first rehearsal with a new troupe:

> A certain creature by the name of R. . . and her female companion Z. . . aimed their poisonous venom at me as vehemently as one might expect from a disgraced penitentiary-candidate, who just a few years ago was sentenced to pulling wheelbarrows with other H. . . [*Huren*: whores].—Many people still remember quite well, how this nice R. . . had to leave P. . . because of her disgusting behavior. (II: 128–29)

Fanny's response demonstrates both her knowledge of, and participation in, the public discourse shaping R. . .'s reputation:

> I have often heard tell of the horrible tricks of that arch-prostitute R. . . . She is known to half the world as the worst whore, whom the authorities should stick in jail again.—What better could be expected from the wife of a cobbler, whose husband was forced to leave his profession because of his wife's wantonness? . . . So much was told to me recently by an impartial connoisseur of the theater. (II: 133–34)

The sharing of opinions and gossip about well-known actors functions to demonstrate women's active participation in the community of spectators who police the stage, its morals, and its employees through verbal and epistolary intercourse. Indeed, rather ironically, these exchanges stand as evidence of women's own participation in the public discourses that defined virtuous, moral behavior; that is, they show women to be active members of the very social audience that is such an unreliable "reader" of female character. While there is no reason not to trust Amalie and Fanny's impression of R. . . and Z. . . , by showing gossip at work in defining those two women, the novel certainly begs speculation about the extent to which they might be victims of the same kinds of misreadings and misinterpretations that cause Amalie so much anxiety and distress.

But, more importantly, the fact that Ehrmann's novel is a thinly veiled autobiography adds another, truly public, dimension to her characters' assessment of actresses like R. . . , for Ehrmann's readers would have readily guessed to whom the initial "R. . ." referred (Madland, *Marianne Ehrmann* 62). The novel thus uses the theater to bring its female reader into the circuit of public exchange of information. While women could not be expected to share knowledge of business, banking, or commerce (public activities from which they were excluded), they could share—as readers, spectators, and critics—in the public formation of ideas about the theater and its practitioners. As a result, Amalie and Fanny's letters about the theater hail the novel's female readership into the real-world community of spectators, by encouraging them to imagine themselves as similarly participant in public life through their attendance at, and knowledge of, the theater.

Contrary to contemporary perception of the theater as a place of potential danger to women, then, Ehrmann positions it as a site of women's civic participation, and as an opportunity for women both to increase their knowledge and exercise their judgment and moral reasoning. Echoing Schiller, Ehrmann has her two protagonists argue vociferously for the value of the stage as a moral and educational institution—both for the public and for the actors—and thereby uses the novel as a means of publicizing her own ideas and plans for stage reform. These plans are detailed in a letter from Fanny that describes "a project for the improvement of the morals of the stage" designed by herself and her fiancé Karl (II: 138–41). The letter is framed such that it clearly aims at reaching the highest possible audience, both within the narrative and through publication in the novel itself. Fanny begins and ends her letter with the hope that her ideas might find their way to the emperor:

> Our great Emperor Joseph has instituted good moral institutions throughout our land, and we hope that he will also eventually turn to the cleansing of the stage, when a patriot finally dares to describe its true conditions to him. (II: 138–39)
>
> What do you think of my ideas?—I've just sort of sketched them above!—If a philanthropist would think them over better—work them

> out—and present them before the great Emperor Joseph, how happy I would consider myself! (II: 141)

This framing of Fanny's reform plan with expressions of hope that it might reach a wider audience reflects Ehrmann's sensitivity to the constraints on women's civic participation in the late eighteenth century, and it calls attention to the strategies of deflection women had to employ in order to get their ideas into public circulation. Because they could not influence public policy directly, women—including Ehrmann herself—had to participate in public life, and the formation of public institutions, indirectly. Hence, she shows Fanny formulating her plans in a "private letter" to Amalie, in which the best she can do is hope for some mediator to bring them to the attention of the emperor. Ehrmann's novel then provides the wished-for mediation, putting the plan into circulation in such a way that both she and her fictional character are distanced from what might be perceived as an unseemly and unfeminine participation in public discourse. Ehrmann's use of Fanny as a private proxy for inserting herself into the public debate on the theater thus not only signals Ehrmann's own experience of the impossible bind the discourse of antitheatricality put women in, but it also represents a performance of virtuous femininity on the part of the author, because it veils her own participation in public discourse as the private correspondence of a (fictional) Ideal Woman.

Beyond giving evidence of the complex web of deflections women needed to employ in order to influence public opinion, Fanny's ideas for theatrical reform model an attitude toward the theater that converges with eighteenth-century ideas about both the potential social utility of the theater and performance and the kinds of performance that are "proper." The reform of the stage laid out in Fanny's letter aims primarily at ridding the theater of "bad" actors—in both senses of the word. She complains that the problem with the current theater is that the behavior of most actors

> is annoying, and when widespread it strengthens the prejudice against better mannered actors and robs the audience of their belief in every moral that is presented on respectable stages because people become accustomed to believing that here, as there, the fox merely preaches to the geese.—. . . [in addition] their debauchery puts them in debt, they cheat good citizens,

> seduce their sons and daughters, frequent beer houses, [and] nourish prejudice and superstition among the common folk, luring them into adventures, treasure hunting, conjuring, and the like . . . . (II: 139)

Fanny argues that because such actors bring the art of acting into shame and disrepute, they prevent the theater from reaching its full potential as a moral and educational institution. What is interesting here is Fanny's determination to rescue the baby from being cast away with the bath water: she sees acting as a noble and moral art that must be saved from the immoral practitioners.

The linking of the usefulness and morality of the art of acting to individual actors' off-stage behavior was common in the eighteenth-century: much of the condemnation of the theater as an institution stemmed from critics' fear and loathing of actors' dissolute, unfixed, wandering lifestyles. Like many eighteenth-century reformers, Fanny locates the problem with the theater at the individual level, with the practitioner rather than the institution as a whole. But, unlike many critics who condemned actors because of the deception they practiced for a living, Fanny argues that, not only can actors be moral, but moral actors, practicing their profession well, are good for society. Her solution is governmental supervision: a board of experts who would "examine the talents and lifestyle of the actor for some time" before approving their engagement with a pre-approved troupe. This, she argues, would not only drive away the dissolute rabble who take refuge in the theater, but would also make it safe for those who take their art seriously and practice what they preach from the stage:

> An honorable actor would no longer be reduced to itinerant beggary by oppression and intrigue; the morals of these people would gradually become purer; the audience would be better served; the good objective of the stage would be fulfilled, and the directors would be saved from so many bankruptcies that are mostly occasioned by the intrigues of such itinerants. (II: 140)

Part of what is going on here is an imagined recuperation of the stage for actresses like Amalie—a group that would include women like (the ex-actress) Marianne Ehrmann herself. By proposing to cleanse the theater of the "bad" actors who make it a place of dissolution (and hence danger to women), Fanny's reform plan dreams of a theater that would not only be hospitable to virtuous women, but also be a place in which they could thrive, and thereby divorces professional acting from immorality per se and rescues actresses from an automatic association with viciousness.

Ehrmann bolsters the case for the proposed reform plan by giving her heroine the opportunity to work with a troupe that is a model for the kind of theater she imagines. Under the direction of Seipp (the only director she identifies by full name), the members of the troupe are held to the highest moral standards, for he "tolerates no bad manners among his people" (II: 135).[9] Amalie describes Seipp as acting like "a true father," distributing roles carefully so as to forestall jealousy among the actors, mediating disputes, banishing visitors from dressing rooms and rehearsals in support of a strict policy against licentiousness, and taking on responsibility for the well-being and education of his troupe members (II: 134–38). Under Seipp's management, women are treated respectfully and encouraged to thrive as artists. Not only does Seipp defend and protect his actresses against the advances of audience members, but he also explicitly values them for their skills rather than their bodies. Amalie quotes him explaining to a man who has complained about the lack of beauty in his company: "I am the entrepreneur of a cultured theater group, not a meat stall where any libertine can get his needs satisfied at will" (II: 138).

The description of Seipp's theater troupe has two functions in the novel. First, it serves as an exemplar of a theater that practices what it preaches—that is, its inner workings model the virtuous behavior it displays to the public on stage. As a result, it demonstrates that the theater can indeed be a proper, antitheatrical, nonhypocritical source of educating the public, just as Fanny envisions. Second, and perhaps more importantly, the description of Seipp's troupe offers an image of the theater as a public space replicating the dynamics of the domestic sphere, in which women have a proper place, a respected role, and paternalistic guarantee—and defense—of their virtue. In contrast to reigning bourgeois ideas about the theater—and in contrast to the depiction of the theater that dominates most of *Amalie*—the episode with Seipp's troupe offers an alternative notion of the theatrical space, one in which the nuclear-family model so prized by society is emulated and reproduced. Ehrmann offers the possibility of a theater that is a haven for unattached women rather than the last refuge of the dissolute.

Consequently, the argument for the reform of the theater proposed in Fanny's letter is linked to the novel's contestation of dominant discourse on femininity because it contributes to the case Ehrmann seems to be making throughout the novel that women's exclusion from the public sphere is necessitated by social conditions rather than "nature," and that *ergo* there is nothing inherently vicious about the public woman, especially the actress. The novel buttresses this claim through its depiction of Amalie as a woman who becomes an actress and remains virtuous despite the temptations of the profession—a depiction that also serves, by way of side effect, to recuperate Ehrmann's own earlier participation in the profession.

Above all, Ehrmann uses Amalie's stint as an actress to draw attention to the social and economic vulnerability of the virtuous person who chooses (or is forced into) the profession of acting. During her employment with various troupes, Amalie must deal with predatory directors who attempt to get her on the casting couch, jealous and vindictive colleagues, and unwanted attentions from fans who assume her sexual availability; she is also under constant threat of disease, unemployment, poverty, or abandonment. "God!" Amalie complains, "what a young woman with no husband at her side must bear!—Seduction, scorn, rudeness are her lot! Every burdensome cad irritates her!" (II: 159). Her experience as an actress supports Schulze-Kummerfeld's assertion that "no woman in the world has more merit, when she remains completely virtuous, than a woman in the theater," but less because the temptation to vice is so strong (as Schulze-Kummerfeld would have it) than because the stress and strain of the lifestyle appears so great (*KSK* I: 60).

At the same time, however, despite Ehrmann's recognition of the pressures bearing upon women who work in the theater, her heroine is quick to condemn immoral actresses and attribute their vices to their own failings. For example, in letter CXXXIV, Amalie is biting in her critique of the moral character of another actress in her troupe:

> Madame K . . .s is a piece of meat, who is at anyone's command. Her disgusting sensuality borders on the most extreme contempt, which falls to her from men who know her—Her addiction to conquest, her vanity, selfishness, et cetera, are evident at first sight. . . . I have always noticed in the world that the stupidest women are in every case the most dissolute. (II: 166)

For another actress in the troupe, however, she has nothing but praise:

> Madame J. . . on the other hand . . . is a good, solid-thinking woman with an irreproachable and honest disposition.—She divides her time between religion and her professional duties, and enjoys the happiest, most satisfied marriage. . . . Misfortune has made the good woman soft and wise; she demands little from fate, and enjoys that little with a pure, blameless conscience. (II: 167)

Amalie's judgments here support Ehrmann's conviction that principles and education can help combat pressures on women to act immorally. The difference between the immoral actress and the moral one (and Amalie) is that the former has not been properly educated to defend herself against the pressures of the profession. As such, by providing both the example of the dissolute actress and the counter-example of the principled, virtuous one, Ehrmann solidifies the point that a woman can become an actress and remain virtuous.

Even more importantly, her equation of good (moral) actresses with good (talented) acting has a crucial corollary: that bad (immoral) actresses are also bad (untalented) actors who—above all—cannot successfully portray noble and virtuous characters. This is a point that is made repeatedly by both pen-pals. For example, Fanny's criticism of the actress R. . . quoted earlier includes the following catty gossip about the actress's limitations:

> [S]he—so people say—plays the roles of vile women, shameless courtesans, comic procuresses, and malicious, quarrelsome, sinful creatures with

> great naturalness; . . . but as honorable characters, in the roles of moral, well-raised mothers, she is said to be unbearable. (I: 134)

Amalie later makes a similar criticism of another actress, who is the "favorite" of a director, and who has an infamous reputation as a prostitute:

> This much has to be said for her: she plays her coquettes with a certainty, with a habituation, with an insolence, with a cold insensitivity, with a cunning spite, with hypocritical self-interest, with a false thirst for conquest, and with a branded heart, as only a person who naturally had such a character could.—She is also successful in some characterized "conversation roles," particularly when they involve deception (*Verstellung*), pride, or envy. On the other hand in all of her good-natured roles she kills each and every passage that expresses feeling; and she is impossible to watch, let alone listen to, in tragedies.—She delivers every moral sentiment of love or virtue so stiffly, so indifferently, and so coldly that it is a distress and shame for the author when his expressive work falls into her hands. . . . Have I not told you before, that *an actress's moral behavior will be most conspicuous to the connoisseur of the stage when she is playing the opposite role?* (II: 183–84, emphasis added)

We can read this insistence that immoral women are incapable of successfully portraying virtuous characters in several contradictory ways. To begin with, it is further evidence of Ehrmann's investment in the ideology of authenticity and her faith in the homology between the inner and outer self. Like Friedrich Ludwig Schröder, the great eighteenth-century actor who granted the audience the power to penetrate into the actor's soul and read his or her "true" character, Ehrmann seems to believe that, in Fanny's words, "experienced sluts can not deny their nature," no matter how good they are at deceiving (II: 187). Amalie emphasizes that the "actress's moral behavior will be *most* conspicuous . . . when she is playing the *opposite role*" (emphasis added). The vicious woman would thus also seem to have an important function in the theater: playing coquettes and villainesses. For if we follow Amalie's reasoning to its logical conclusion, good women, whose moral behavior would be "most conspicuous" when playing vicious characters, would be unable to play those roles successfully. As a result, we might want to read Amalie's theory of acting reception here as an explanation for why her own moral behavior is so rarely "conspicuous" to her social audience in the novel: because she eschews performance, she has no opportunity to play at all, let alone play her "opposite role."

Even given such an explanation, the novel's expressed faith in the transparency of vice seems at odds with its portrayal of the opacity of Amalie's virtue, for it begs the question, why is the nature of the immoral woman self-evident and that of the moral woman so easily misread? Ehrmann's figuration here of the way in which women are impacted by the discourse of antitheatricality seems designed to reveal the illogic of that discourse. The virtuous woman may not make the truth of her "self" readable (except, perhaps, on the stage, and, most conspicuously, when playing an immoral character), and the immoral woman cannot hide the truth of her "self": making ideal femininity an impossible act indeed.

We can read the novel's insistence that bad women make bad deceivers differently, however. For what bad actresses are bad at performing is, precisely, virtuousness. By linking immorality with bad acting, Ehrmann reveals the Lady Marwoods of eighteenth-century fiction to be a masculine fantasy that perpetuates a myth of female power located in woman's ability to perform ideal femininity. Discourse that framed the performance of femininity as the refuge and recourse of villainous monstrous women provided a powerful negative example to women, encouraging them to adopt the naive antitheatricality that was its opposite (even as—or perhaps because—it fashioned the antitheatrical character as victim). In such discourse, as in Rousseau and other proponents of antitheatricality, immoral people make particularly *good* deceivers—in fact, their ability to deceive well is part of what makes them immoral. But Ehrmann seems to recognize such discourse as a vehicle for policing women's behavior and keeping them socially powerless: the social deterrent against performing femininity that emerges from such texts puts women even further at the mercy of a patriarchal society that abrogated to itself the privilege of reading and interpreting their "character" and determining their fate.

Ehrmann completely reverses the terms. Her novel argues that in order to act well—both on stage and in life—one must already be moral, which leads logically to the proposition that all good actors are moral people. I have already noted in this book that this is an argument in service of recuperating the profession of acting; but Ehrmann takes it even further in *Amalie*. For her novel does not only demonstrate that moral women make better actresses in a variety of ways, it also somewhat contradictorily proposes that the skills of the actress are useful to the moral woman, especially in her relationships with men. Despite the novel's ambivalence about the performance of femininity, it shows that acting is a useful art—not just as a means of educating the public (as Schiller would have it) but also on a personal level, as a way of gaining skills that serve the Ideal Woman well. Right after the breakup of her first marriage, Amalie stays at a convent where she staves off melancholy by creating an amateur theater among the female students. Although all of the girls are totally inexperienced at acting, she manages "to bring them to a tolerable perfection" through drill and repetition (II: 38). When two of the nuns challenge the seemliness of the activity, Amalie defends it by pointing to its educational value and usefulness: "This activity belongs to education, and builds heart, head, and reason in the pupils" (II: 41). Fanny's later description of the qualities necessary for a good actress read like a description of Ehrmann's conception of ideal femininity:

> A good tragic actress absolutely needs brains, knowledge of literature, education, feeling, lively passions, a smooth voice, a strong imagination, a soft receptive soul, good command of German, good breath, enthusiasm for virtue, melancholic tendencies, a good memory, industriousness, and sufficient power of discernment to be able to imagine herself with liveliness into the given situation! (II: 164)

It is thus, perhaps, important that Amalie must first prove herself to be a good actress—good in both senses of the word—before she is permitted to marry and live happily ever after. Erhmann's novel thus not only recuperates acting as an appropriate and moral profession for a woman, but also implies that, in fact, the education necessary to produce good actresses is the same as the education necessary to produce good women.

Through her novelistic depiction of the life of a woman who negotiates the public sphere as an actress, Marianne Ehrmann exposes many of the contradictions and paradoxes that the discourse of antitheatrical subjectivity posed for women in the public sphere. While she is committed to presenting ideal femininity in terms of sincerity and transparency, she rejects the notion that women are naturally so, insisting that what women need is not naiveté but an educated self-awareness. Moreover, she also reveals the social dynamic that makes it difficult, if not dangerous, for a public woman *not* to produce an audience-oriented performance of her self. The conflict between Amalie's commitment to antitheatricality and her failure to be properly "read" by her social audience is one that is left largely unresolved. But Ehrmann is not alone in her interest in problematizing the reception of sincere being; as I argue in the next chapter, the issue of the social audience also looms large in works of her contemporaries Elise Bürger and Friederike Helene Unger.

5. The Eye of the Beholder

Elise Bürger's "Aglaja" and F. H. Unger's *Melanie, the Foundling*

In this chapter I turn my attention to two works that foreground the role of the social audience in the construction and reception of female identity. The two texts I consider here—Elise Bürger's story "Aglaja," which appeared in a book entitled *Labyrinths of the Female Heart* (*Irrgaenge des Weiblichen Herzens*, 1799), and Friederike Helene Unger's *Melanie, the Foundling* (*Melanie, das Findelkind*, 1804)—are very different in both style and content from the works considered in previous chapters. Formally, both reject aesthetic transparency in favor of a theatricality that mitigates against the reader's hallucinatory absorption into the narrative's scene. Both texts offer a series of often disconnected—or, at best, loosely connected—events that do not "add up" to a conventional narrative, much less a neat moral ending. In place of deep interiority, these texts offer female characters who enjoy great geographic and social mobility and survive a variety of adventures, partly, if not largely, by dint of their ability to perform and masquerade femininity.

This has a number of interrelated effects, in both texts. By calling attention to the artificiality of its own image of ideal femininity, each work urges the reader to consider the extent to which ideal femininity itself is also merely a fictional construct. At the same time, the inherent theatricality of these texts also clearly positions the reader as audience to the text, that is, as public reader both of the women who wrote the narratives and of the female characters they created. As a result, the formal theatricality of both these texts points to, and mirrors, their thematic concerns. In particular, each of these works problematizes the equation of virtuous femininity with antitheatrical subjectivity by demonstrating the complex ways in which the expectations, desires, perceptions, and, above all, *misperceptions* of the social audience—in German, *das Publikum*, the public—define female subjectivity and experience.

By calling attention to the unreliability of audience response as one of the reasons ideal femininity was essentially an impossible act, these works expose the utterly untenable position into which the discourse of antitheatrical subjectivity placed women. For while each of these works accepts the premise that the Ideal Woman simply "is" naturally good, honest, sincere, and authentic, each also presents a heroine who is forced to perform what is actually natural to her because, in fact, her audience does *not* possess the "penetrating glance of the virtuous" theorized by Gellert and other eighteenth-century proponents of the project of sincerity. Both of these texts implicitly argue that, while it is important for a woman to be transparently virtuous, it serves no purpose unless the audience sees it, and hence, in fact, women must take proactive and paradoxical steps—such as performing the sincere and honest person they really "are"—to ensure the desired audience response. In addition, by foregrounding the importance of audience response, each of these texts also implicitly exposes the fact that the definition of ideal femininity in terms of antitheatricality was contingent on woman's confinement to the domestic sphere. It is only by relegating woman to the home that theorists like Rousseau can essentially sidestep the issue of whether or not audiences can be trusted to properly read the Ideal Woman's virtue. As a result, these texts also alter the terms of the debate: they call the reader's attention to the power of the social audience and demonstrate how the public's (inevitable) misreadings and misinterpretations can compel a performance from even the most sincere and antitheatrical woman.

* * *

ELISE BÜRGER: "AGLAJA" (*LABYRINTHS OF THE FEMALE HEART*)

Elise Bürger published *Labyrinths of the Female Heart* in 1799, seven years after her scandalous divorce from the well-known poet

Gottfried August Bürger.[1] It was one of her earliest publications, appearing in the same year as her very popular drama, *Adelheit, Countess of Teck* (*Adelheit, Gräfinn von Teck*), and coinciding with her first great success as an actress on the Bremen stage (Ebeling 198; Rüppel 227). *Labyrinths of the Female Heart* is a curious work: it consists of two distinct prose narratives, "Dirza" and "Aglaja," each of which tells the story of its eponymous heroine. The stories have nothing in common, other than the fact that each traces the life of an unconventional woman, and Bürger provides no apparatus to guide her reader's reception of the work: it is up to the reader to discern what, if anything, links the two narratives. But what is perhaps most curious about this text is that while the book's title promises an exploration of the inner workings of female identity and experience—insight into the "labyrinths of the female heart"—it in fact presents precisely the opposite. In both narratives, Bürger determinedly avoids giving psychological depth to her characters, presenting instead two women whose "interior selves" remain opaque to the reader. Instead, Bürger directs the reader's attention to the role of the social audience in defining "ideal femininity," demonstrating in the process that, in the public sphere, what matters is not subjective antitheatricality but audience response. The effect of Bürger's narrative strategy, then, is twofold: on the one hand, it discounts the importance of subjective transparency as a defining feature of female virtue, and on the other, it highlights the impossibility for women of making their interior "being" readable and knowable in the public context, given the ungovernability of audience reception.

While both texts share a narrative strategy that eschews depth, I focus my attention here on "Aglaja" because—along with Ehrmann's *Amalie*, Unger's *Melanie*, and the two short stories by Sophie Mereau discussed in chapter six—it is one of the few works by an eighteenth-century German woman author in which a female protagonist takes up acting as a profession, and because, unlike Dirza, who is a negative example, the character of Aglaja is presented as essentially virtuous. The story begins with a graveside tribute to Aglaja from her friend, the story's narrator:

> Aglaja, dear unhappy woman! Look down from the fields of peace, smile upon the woman who tells the story of the happy and sad hours of your

> prematurely ended life . . . and forgive, if, in my desire to fulfill the demands of truth, things slip from my pen that you entreated be committed to silence! Few were like you, good and unhappy! (36)

The narrator, an old friend, then begins to recount Aglaja's story, divided in three parts: "First Love," "Labyrinth," and "Death." "First Love" tells how Aglaja, a beautiful orphan from a wealthy, honorable, bourgeois family, becomes a lady's companion at the court, where she falls in love with the nobleman Ludwig. Aglaja is mocked and vilified for aiming to marry above her station, but after several years of secret courtship she and Ludwig prevail upon his family to approve of their union. However, shortly before their marriage Ludwig is killed in a riding accident, and Aglaja, devastated, spends a year in mourning, withdrawn from society and longing for death herself.

"Labyrinth," the longest section, begins with her return to society. Aglaja has vowed never to love again, but when her aunt dies and leaves her penniless, she enters into a marriage of convenience with a wealthy banker. While married, she meets and falls in love with Prince Eugen. When her husband dies suddenly, leaving her bankrupt, she moves to court at the prince's invitation. They embark upon a relationship that she hopes will eventually lead to their marriage, but her plans are thwarted by intrigues instigated by the prince's uncle, who wants Aglaja as his own mistress. The details of these intrigues take up most of this section, as the uncle repeatedly manipulates appearances to make it look as if she is having an affair with another man. His machinations work: Aglaja's reputation is destroyed, and the prince, believing her to be unfaithful, marries a princess. Driven from the court by the uncle's smear campaign, Aglaja retires to a small town where she starts a small business with her faithful servant, Leonora. When Leonora dies, the business folds, and Aglaja becomes ill. While recuperating at the baths, she meets an actress, Mme. B. Against Mme. B.'s advice, Aglaja decides to become an actress too. Under Mme. B.'s tutelage she quickly gains success on stage, and she and Mme. B. become good friends and—against stereotype—work harmoniously together for two years.

The final section, "Death," begins with Aglaja's decision to return to her hometown to perform. Her reception there is not what she had hoped for: the false rumors from the court have preceded her, and the townspeople consider her shameless for returning as an actress. She is followed there by Prince Eugen, who has begun to harbor doubts about his decision to abandon her and seeks her out at the theater. Her debut is a failure, and she is humiliated by the hostile reception she receives from the audience. After the performance she is seeking solace with Baroness X., her longtime, loyal friend, when the prince suddenly appears, begging her forgiveness and promising to leave his wife and child to be with her again. Although her love for the prince is rekindled, she realizes that she cannot break up his marriage and so flees in the middle of the night, coincidentally sharing a coach with a theater manager from another town, who had seen and admired her performance in her hometown. He engages her to perform in his troupe, where she wins instant acclaim among the audience. Unfortunately, her success and popularity arouse the jealousy of another actress in the troupe, who exacts revenge by sabotaging a piece of scenery that sends Aglaja crashing to her death in the middle of her performance as Medea. The story ends with a description of the exceptional honors posthumously bestowed upon Aglaja (including a yearly ceremony marking the anniversary of her death) and, in a final paragraph, a confirmation of her essential virtue:

> Some years later chance happened to also bring Madame B. and the Baroness X. to D., we all three walked hand in hand to that place of rest that enclosed our favorite memories, and there, on the grave of our loved one, we formed a band of faithful insoluble friendship; her spirit hovered around us in blessing, and we turned to turned to each other with the cry: She was indeed a good woman! (118)

As with *Amalie*, it is tempting to read "Aglaja" in light of its author's biography. At the time of the story's publication, Elise Bürger was in the early stages of both her acting and writing careers and had personal knowledge of the difficulties women faced when they chose, or were forced by circumstances, to live their lives outside the confines of the domestic sphere. Bürger herself was an unconventional woman: her relationship with the celebrated "folk" poet Gottfried August Bürger had been instigated by a love poem she had written and performed at a party—as a "joke," she later claimed—which was then published anonymously and purportedly without her permission by Marianne and Theophil Ehrmann in their weekly journal *The Observer* (*Beobachter*).[2] The poem itself caused something of a sensation: in it, Elise Hahn, referring to herself only as a "Swabian girl" (*Schwabenmädchen*), describes her sensual response to G. A. Bürger's poetry and audaciously offers herself to the poet. As she read his poetry, she claims, her heart throbbed, tears ran down her face, and "an 'Ach!' full of sweet desire stole quickly from my soul" (Kinder 9). She ends the poem with a bold declaration of her desire for his courtship: ". . . if you'll woo once more again / Then let it be a Swabian girl, and choose me!" (Kinder 13). G. A. Bürger's interest was so piqued by the poem that not only did he send Marianne Ehrmann several letters begging her to reveal who had written it, but also engaged in some ingenious sleuthing himself to discover its author's identity. Once he had, a brief epistolary courtship ensued; their first face-to-face meeting resulted in a marriage engagement.[3]

The highly unusual nature of the courtship between the beautiful twenty-year-old Elise Hahn and the recently widowed forty-year-old Bürger was the stuff of eager and, in some cases, malicious gossip in Stuttgart and Göttingen (Ebeling Ch. 1). But aside from the fact that her marriage added to the general scandal surrounding her reputation both as a young woman and in later life, the circumstances under which Elise Hahn met and married G. A. Bürger are also worth noting because of the way in which they intersect with the larger concerns about gender and transparent subjectivity that animate this book. For as Ulrike Weckel points out, their engagement may very well have resulted from G. A. Bürger's successful performance of transparency and authenticity in his correspondence with Marianne Ehrmann and Elise Hahn during their courtship. From a close reading of G. A. Bürger's letters, Weckel argues that their courtship rested on G. A. Bürger's mobilization of a "complicated . . . literary-gallant play of representations of spontaneous expressions of feeling and personal intimacy" (165). But while Weckel seems to argue that both members of the pair were complicit in this game of representation—she concludes that "despite all their sophistication Elise Hahn and G. A. Bürger might in the end have taken gallant appearance for real feelings" (166)—she presents no evidence that Elise Hahn was as calculated in her self-presentation as her husband. Rather, contrary to the story that circulated both during and after her lifetime, Hahn might herself have been the victim of a false performance of self on the part of her future husband.

In fact, the circumstances surrounding their courtship continue to remain open to a multitude of interpretations. For example, Hahn's original "playful" ode to Bürger might indeed have been an honest, direct, and sincere expression of the love his poetry and image inspired in her, as the poem's language indicates in its final verse:

> With genuine Swabian-Sincerity
> With German sense and openness
> The writer [of this poem] loves you. (Kinder 13)

At the same time, such an emphasis on sincerity and honesty can also be read as merely a mobilization of the trope of sincerity, and as a front covering coquetry and seduction. The fact that the poem was originally performed by Hahn as part of a parlor game—and only later found (at first anonymous) publication—further complicates the issue. On the one hand, Hahn might indeed have been the victim of a practical joke by guests at the party who took her poem to the Ehrmanns without her knowledge; on the other, the poem's indirect route toward publication might have been a strategic maneuver on Hahn's part to get the poem into the hands of its intended audience with the minimum of scandal and social consequences. Given the documentary evidence, the question remains an open and debatable one.[4]

In any case, what would undoubtedly have been important to Hahn in this socially fraught situation would have been to maintain an image of herself as naive, an image that the prevailing story about the means by which the poem came into circulation served to confirm. But later reinterpretations of their courtship (by Bürger himself, and by literary historians following his lead) favored a reading that cast Hahn's innocence and naiveté in doubt and figured G. A. Bürger as an honest victim to Elise Hahn's cunning performance of seduction. Such a multitude of interpretations and reinterpretations speaks to the paradoxical position an audience occupies when presented with claims of sincerity and transparency and to the difficulty of both presenting one's self as "true" and discerning truth from appearances in a cultural setting in which the social consequences of *not* being perceived as authentic can be dire. Elise Bürger's firsthand experience of these paradoxes and difficulties, in the event that would mark the rest of her adult life, finds expression (as I describe in more detail below) in "Aglaja" 's preoccupation with the relationship between self-presentation and audience response.

The Bürger marriage was doomed virtually from the beginning by difference in age and temperament. G. A. Bürger sent Elise Bürger home to her mother just eighteen months after their wedding, accusing her of being a bad housekeeper, a distant mother, and a social butterfly and making public his suspicions that she had been committing adultery as well (Kinder 65–88). One of the conditions of their divorce agreement was that Elise Bürger was forbidden to remarry, which had the effect of excluding her from conventional domesticity and consigning her to a life in the public realm (Kinder 151). Left to support herself, Bürger turned to acting and writing and also established herself as a teacher of acting and declamation. She had success in all three areas: her plays were frequently performed, she found steady employment as an actress throughout most of her youth, and she tutored several famous actors.

However, as a public woman with a scandalous past she was continually dogged by criticism of her character and virtue, and she became the object of several widely circulated calumnious attacks in print that gave her an infamous reputation in literary circles, and literary history, well into the twentieth century (she is often cursorily referred to as "the Swabian Girl" (*das Schwabenmädchen*), an appellation that immediately evokes the audacity and scandal of her poem).[5] In addition, like most self-supported women of the eighteenth century, she barely eked out an existence in her later years: at the end of her life, blind and impoverished, she supported herself by writing occasional verses commissioned for anniversaries and birthdays.

While "Aglaja" is by no means an autobiographical tale, the protagonist's experiences resonate with those of the author. In particular, the story's depiction of Aglaja's victimization by public opinion, its dramatic presentation of the vicious effects of backstage jealousies, and its sympathetic portrayal of the difficulties actresses faced when confronted with public stereotype were important issues in Bürger's personal life. As such, and very much like *Amalie*, the story can be read in part as a fictionalized public description, explanation, and justification of its author's own conduct and choices.

But unlike the earlier works discussed in this book, which are antitheatrical both in form and in attitude toward subjectivity, Bürger's "Aglaja" is determinedly theatrical in both its form and its presentation of the self. Where those works gave full access to the protagonist's interior subjectivity, created the illusion that the main character was presenting her "real" self through her own words and thoughts, and defined female virtue partly in terms of authenticity and "natural" being, in "Aglaja" there is no interest in illusionism, in drawing the reader into Aglaja's interior identity, or in exploring her subjective depth and authenticity. On the contrary: the picaresque nature of the narrative style, in which we are given a series of life-events without any real sense of who the main character "really" is, how she feels, or why she chooses to do what she does, serves to emphasize the unknowability of the "truth" of a woman's experience and highlight the extent to which a woman's "being" is dependent on public perception of her performance of self.

Such a narrative strategy, in combination with Bürger's reputation, has made *Labyrinths* a steady victim of neglect and mischaracterization.[6] There is only one scholarly work that takes this text seriously, Karin Wurst's essay "Elise Bürger and the Gothic Imagination," and here the focus is exclusively on the first of the two prose narratives, "Dirza"; the much longer "Aglaja" is not even mentioned. Christine Touaillon (wrongly) assumes from Bürger's title that it is a sentimental novel; on the fact that the text could not, at the time, be found, she comments: "The personality of its author leaves us with no regrets as to its loss" (228). Touaillon's conflation of the quality of Bürger's work with the quality of her life ironically recapitulates assumptions about the "natural" correspondence between a woman's interior "self" and its exterior expression: Bürger's fictional writing is disdained, even in absentia, on the supposition that it would be a performative representation of her "self" that would, if found, continue to enact the unconventional and "unnatural" womanhood that Bürger herself came to symbolize.

Even critics sympathetic to Bürger find little of value in this text. Friedrich Ebeling, who imagines himself as something of a knight in shining armor rescuing Bürger from the character defamation that had dogged her throughout her life, dismisses her writing as trivial in general and mischaracterizes *Labyrinths* as a book "that uses a purposeful and winning writing style to achieve its goal of leading women through the maze of their own follies, weaknesses, and caprices . . . and of letting them recognize their true vocation" (198). Hermann Kinder, who also attempts to be evenhanded in his history of the Bürger marriage, provides a summation of Elise Bürger's oeuvre that is both typical and revealing: "[T]here is something kitschy in all of [her works], something of a pose-like nature, a dishonest drapery. Salon painting, and not of a very brilliant kind." He then goes on to note that the nearest her work comes to expressing "that trace of personal engagement, which makes literature 'genuine' and 'true' " is in the patriotic songs that she donated to the Wurtemburg army in support of their war for freedom (178).

In light of my argument about the precarious position women occupied vis-à-vis demands for subjective antitheatricality, however, such an association of "good" literature with the expression of an author's personal self becomes suspect. For the naiveté that was proper to the Ideal Woman precluded, by definition, such an exposure of self through literary production. The fact that Bürger's narrative deliberately refuses to make that move raises the question of what might be the proper literary form for expressing the "truth" of women's experience of public life in eighteenth-century Germany, given that—again, by definition—such experience automatically rendered women suspect and "unnatural." Thus, like Wurst, who sees Bürger's importation of the Gothic as an expression of "formal displeasure with . . . realistic writing conventions at the end of the century," I prefer to read Bürger's narrative strategy not as a "failure" to produce good literature, but rather as a deliberate attempt to counter dominant discourse (Wurst, "Elise Bürger" 11). As such, the disjointed nature of the narrative precludes any interpretation of its protagonist's subjectivity as one that is continuously, organically, and teleologically coming into being. The narrative style, which is stubbornly superficial, purposefully rules out any deep investigation or excavation of Aglaja's interior "self."

The story's tone is set at the outset: after the initial tribute to Aglaja cited above, Bürger launches into a description of Aglaja's external characteristics:

> Aglaja was no beauty, but she was exceptionally attractive; her physique was perfect; her eyes spoke; her mouth smiled softly; dark hair fell in full waves around her white neck; she bloomed! She was a lovely girl! (36)

This description is notable not only for the focus on how Aglaja appears (as opposed to what kind of person she is), but also for the attribution of agency to her body parts. It preemptively disassociates Aglaja's body—and in particular her eyes and mouth, conventional gateways to a person's interior thoughts and feelings—from her inner being. Aglaja does not smile, her mouth does, and her eyes "speak" seemingly of their own accord.

Such a description of the protagonist—coming, as it does, in the first paragraph of the story proper—is symptomatic of the narrative's lack of interest in linking Aglaja's interior "self" to what can be known—or, more precisely, told—of who she was. Instead, the story consistently foregrounds the exterior events of Aglaja's life, giving us a picture of a character as she might be seen by her audience rather than as she understands herself. Aglaja's interior thoughts and motivations crop up in the story primarily at the moment of their disappearance, as in this description of her return to society after a year of mourning Ludwig's death:

> Aglaja lived once again in the social circles in which she had once shone, and which really had lost something through her removal; her sorrow had brought forth no unpleasant effect to her appearance; on the contrary, she had become only more interesting as a result of the softness imparted to her eyes by a heavy spirit . . . . (50)

Information that might give the reader access to Aglaja's feelings and inner "truth" is quickly pressed into the service of providing a picture of her appearance, her behavior, and her reception by the social audience, further underlining the reader's position as spectator to Aglaja's performance of self rather than as privileged sharer of her subjective truth.

In lieu of presenting the "truth" of Aglaja's life through an exposition of her interior "self," the narrative emphasizes the ways in which public perception of Aglaja's actions buffet and shape her experience and thereby condition and construct who she "is." Aglaja can only "be" the sum total of countless public (re)presentations, most of which result from other people's manipulation of, and (at times willful) misinterpretation of, her motives and character. Bürger highlights the function of gossip, rumor, jealousy, and intrigue in the shaping of Aglaja's life and experience, calling attention to the active role her public audience plays in determining who she is. This plays out across the social spectrum, from the envious bourgeois women who spread rumors that she had been a wasteful wife and blame her for her husband's bankruptcy, to the elaborate courtly machinations and improvisations perpetrated by Prince Eugen's uncle in order to separate her from Eugen and (above all) destroy her reputation.

The power of public opinion to determine a woman's "being" is perhaps most evident in Bürger's portrayal of the world of the theater and Aglaja's experience as an actress. When Aglaja expresses her desire to become an actress, Mme. B. (the veteran actress who shares Bürger's initial), tries to convince her to avoid the profession, warning that she is too old, too unaware of the rules and systems that govern theater work, and too seduced by the glamour that seems to inhere to the stage:

> You do not know the inner side of the theater and its players; oh my friend, things in the world are not as they seem; if I could represent this profession to you as it is, with all of its thousands of evils, you would gladly rush back to your sewing needle and prefer a calm peaceful industrious existence to the more glittering one that shimmers opposite you! (96)

However, this fairly conventional image of the theater as a den of evils is quickly contradicted by the depiction of a utopian and harmonious working relationship between the two women, who not only develop a bond of friendship but also become a professional team:

> Madame B. led [Aglaja] to the director, and they reached an agreement. Aglaja's exterior was advantageous, and she debuted as the Queen in Schiller's Don Carlo. Madame B., who played the Princess Eboli,

> supported her by virtue of her esteem among the company, and Aglaja reaped great applause. This gave her confidence, and soon she was able to shine next to the magnificent B. She, for her part, disavowed all pettiness, praised Aglaja's achievements, and never expressed the slightest envy over the developments in the audience's favor; indeed, two women of the theater, both still under thirty, both beautiful, both intelligent and full of spirit, both worshipped and adored—what a miracle of mutual resignation! They were a phenomenon on the theatrical horizon; they spent two peaceful years in this manner . . . . (97)

Despite Mme. B's confirmation of the prevailing assessment of theater as a dangerous place for the virtuous woman, the narrative provides evidence that it need not be, and that good women can and do thrive within the institution.

But this presentation of Aglaja and Mme B. as miraculous exceptions to the rule of backbiting and vicious intrigue in the theater serves primarily to bring the power of stereotype and prejudice into relief, for despite the fact that Aglaja is a "good" actress—in both senses of the word—she receives a cold and hostile reception from the citizens of her hometown, who consider her return as an actress tacit confirmation of all of the vices attributed to her by the rumor mill. The conversation she overhears between two old acquaintances reveals the category slippage that determines her reception, and identity, upon her return:

> *Captain:* . . . she has the *Effronterie,*—for of course you know, Friend! That she is an actress——
>
> *The Other:* What? Well, well, nothing in the world is impossible; the beautiful Aglaja!—and she was so proud—she would hardly allow one to kiss her hand.—
>
> *Captain:* Pah! First she ruins her husband, then becomes mistress of the Prince of *—then chased from the court—and then she kept a *petite Maison* in F., which the police shut down, and in despair she turned to the theater [. . . and now she has the *Effronterie*] to come here, I mean, to play a guest role here, to present herself *en Public*; can one be any more shameless? (104–05)

Even though all of the captain's assumptions and accusations are false, they are nonetheless powerful, and that is precisely the point.

All of her former acquaintances believe the rumors and attend her performance solely in order to mock her and witness her humiliation and failure.

Bürger is ruthlessly unsentimental and unromantic about the power of Aglaja—or any woman—to combat negative public opinion through virtuous, authentic living. On the contrary—and this, perhaps, is where the story most closely intersects Bürger's own experience of public (re)constructions of herself—the narrative convincingly demonstrates that the "truth" of a woman's self is, to a very real extent, immaterial in light of, and when set against, the social assumptions and material conditions that determine and overdetermine the production and reception of that "self." Who Bürger "was" was, ultimately—like her heroine—the sum total of appearances and representations. And like her heroine, Elise Bürger herself remains, in literary history, an enigma: what we know of her is the result of a concatenation of others' (often untrustworthy) assessments of her and her own (self-interested, and therefore equally untrustworthy) self-representations.

As a result, in contrast to the epistolary novels of La Roche and Ehrmann, which excavated a woman's thoughts to demonstrate her naive, natural virtuousness, Bürger's story emphasizes the extent to which a woman's "being" depends—precisely as Rousseau proclaimed—upon her reputation. But in opposition to Rousseau, Bürger's narrative fundamentally challenges the criteria by which women are judged to be virtuous and good, through its discounting of the discourse of subjective antitheatricality as a criteria for virtue. By insisting that her protagonist is "good" and "virtuous" despite the fact that she neither remains properly in the domestic sphere nor is subjectively authentic in the traditional sense, Bürger challenges her readership to recognize the coercive and prejudicial nature of the cultural association of virtue and subjective authenticity with domesticity. That is to say, by incorporating publicity and subjective performance into its definition of a "good" woman, "Aglaja" not only argues that the public woman—and particularly, the actress—can, indeed, be "virtuous," but also starkly reveals the impossible tautology that governed the lives and reputations of women who lived their lives, by choice or circumstance, outside their "proper" sphere: that is, the tautology in the Rousseauian notion that any woman who displayed herself outside the domestic sphere could not possibly be a naive, authentic, natural woman, because such a woman could exist only within domesticity.

In addition, Bürger also discounts the importance of subjective antitheatricality by undermining the conventional association of virtue with naiveté. She does this by revealing the powerless and vulnerable position naive women occupy outside the domestic sphere, and by demonstrating that self-awareness and conscious self-performance are not necessarily incompatible with "virtue." Thus, for example, early in the story Bürger establishes Aglaja as a naive girl who cannot even recognize that she has just fallen in love:

> At home, Aglaja's aristocratic friends, more sharp-eyed than their playmate, explained to her what she felt; the lovely girl took an unconstrained delight in the sweet first feelings of her pure heart, and, dreaming, forgot the future in favor of the beautiful present. (39)

The conventional image of bourgeois innocence invoked here is then cemented in the narrative by a recounting of how the young and inexperienced Aglaja is tricked into inadvertently revealing her love for Ludwig by a clever baron (at the theater, of course):

> Ludwig was an officer; it was wartime, several regiments were to march, he perhaps with them. Aglaja sat in the theater, Ludwig stood opposite her, the Hussar cavalry Captain von Kühnöhl behind her chair: "the B—sche regiment will also march!" he whispered in Aglaja's ear . . . Aglaja became pale, and her eye rested questioningly on her loved one: "What is the Captain saying about my regiment?" asked Ludwig; "it will—unfortunately—not march."
>
> "Praise God!" cried the indiscreet Aglaja! The Hussar turned away, stroking his red moustache . . . and laughed scornfully at the stupid little bourgeois goose! (40)

The innocence and naiveté that might mark Aglaja as "virtuous" become, at one and the same time, the means by and through which Aglaja is defined and shaped in the public eye: the baron leaves the theater and spreads the story widely, rendering Aglaja the laughing-stock of good society. Bürger thus subverts the usual association of innocence and naturalness with goodness, by showing the bad consequences that can result from acting "naturally."

In Bürger's narrative world, innocence is not only not a virtue, it is a liability. The Baron's discovery of Aglaja and Ludwig's affair quickly leads to their separation by Ludwig's parents, who disapprove of his match with a bourgeois girl. But, the narrator tells us in an approving tone, "love makes even innocence cunning and deceitful" (43): Ludwig and Aglaja meet in secret for the next three years, disguising their relationship by outwardly flirting with others. This pragmatic deployment of performance is presented as a matter-of-fact necessity that in no way detracts from Aglaja's virtue. On the contrary, it is presented positively, as evidence of her cleverness and her triumph over prejudice:

> [S]he capitalized on the disposition to coquetry that, displaced by love, lay hidden in the background of her soul, and—in defiance of the aristocratic family—conquered one man's heart after another. (44)

The attitude toward coquetry in this text is in stark contrast to that demonstrated in the earlier works discussed in this study: rather than seeing it as one of the vices to which women are prone, Bürger presents coquetry as one of many skills a woman needs in order to successfully negotiate the public sphere. Every woman, the narrator notes early on, "brings her own, small or large, portion [of coquetry] with her from her mother's womb" (38). Aglaja's use of coquetry as a smokescreen against discovery of her ongoing relationship with Ludwig is presented as a justifiable use of her inborn talents rather than a vicious indulgence of sensuality. In insisting that a deliberately coquettish woman can still be considered "a good woman indeed," the story ultimately demands a reexamination of why, and for whom, naiveté is "good."

In fact, in its dismissal of naiveté "Aglaja" could be read as a throwback to baroque society's blunt acceptance of the idea that people act as players on a politico-social stage. But Bürger is writing within a discursive setting in which authenticity, sincerity, and antitheatrical subjectivity do indeed matter, and in which deliberate performances of "self" are condemned as immoral, *particularly* when the performer is a woman. As a result, her exposure of the pitfalls of naiveté and her insistence on the necessity of managing one's appearance and image in the public sphere represent a challenge to notions of ideal femininity that associate virtue with naiveté. In its place, Bürger proposes a definition of virtuous womanhood that takes publicity into consideration and understands that women must account for, and, at times, manage an audience that may be responding and reacting as much (if not more) to other's representations of her actions as to her actions themselves.

The complexities of that audience's response are exemplified in the prince's reaction to a letter Aglaja writes after she has been victimized by his uncle's intrigues, forced to flee the court, and had her name and reputation destroyed by rumors that her flight was necessitated by pregnancy. Her letter to the prince accurately represents her side of the story:

> Dear Prince!
>
> You receive here the farewell letter of a love that I, fool! believed would make me happy, and which was destroyed through base intrigue, the victim of an evildoer whom I forbid to name out of respect to you. My heart's peace is gone, my hopes destroyed, I joyless, and Eugen free! Yes, take all of your holy oaths, along with your letters, back; from this beautiful and heavy dream I keep only your picture, which will forever live in my heart. Live well! Still and always my beloved Eugen! Be a wise Prince to your country, a true and gentle husband to your wife; do not completely forget the unhappy Aglaja—you were too loved by her! (92–93)

The prince's immediate reaction, however, shows that under the right circumstances truth can be taken for appearance as readily as appearance is taken for truth: " 'The hypocrite!' cried the Prince, when he had finished reading; 'Nature has thrown the loveliest cover around the falsest heart!' " (93). While the narrative's reader might "know" that Aglaja's heart is not "false" in this affair, Bürger has also deliberately refused to provide any substantial evidence as to the "truth" of Aglaja's heart. In fact, the prince's misreading of Aglaja's motives and sincerity here are reminiscent of G. A. Bürger's retroactive rereading of Elise Bürger's motives after the failure of their marriage and his casting of her into the role of devious seductress who used a show of naiveté to dupe him into marriage. Rather than recapitulate her own futile efforts to convey the truth of her "self" to a hostile public, Bürger uses "Aglaja" to demonstrate the impossibility of truthfully conveying female subjectivity to an audience at all, particularly in the face of a culture that automatically conflates female independence and publicity with vice.

* * *

FRIEDERIKE HELENE UNGER: *MELANIE, THE FOUNDLING*

Friederike Helene Unger's novel *Melanie, the Foundling* tells the story of a young woman of unknown origins who is cast out into the world to make her own way. The novel traces her journey as she moves, with greater and lesser degrees of success, between and among several social circles and occupations. The novel's plot and its complications revolve around the central problem of who Melanie really "is": her lack of a proper place and identity in society compel her to assume a series of roles—including that of actress—in order to survive. Like "Aglaja," Unger's novel embraces theatricality and performance in both form and content. Formally, the novel calls attention to its own artifice, rejecting realism in favor of a theatricality that mitigates against the reader's absorbed identification into the novel's scene. Because Unger continually reminds her reader that the female protagonist is a construct of her pen, she enables us to recognize the extent to which female subjectivity is likewise a construct.

My reading of *Melanie* proposes that the novel anticipates Butlerian notions of gendered identity as a compulsory performance by revealing the complex interplay between culturally available social scripts and a woman's ability to enact and/or resist them. As a result, the novel departs from reigning conceptions of ideal femininity as grounded in nature by clearly presenting femininity as an "act." At the same time, Unger's novel draws on eighteenth-century theories that argued that good acting is grounded in sincerity as a means of recuperating Melanie's performance of femininity back into the ideal. But the novel is, above all, a satire, and in the realm of satire any recuperation serves in the end to destabilize what it seems to affirm. As a result, ultimately Unger offers us no firm ground to stand upon, presenting us with what appears to be a set of endlessly reflecting mirrors bouncing "natural" identity against its performance. Like many of Unger's other works, *Melanie* is riddled with contradictions and inconsistencies that resist full resolution or reconciliation.[7] For while her narrative depends to a certain extent on the notion that Melanie has a stable core of identity that remains unchanged throughout her life and thus represents the ideal antitheatrical woman, it also continually reveals the essential fictionality of femininity, and demonstrates the complicated ways that the performance of ideal femininity was pressured and policed by the expectations and desires of the social audience.

Friedrike Helene Unger has been the subject of a growing body of research in recent years.[8] Feminist scholars in particular have "rescued" her from literary obscurity, arguing that her novels are both important in their own right and as evidence of women's engagement with the literary scene around 1800.[9] In addition, recent scholarship has also focused attention on the satirical aspects of Unger's work, on its function as social critique, and in particular on its proto-feminist agenda.[10] But despite increased interest in Unger's work in general, little attention has been paid to *Melanie*. Touaillon dismisses it out of hand as a novel whose subject is "the fight against sentimentality" (253) and only two other twentieth-century critics, Zantop and Giesler, devote any significant attention to the novel. Zantop reads the novel in terms of its engagement with the "roles" for women laid out by Goethe and as a work that reveals the impossibility of a female *Bildungsroman*. While her analysis of the novel's engagement with performance and theatricality dovetails in many respects with my own, it is aimed at demonstrating Unger's relationship as a writer to contemporary literary models, in particular to Goethe. Giesler largely follows Zantop in her brief treatment of *Melanie*, describing the book as a "theater novel, which conspicuously links the metaphor of theater with the problem of identity" and noting both the inherent theatricality of Unger's writing and the satirical edge to the novel (69). However, in line with the argument of her book, the emphasis of Giesler's analysis of the novel is Unger's use of intertextual references in her writing. My analysis takes up some of the same threads of Zantop and Giesler's arguments and pulls them in a different direction, in order to show how this novel uses the theater and acting to reveal the untenability of bourgeois demands for subjective authenticity and sincerity in the "ideal woman."

Melanie, the Foundling tells a familiar "princess" fantasy. Mysteriously abandoned as a baby, Melanie is found in a basket by Princess Aurore, who brings Melanie up as one of her own children. When Melanie is eleven years old, her status as a foundling is revealed to her by a mean-spirited servant, and Melanie's relationship to the royal family is forever altered. No longer seen as a genuine member of the family, she ceases to be addressed as "Miss" and begins to feel distanced from her former "sisters" and Aurore. The distancing reaches a peak when Aurore begins to suspect that her husband, the Prince, has fallen in love with the teenaged Melanie. When, through a series of misunderstandings, Aurore catches her husband in Melanie's room one evening, Aurore casts her out of the castle. Melanie is rescued by Aurore's brother, Prince Rudolph, who is in love with Melanie, and who spirits her away to his hunting lodge, where she remains under the supervision of an ex-mistress of Rudolph's father.

Melanie is not a particularly welcome guest at the lodge, however, and she becomes less so when news arrives that Aurore has issued an order for her arrest and imprisonment. Thus, when she encounters a troupe of actors while walking in the forest near the lodge, she joins them. She has a natural talent for acting and quickly becomes the star of the company. Among her admirers is Count Wilhelm; they fall in love, and he declares his intention to marry her. But his mother intervenes and forces Melanie to give up acting, go into hiding, and renounce her claim to him, leaving him free to marry his intended bride. Wilhem's mother sends Melanie to live as companion to her odious sister, the Countess Ottenburg; Wilhelm, meanwhile, kills his fiancée's brother in a duel and is forced into exile himself, with the Austrian army. From this point on Unger puts

Melanie into the care of a series of widowed or otherwise unattached women, who serve both as caregivers to Melanie within the diegesis and as literary foils to her character.

At Countess Ottenburg's, Melanie is befriended by the Baroness Helene, who takes pity on her and invites her to become her companion for a while before sending her to live with a bourgeois friend, Mme. Leerheim. Things go awry with Leerheim when the organizer of an amateur theatrical event discovers Melanie's acting talent and replaces Leerheim with Melanie in the role of Emilia Galotti. Leerheim banishes Melanie, and she returns to the care of the baroness, where she becomes friends with Cölestine, Count Wilhelm's intended bride, and Cölestine's mother, the Countess Löwenheim. When Melanie's old acting companion Mariane suddenly arrives and reveals Melanie's identity to them, Melanie is forced to tell Cölestine and her mother her entire life story. At this point Countess Löwenheim realizes that Melanie is the daughter of her deceased sister (who had also been named Melanie) and therefore her niece. A letter from Aurore's daughter (which has coincidentally arrived that very day) gives further detail, as the midwife who delivered Melanie has finally revealed the secret of her birth: the countess's sister had been one of Aurore's ladies in waiting. During a ball at the castle she accidentally "got herself into the wrong room," where she had a sexual encounter with Aurore's husband, the Prince.[11] The mother's fate is vague—it is clear only that she died some time after Melanie's birth—but the mystery of why Melanie was abandoned to the care of Aurore and the prince is finally resolved: her mother left her to be brought up by her natural father.

The novel thus ends happily. Melanie discovers that she is indeed of royal blood; at almost the same moment she wins a large sum of money in the lottery, and after she proves her love for the count by being willing to marry him even though she thinks he has been crippled in the war, the two are married. Melanie is reunited with her family, and her identity—as a "princess"—is finally (re)confirmed.

That the novel foregrounds the complexity of the relationship between "natural" identity and role is evident even from this brief plot summary—Melanie both always was a "princess" all along (or of noble descent, at least, by right of birth and blood) and, except for a brief period in childhood, not a "princess" (in social status and role). On the one hand, Unger seems to present us with an utter stability of "natural" identity—for throughout, Melanie "is" persistently the figure destined to be revealed as really a "princess," a fact that explains why most of the other roles she must take up in the course of the novel fail to fit her well. But on the other hand, that moment of revelation seems not to produce, in Melanie, a sense of identity and wholeness but rather its opposite: upon hearing the news she experiences a profound psychic and physical alienation, appearing to the countess as a "cold, lifeless image" and almost immediately falling into a death-like faint (206). Even when firmly installed in what has been revealed as her "natural" role as the daughter of the prince, Melanie continues to be compelled to perform a number of other roles, including reluctantly pretending to be in love with another count in order to preserve the honor of Aurore's daughter (240–42). Finding out who she really "is" thus only confirms the role Melanie must forthwith play, it does not relieve her of the necessity to perform, for—as the Countess Löwenheim announces once Wilhelm is revealed to be unharmed and Melanie has accepted his offer of marriage—"It seems we are playing comedy here!" (248).

The countess's announcement seems to indicate that none of the characters in the novel questions the necessity or naturalness of performing; the problem throughout is, rather, whether or not Melanie's "performed" identity matches her "natural" one. As a result—and here we seem to be presented with an irreconcilable contradiction—the novel seems to want to both figure ideal femininity as quintessentially antitheatrical and insist that all subjectivity has a performative dimension. The novel presents subjective identity as something that does not only depend on transparency of motive, thought, and feeling but also on social standing, class, and occupation. Thus Unger complicates her own equation of ideal femininity with antitheatricality by emphasizing the powerful influence external factors have on an audience's reception of female subjectivity and virtue. Who Melanie "is" on the inside does not seem to change in the novel (although, as I note below, we do not receive much information on her interiority to begin with); but who she is perceived to be socially does, and it changes so substantially that for the Countess

Löwenheim what was sure tragedy—having her daughter's fiancé fall in love with an actress—gets transformed into comedy.

The narrative trope of the "unrecognized princess" that Unger draws upon (and largely satirizes) in this novel immediately invokes one of the chief paradoxes of antitheatrical subjectivity, namely: how, in the absence of a proper, and properly contextualized, performance of one's essential "self" can one have one's "true" nature recognized by others? Consequently, an exploration of the relationship between identity and performance is built into the narrative structure Unger adopts for her tale. At the same time, because Unger continually draws our attention to *her* role as writer in determining both Melanie's "fate" and "character," the narrative insistently refuses to let us imagine Melanie as a stable character who preexists her narration in the tale. In fact, much of the novel's satire depends upon our recognition that who Melanie "is" is, first and foremost, an effect of writing.

From the outset of the novel, Unger foregrounds her presence as author and creator of the characters in the story. Shortly after introducing two of the main characters—Melanie, the found baby; and Princess Aurore, who quickly embraces Melanie as her child—Unger interrupts the flow of the narrative with an aside to her reading audience. Aurore, she tells us, is a woman who loves to have fantastic, romantic events in her life. "But," Unger writes, "we must say—as with all such characters of this mixture, the fire burned brightly enough, for the time it warmed enough; but—it tended to die out quickly and soon. Yet in this case we don't want to be anxious about it, for the sake of our little Melanie, whom we dearly love" (7). The reference here to "we" and "our" is an early signal of the novel's interest in calling attention to its own artifice and to the fictionality of its characters: it is both the royal "we" of the author, who wants to remind her reader of her control over the fates of her characters, and the collective "we" that makes the reader complicit in that control, through the act of reading and (re)creating the story.

Likewise, Unger takes advantage of the structural familiarity of the story to play with her reader's expectations and heighten the sense that the novel itself is a performance on the theme of "unrecognized princess." Thus our suspicion as readers that Melanie will turn out to really "be" the princess she only gets to "play" at being during her childhood is encouraged not only by our knowledge that this is the way such stories tend to go, but also by a couple of hints dropped by the narrator that seem intended to encourage us to appreciate how well Melanie is performing, for us, the role of "unrecognized princess"—and that simultaneously draw our attention to the narrator's performance in crafting Melanie's tale. So, for example, when Melanie finds herself feeling at home upon her arrival at the Countess Löwenheim's estate, we are told,

> [T]he title "Miss," with which she was introduced here, had a pleasing sound to her little heart that—despite all objections of her reason—her heart did not entirely resist; for ideas of high rank and hopes for a favorable revelation of the secret of her birth still haunted her romantic little head. (182)

The narrator's mockery of Melanie's hopes that she might indeed be entitled to be addressed as "Miss" seems to be a wink and a nod in the direction of the reader, who would already be anticipating that those hopes will in fact be fulfilled by novel's end. Moments like this in the text call attention to the writerly craft that allows Unger to play with her reader's expectations while at the same time revealing the mechanism at work in that play. As a result, the "doubled" reading of Melanie encouraged by both the narrative structure and the narrator's hints about her "real" identity adds a level of theatricality to the text, as it heightens our awareness not only of how Melanie continually performs (that is, both within the diegesis itself and as a character functioning in a particular role within a familiar narrative form, as "unrecognized princess"), but also of the author's performative manipulation of her narrative material.

Unger's choice seems deliberate here: as Susanne Zantop notes, by the time Unger wrote *Melanie* she was not only a confident and accomplished writer, but was also developing her own literary style ("Nachwort" 394). By calling attention not only to the artificiality of the narrative but also to the reader's role in (re)creating the story, Unger precludes the hallucinatory, identificatory response that was so crucial to the ideological project of transparency as described in the opening chapter of this book. In its stead, she encourages her reader to take up a theatrical relationship to the text, to recognize and affirm the novels' status as a performance, and to engage in critical dialogue with the novel.

In fact, this is a dialogue that Unger at times writes into the novel itself, as when she scripts her reader's response to a plot twist:

> "Oh, I don't want to interrupt you," says one of my lovely readers, who with many others has the habit of assuring that she doesn't want to interrupt while in the process of interrupting. Well: "Oh, I don't want to interrupt you; this is going to be, it seems, a novel without love. How can you expect us, my Sir or Madame, to enjoy such a stale and clumsy piece of work? A novel without love is like a face without a nose, which thus loses all physiognomy."
>
> I would be happy, my lovely readers, if I could succeed at a novel without love; for love—is love. (184)

The satirical edge to Unger's observations about her reader's expectations is unmistakable—she is clearly poking fun at the traditional sentimental novel and its timeworn plots. At the same time, however, speaking directly to her reader in such a way is the equivalent of breaking the theatrical fourth wall, and it indicates that we should be alert to the many ways in which the novel employs theatricality, not only in its aesthetic form, but also in its engagement with received notions of ideal womanhood.

Put bluntly, the novel's formal artificiality and theatricality point to the artificiality and theatricality of its main subject: virtuous femininity as exemplified by the main character, Melanie. In contrast to the realism of novels like *Sternheim* or *Amalie*—which encourage us to enter into the illusion that the heroine is a "real" person whose history is being "truthfully" represented by the novel itself, in the form of her "real" letters—Unger continually inserts herself into the narrative and reminds us that "Melanie" is a construct of her pen and hence, in every sense, exists *as* and *as a consequence of* performance. The stability of identity—that is, the narrative of origin and biographical history—that grounds the illusory aesthetic of the epistolary novel is wholly absent here. In its place, Unger presents us with a character who must continually construct and reconstruct her identity.

Melanie begins the novel with, essentially, no proper identity: the basket in which she was abandoned to Aurore's care by her mother contains no clues to her origin, only a brief note containing her name and the hope that "Melanie will, if she has her creator's heart (*das Herz ihrer Urheber*), requite her noble benefactress love for love, and joy for joy" (5). The ambivalence of the German original here is noteworthy: where one would expect to see the word *Vater* ("father") or even *Mutter* ("mother"), Unger uses *Urheber*, which can mean parent, creator, author, or originator, indicating a conflation of "Melanie's" mysterious parents and her "author" and underlining the novel's self-reflexivity vis-à-vis its own deployment of artifice.[12] Melanie's lack of identity is thus formulated at the outset not only as a narrative plot element, but also as the effect of authorial performance. The theatricality of Unger's writing is inextricably linked with the novel's investigation of the theatricality of female identity.

That investigation involves, above all, an emphasis on the extent to which female identity is an effect of role-play. Role playing is the major female activity in the novel: not only do all of the women characters in the novel seem to be playing a socially prescribed role, but during the course of the narrative Melanie takes on a series of roles, including that of a young princess (before her exile from Aurore's court), virtuous maid in distress, "other" woman, lady's companion, ghost writer, and, in the end, noblewoman and wife (cf. Zantop, "The Beautiful Soul" 41, 43). What is important to note is that all the roles she takes up are always already predetermined: there are only a limited number of social scripts available to Melanie. In essence, the novel is about Melanie's successful enactment of or—where appropriate for the "ideal" woman—resistance to those scripts.

Accordingly, and—given the eighteenth-century bourgeois prejudice against performance—remarkably, Unger's novel does not automatically associate performance with viciousness and deception. This is partially attributable to the novel's setting in the aristocratic milieu, where acting and performance are less derogated than in the bourgeois setting. But although Melanie represents a bourgeois ideal of womanhood—that is, she is virtuous in the expected ways—Unger is less interested in using the presence or absence of performance to *oppose* aristocratic and bourgeois cultures than in exploring and investigating how performance mediates the complicated relationship between interior subjectivity, social role, and audience expectation.

Consequently, she shows that there is a similar set of pressures at work in both the aristocratic and bourgeois cultures that compel and constrain Melanie's performance of self and in the process reveals the hypocrisy behind bourgeois demands for authenticity and sincerity. This is perhaps most evident in the (satirical, and very funny) episode in which Melanie goes to work for the bourgeois writer and "intellectual" Mme. Leerheim (whose name translates as "empty home"). Leerheim is a fake: her philosophical writings are plagiarized translations, and she props up her identity and reputation by surrounding herself with posers. Her *salon* is a scene of bald pretension—the narrative even deploys theatrical metaphors in describing her retinue so as to leave no doubt as to the level of insincerity at play in this setting:

> The best that can be said of the other gentlemen and ladies of this circle is, that they always waited in pious resignation to find out what kind of role the head actors would give them; in fact they were simply extras, even just gap-fillers, who were shoved and turned about upon this small stage of vanity wherever and however it might please [the principals]. (156)

Melanie's "role" in this setting quickly becomes that of the naive, ignorant girl—a blank slate to Leerheim's sophisticated woman of culture—despite the fact that, at this point in the narrative, she is fairly well acquainted with the world, having had experience both in several courtly settings and as an actress. The episode provides Unger with the opportunity to demonstrate not only that the performance of identity pervades all social levels, but also that such performances are interrelated and can serve both social good and ill. Thus, while Leerheim's artificiality is facile and detestable, it has the positive consequence of providing Melanie with a social script that gives her the opportunity to shine in the role of the good, innocent, sincere, and naive bourgeois girl.

For Melanie, this is not a particularly difficult role to play—in fact, the narrative presents her as "born" to it. This is different from saying that the novel presents Melanie as "naturally" and transparently good, innocent, sincere, naive, et cetera: on the contrary, what is foregrounded throughout is the complicated relationship between Melanie's "nature," her propensity for acting, the roles she takes up or is pressed into, and her social identity. Very early in the novel Melanie is presented as a girl who imitates others well and has a natural talent for acting:

> Among this blossoming virgin's talents . . . the favors of the both the tragic muse and the joyful, playful Thalia were the most striking. . . . [Melanie took part in the tasteful spectacles organized by Aurore and] was always the Grace of the party, the one whom all hearts, even the women's, praised; and she elicited the wish from many connoisseurs that she might devote herself entirely to the art [of acting]. (13–14)

Yet, contrary to reigning discursive notions about the morality of performance, Melanie's natural talent for acting does not make her vicious or dangerous. Rather, Unger emphasizes that she uses her talent only and always in the service of sincerity. Thus, for example, we are told that in her professional debut she "had to be Klärchen, and was so completely, that there would never be another like it" (64); that unlike other actresses she never "only pretended" on stage (189); and that in addition she not only personifies but is the personification of the virtuous bourgeois heroine: "Even Lessing would have seen his own Emilia completely clearly for the first time [in her performance of the role]" (70). This configuration of the relationship between Melanie's innate virtue, the naturalness of her performances, and her ability to successfully portray virtuous characters meshes with "intuitive" acting theories, which posited a similar connection between the actor's interior state and his or her skill at convincing an audience of the "truth" of the performance of a role. As in that theory, in Unger's narrative world authenticity and performance are not mutually exclusive but rather mutually enabling.

At the same time, however, the narrative also underscores the fact that it is not enough simply to have a natural propensity for acting: the talent must be trained and channeled. For Melanie, acting is *work*. Unger shows her assiduously studying the craft in order to perfect her talent:

> Now the studying began in earnest. Flattery called Melanie perfect; fortunately she didn't believe this and took every hint, every bit of advice of her teacher, the director. To be the creature of shallow criticism of the day, the idol of frivolity, was meaningless to her; she wanted to thoroughly explore her profession and exploit, not waste, the lovely gift of nature. She read the memoirs of Hippolyte Clairon[13] with delight, and tried to apply her observations to the more recent breed of literature. (63)

Unger's description of successful acting as resulting from a combination of virtue, natural talent, and hard work is reminiscent of Schröder's gloss on Riccoboni: he, too, advised young actors to cultivate both their own moral center and their technical craft.[14] The narrative's emphasis on the work involved in successfully filling a role belies the "naturalness" with which it also shows Melanie taking up the various social roles she fills, raising the suspicion that similar work is involved in her performance of off-stage social roles and thereby undercutting its own presentation of Melanie as "naturally" genuine and naive. Consequently, the novel's deployment of the relationship between authenticity and performance in terms of intuitive acting theory helps explain the apparent (and essentially unresolved) paradox inherent in the novel's depiction of Melanie as both virtuously antitheatrical and a consummate performer of roles.

Unger is, in effect, using acting theory as a means of re-presenting female subjectivity "off stage." That is, rather than positing ideal femininity in terms of a natural identity that is immediately and transparently expressed in some naive, mystical way, the novel shows that Melanie's "natural" inclination to virtue and sincerity helps determine how she interprets and enacts the social scripts made available to her. Some seem to come "naturally," others present what can only be termed an "acting challenge," and in still other cases her "natural" virtue compels her to resist a given script.

As I have already mentioned, the role of innocent and virtuous girl, in a variety of settings, both on and off the stage, fits Melanie like a glove. "Lady's Companion," however, requires a bit more work. As companion to the Countess Ottenburg, Melanie feels wrongly relegated to a role among the servants: the countess has her serving tea to guests and cleaning up after her dog, Mops. Unger uses the scene to reveal both the difficulty such a role presents to Melanie and the way that the different perspectives on her "proper" role impact her construction of self. Generally Melanie is ignored by the countess's company; one day, however, she attracts the attention of a female guest, who asks the countess where she "found this rare beauty?—She inquired in precisely the same way one might ask, if one wanted to buy similar goods at a similar price" (104). The countess tells the guest that Melanie is an orphan of unknown origins, who has been placed in her care by her sister and who had been an actress before coming to live with her. The guest's response interpellates Melanie into the scene in what is, for her, an ill-fitting role:

> She called Melanie, who was serving biscuits to her Countess, to bring her something too, and then left Melanie standing a good long while with her tray, during which she conversed quite calmly with her neighbor. Melanie trembled almost to a faint, sent a tearful look towards heaven, gave the tray to a servant and left the room. "I did it purposefully!" said the young lady, watching Melanie stagger away. "That thing strikes me as full of pretension and self-conceit with her courteous little mask. Such behavior must be reprimanded." (105)

The gap here between Melanie's own conception of her role in this company (as an equal, if not in social standing, at least in upbringing and character) and the attitude of the countess and her guests—who not only interpret her lack of concrete social standing and status as "ex-actress" as a sign of social inferiority, but also treat her as such in a deliberate attempt to put her in her proper place—demonstrates Unger's understanding of the complex interplay between script, role, and audience response that goes into constituting "identity." On the one hand, Unger evokes her reader-audience's sympathy for Melanie's situation: Melanie is, after all, only trying to do her best to survive, and her feelings of indignity at her treatment are fully understandable, especially as the narrative has us suspecting that she is indeed of noble birth. At the same time, Unger makes it easy to understand the perspective of the Countess's guests, who see Melanie's reluctance to serve not only as a refusal to inhabit her proper social role but also as an arrogant pretension to a social standing that her past history can not possibly support. The role Melanie is constrained to play in this context is challenging not only because it doesn't "fit" her, but also because her immediate audience—the countess's guests—misread one performance (virtuous suffering) for another (arrogant pretension). The scene thus reveals Melanie's difficulty in enacting certain social roles, given both her personal inclination toward sincerity and the unpredictability of audience response, and, in so doing, clearly gives the lie to the notion that the virtuous woman's natural "being" is transparently readable. Instead, this scene highlights both the opacity of Melanie's "self" to her audience and the power of that audience to determine her success or failure in a given role.

Where the role of "lady's companion" represents a challenge for Melanie, the role of actress, at least as it is defined by eighteenth-century stereotype, is one to which she is completely unsuited, despite her natural talents as a performer. Indeed, from the moment Melanie chooses to join the acting troupe, she not only resists, but also fundamentally redefines the role of the actress both within the troupe and in relation to her audience and admirers. Once again, we see Unger presenting us with an interrelationship between "natural" inclination and social script: she insists that Melanie's resistance to the "role" of the actress stems from her innate sense of virtue and morality and yet simultaneously presents her conduct as a deliberate, performative choice:

> Melanie had not made any special plan regarding her conduct. She knew of no other, than that sanctioned by honesty and uprightness (*Rechtschaffenheit*) and morality (*Sittlichkeit*); but accustomed as she was to the highest decency of decorum, she found it proper to move into an apartment in the Director's house and to arrange for a place at his table, which was granted her in return for a deduction from her wages. Her female compatriots took a *chambre garnie* and distanced themselves as far as possible from the very supervision that our Melanie never would have imagined she needed to avoid. (61)

Melanie's "performance" of the role of actress, inflected as it is by her natural inclination to virtue, not only sets her apart from the other women in her troupe but also sets a higher standard of conduct for both troupe and audience. When, at her debut, she refuses to take a curtain call because she feels that it would be indelicate to allow herself to be called forth in order to be praised, "it succeeded so well that since that day all other actresses followed her example, and the audience was sophisticated enough to accept this, even if it was exaggerated delicacy" (64–65). Her graceful handling of the male admirers who swarm her dressing room also draws approval: "A new miracle! [She even has] intelligence and fine manners! Absolutely no impudence, no derision! Some even considered it dowdy and prideful, that she hadn't responded saucily" (65). And although two of the other actresses in the company conduct love affairs that result in illegitimate pregnancies, Melanie's chaste and respectable affair with Count Wilhelm wins her the respect and trust of the community and alters their attitude toward actors in general:

> Her beauty, her moral value, which were made evident by the respectful love of the universally esteemed Count, these were recognized everywhere. The audience brought delicacy to the manner of its admiration, and this made Melanie employ her powers and talents to please them even further. Mothers allowed their daughters to seek her company; and that was no small thing in a city in which there was still plenty of room for the modernization of ideas. Even young wives allowed their husbands to pay homage to the beautiful Melanie, because in this case the fear that she might seduce or swindle them fell away; for Melanie's generosity and liberality leant her character a unique worth, all the more so because these lovely virtues seldom tended to show themselves in this sphere. (83)

This description of Melanie's ability to shape her performance of a social script in such a way as to change the audience's opinion of actresses contrasts sharply with the portrayal of her treatment at the hands of the countess's guests (which comes later in the novel), and can be read as evidence of Unger's sophisticated understanding of the shifting power dynamics that might come into play for any given performance of identity. The social position of the actress was, for the most part, not a particularly powerful one, but, as we have seen from the memoirs of Schulze-Kummerfeld, some actresses took the lofty moral goals of the theater quite seriously and aspired to serve as community role models. Melanie's "interpretation" of the role of actress runs along similar lines, and this, in combination with her connection to the socially powerful count, accords her the ability to shape and direct audience response to, and reception of, her identity. What is interesting is that in both cases—as a member of the acting troupe and in the countess's tearoom—Melanie produces a performance that does not match audience expectations. Her different reception in the different settings reflects less the quality of her performance, or the extent of her resistance to the "role" she is given to play, than her status relative to her audience.

Melanie not only successfully stays within the parameters of ideal femininity while in the role *of* an actress, she also specializes in the role of virtuous bourgeois girl *as* an actress: her "master role" is the virtuous, innocent, openhearted Emilia Galotti. The fact that Melanie has the same "role" both on and off the stage gives the inescapable impression that Unger imagines acting on stage as simply one end of a spectrum of performance, rather than as the opposite of "real" identity. For, once again, the issue here is not the legitimacy or illegitimacy of performance per se, but rather whether, and to what extent, her performance matches—or grants her an opportunity to express—who she "naturally" is. Melanie's success on stage is predicated on the same conditions as her success in the various social roles she plays, and, as such, becomes only a more visible and easily recognizable (because aestheticized and codified within the parameters of "theater") manifestation of the same set of conditions. Her successful performance of ideal femininity in both settings requires putting "innate" virtue, goodness, honesty, and authenticity into the service of an audience-oriented representation of character. Once again, Unger's conception of performance links up with those eighteenth-century theories of acting that posited it as fundamentally a sincere endeavor.

The novel thus departs from contemporary conceptions of ideal femininity by accepting it as an "act," but it recuperates that act back into a moral system grounded in authenticity by recognizing that there are different *kinds* of performance, and that some are better than others. Melanie consequently represents a model for the *proper* performance of ideal femininity, both on the stage and off. The novel underscores the correctness of her acting choices by opposing her to female characters whose enactment of their roles as women is considerably less ideal.

The first of these oppositions requires us to return to the *salon* of the bourgeois plagiarist, Mme. Leerheim. The character of Leerheim is a satirical portrait of the educated, learned woman (and, as Zantop suggests, might even represent a moment of self-mockery on Unger's part ["The Beautiful Soul" 44]). Leerheim's modus operandum is the complete opposite of Melanie's: rather than framing a performance of self from the inside out, Leerheim puts on a false persona and props it up through setting, costume, and a cast of supporting actors. Thus, the novel not only opposes the two women's characters—Melanie, naive, innocent, sincere, versus Leerheim, sophisticated, shameless, fake—but even more importantly it opposes what can only be called their performance "styles." Simply put, Leerheim is not well served by engaging in a mode of performance that is devoid of any innate commitment to honesty or sincerity. In what is one of the cattiest moments of the novel, Unger reveals the gap between Leerheim's pretensions to represent the ideal bourgeois woman and her ability to do so, by demonstrating Melanie's superior ability to act the role of the ideal woman on stage.

In a scene of both high comedy (for the reader) and great tragedy (for Melanie), Leerheim—"with the confidence of an eighteen-year-old"—proposes to perform the role of Emilia in Lessing's *Emilia Galotti* in a celebratory amateur performance of the play. "Out of honesty and respect Melanie had not even taken the liberty of secretly mocking this blunder on the part of her Lady," Unger tells us, and then continues, once again calling attention to her own writerly performance: "thus the scene she had to suffer and that we must narrate was all the more undeserved" (167). Melanie and a friend find Leerheim's costume lying in the front parlor; Melanie puts on Emilia's veil and begins to act out the role, when the Privy Councilor Tauchwitz, a member of Leerheim's *salon*, steps into the room. He is impressed, and encourages Melanie to continue:

> Somewhat recklessly, perhaps arising from hidden motives of girlish vanity, she fell into her master role with great affect, and the Privy Councilor and

> her young friend stood there astonished, surprised. "Are you she, or are you not?" cried the Privy Councilor. "Mademoiselle, where does this come from? The Muse herself is appearing to us!" Melanie continued, turning to him, as her father Odoardo. His admiration pleased her girlish feelings. Her performance took his breath away. Finally he cried out, full of enthusiasm: "No other, but you, can, may play Emilia. It would be a crime against all the Muses, to give this role to another . . ." (168–69)

Unfortunately for Melanie, Leerheim witnesses this exchange and immediately takes Tauchwitz's declaration as a personal insult. In spite, she withdraws from the production, and Melanie takes over the role to universal acclaim; in turn, Leerheim is so incensed by the incident that she banishes Melanie from her house.

There are a number of contradictions and paradoxes revealed by this small scene. First, this is one of the many places in which the narrative intimates that Melanie in fact occasionally acts with less than complete sincerity and honesty. The references to "hidden motives of girlish vanity" and the fact that she plays her role "with great affect"—all registered without the least tone of disapproval—point once again to the novel's refusal to adopt the notion that subjective integrity and authenticity require a complete repudiation of affect and show. In other words, the acknowledgment that Melanie might be acting from vanity functions to counter the linkage between ideal femininity and naiveté, much in the same way that the novel demonstrates that Melanie can be both knowledgeable about the ways of the world and conscious of her performance of her role in it, and at the same time ideally antitheatrical and sincere. Unger's willingness to admit that Melanie is not always completely and fully transparent to herself is therefore consistent with her efforts, throughout the novel, to disconnect ideal femininity from total naiveté.

At the same time, this scene further engages the novel's figuration of Ideal Womanhood in terms of a performance of sincerity by calling attention to Leerheim's perceived inappropriateness for the role. For although Leerheim imagines herself right for the part, other characters—including Melanie, the privy councilor, and the members of the audience who eventually attend the play and gossip about how bad Leerheim would have been in the role—disallow even the possibility of Leerheim's success in the role because of the clear disconnect between her character and the character of the ideal bourgeois woman as represented by Emilia Galotti. The idea that Leerheim could not pull off the role of virtuous bourgeois woman because she lacks interior sincerity is reminiscent of the actor Schröder's admission that, despite his consummate technical skills, he needed to really "be" honest in order to portray an honest man. What is particularly interesting here is that Unger thus uses a stage role as a kind of limit test for Ideal Womanhood: that is, contrary to eighteenth-century *Kardiognostik* theories, Leerheim's lack of the qualities that pertain to Ideal Womanhood become most visible and readable at the moment she proposes to fill the role on stage.

It is, of course, by no means insignificant that the fictional model for ideal femininity invoked here is Lessing's Emilia Galotti. As a literary "sister" to Sara Sampson, to the eighteenth-century German imaginary Emilia likewise represented a cluster of virtues associated with ideal femininity—sexual chastity, obedience, subjective transparency, innocence, et cetera—within a play that demanded a realistic, aesthetically "transparent" performance style. Unger's mobilization of this figure within her novel represents a sophisticated and complex instance of intertextuality.[15] On the one hand, the repeated reference to Lessing's bourgeois heroine speaks to the power of discursive models, and, in particular, to the power of a specific kind of illusory theatrical performance of those models, to shape and police female identity. Unger's invocation of Emilia Galotti thus acknowledges and to a certain extent honors the potent social script that Lessing's character represents.

At the same time, however, Lessing's powerful and pervasive model of transparency is challenged and undermined by Unger's insistent reminder that Emilia is nothing more than a theatrical role, a character in a play. As a result, the emphasis on Emilia's fictionality dovetails with the novel's conception of ideal femininity as a fictional construct, and as a social script to be performed. Moreover, by revealing the mechanics of acting and the acting theory that go into creating an illusory performance of femininity, Unger also calls attention to the politics of the project of aesthetic transparency: that is, to the pressures it brought to bear on women to take fictional characters for "real people" and model themselves accordingly. Unger's challenge to discursive constructions of ideal femininity thus strikes at the very heart of the project of transparency, by making visible the fictionality and discursivity it sought to erase in its quest to "naturalize" what were essentially cultural constructions of gendered subjectivity.

At the same time, however, Unger also imagines Emilia as a role that must be performed in a certain way in order to be convincing—that is, it can only really be played successfully by a "real" Emilia. Her novel thereby contradicts its own figuring of ideal femininity as a discursive construct by also imagining an essential "idealness" for the role, possessed by some women (Melanie) and not by others (Leerheim). Consequently, Unger's intertextual reference to the role of Emilia Galotti, and her use of it to demonstrate that only a virtuous and sincere woman can "play" the virtuous and sincere woman, stand as evidence of the complexity and contradictoriness of her novel's engagement with the relationship between interior "being," social role, performance, and audience reception. For it would seem that Unger proposes that Melanie *can* play the role, and Leerheim *cannot*, because of who they "are": that is, Melanie's success, and Leerheim's failure, seem predicated on the idea that their interior selves are readable "through" the role, by that penetrating glance of the audience who knows, in Schröder's words, "how to evaluate your worth as a human being through your acting" (Riccoboni and Schröder 78). In other words, Unger seems to be taking up, and promoting, notions that regarded ideal femininity as something that could not be performed (particularly through the negative example of Leerheim).

But such an interpretation is further complicated and contradicted by Unger's persistent reminders, throughout the novel, of the audience's failure to recognize Melanie's inner virtue and morality when she is not properly "cast"—that is, by the fact that who she "is" is not consistently readable by her social audience no matter what social role she plays. By portraying a virtuous woman whose inner worth is only readable when she has the "right" role to play—and by contrasting her with a woman who cannot play femininity "right" by dint of her lack of interior sincerity and virtue—Unger seems to be making the case that ideal femininity *must*, in fact, be performed, but that it is a role that can only be successfully played by a woman who is sincere.

The novel's implicit argument that femininity is a role that demands a particular kind of performance, by a particular type of woman, becomes even more visible, and more complicated, when we consider the other main opposition it sets up, between Melanie and the carefree actress Mariane. The character of Mariane represents yet another intertextual reference: eighteenth-century German readers would have immediately made a connection to Goethe's *Wilhelm Meister's Apprenticeship*, in which the young bourgeois hero falls passionately in love with an actress also named Mariane. Unger plays on the stereotype established by Goethe's novel: her Mariane is, like Goethe's, sexually liberated, and, like the character in *Wilhelm Meister*, she becomes pregnant by one of her suitors. But while Unger's Mariane shares many characteristics with her literary predecessor, Unger presents her behavior from a different perspective and uses her to very different effect.

Mariane functions in Unger's narrative as both the embodiment of the stereotype of the "actress" and the chief representative and champion of a philosophy of subjective "naturalness." And somewhat paradoxically, the two are inextricably linked. Mariane has precisely the attitude towards morality that brought actresses into such ill repute: she is sexually promiscuous, unconcerned about her public reputation, vain, careless, manipulative, deceptive, and motivated primarily by money and praise. But she is not simply immoral; rather, she justifies her unconventional behavior on the basis of a "philosophy" that she articulates to Melanie accordingly:

> I follow Nature, follow her impulses everywhere, and only consult her laws! . . . Everything I have comes from Nature. She made me the way I am; why should I want to improve on her clumsy piece of work? She put my lively passions into a form that was properly made for them. If I pull out one of the threads that she wove together so delicately and so skillfully, then the whole fabric is ruined! . . . Take me as I am. (69)

Where eighteenth-century moralists like Rousseau would attribute an actress's immoral behavior to the fact that what she did for a living was to perform, to excite desires, and to "set herself for sale" on stage (*Letter* 90), and where the Rousseauian condemnation of the actress was grounded in a suspicion that she did nothing *but* perform, Unger reverses the terms and blames Mariane's "looseness" on an unrestrained naturalness—that is, on the very transparency and immediacy that was supposed to mark the proper, innocent, naive bourgeois girl. The novel thus once again reveals the fictionality of the ideal in the depiction of its opposite, as what is "natural" to a woman is shown to be precisely the opposite of what discursive representations of the transparently antitheatrical woman constructed her to be.

The fact that Mariane is—in stark contrast to Leerheim—a largely sympathetic character further complicates the novel's engagement with notions of ideal femininity and performance. For despite Melanie's rejection of Mariane's "philosophy" and the sexual freedom it licenses, the two women remain good friends, and Mariane is one of the few constant pillars of support for Melanie through all of her trials and tribulations. In addition, even though the novel wants to put Mariane forward as a negative example and partially achieves this by showing the undesirable consequences of Mariane's philosophy (i.e., illegitimate pregnancy), it never quite strikes the proper disapproving tone and at times even leaves the reader suspecting that there might be aspects in Mariane's approach to life deserving of admiration, or, at the very least, acceptance. So, for example, when Melanie has been expelled from Leerheim's home after the *Emilia Galotti* debacle, the narrator muses that

> [t]he Marianes . . . skip through roses down the path of life, to reach its end in a bower of myrtle. [Melanie], who had sacrificed so much to virtue, didn't know in the end where she could lay her head. (175)

Thus, even though on the one hand, Unger presents the "natural" woman as also "naturally" prone to making disreputable choices, on the other hand, she also refuses to categorically condemn her and even hints that the freedom such a woman enjoys to express herself and live her life according to "natural" impulses might have its advantages and benefits. As a result, the move to counter prevailing notions of what is "natural" to women functions, at one and the same time, to point to an alternative mode of being for women, one that imagined itself free of the restrictions, pressures, and expectations of patriarchal discourse: in other words, free of the pre-scripted social roles for women as only—ironically—the actress could be. But Unger only hints at such possibilities: as my next chapter demonstrates, the use of the actress to imagine into existence an alternative mode of being for a woman gets its most radical treatment from the pen of Sophie Mereau.

That Unger might have been making at the very least a surreptitious case for Mariane's "philosophy," however, is evidenced by the fact that both Melanie and Mariane receive the same reward at the end of the novel: marriage to a wealthy aristocrat. They get to their goals quite differently: Melanie ends up with her beloved Count Wilhelm only after having shown steadfast devotion to him through thick and thin, while Mariane becomes an "English Lady" after a series of romantic affairs with wealthy admirers. Unger clearly wants her reader to view Melanie's fidelity and sacrifice as the more noble and correct choice, but at the same time she does not particularly go out of her way to vilify Mariane's golddigging. In fact, the narrative presents Mariane's rise to the status of "Mylady" as a comic (and highly satiric) triumph of female performance over looming adversity. Mariane, having realized that her best days would soon be over, uses her talents as an actress to snare a rich British husband. It is noteworthy that, given the discussion of her "philosophy" earlier in the novel, she achieves her final status not by living according to natural impulse, but rather by deploying a performance that accords with her future husband's desire:

> Mariane had toyed with him cruelly, had treated him disdainfully. He took this for German honesty, her extravagance for a sense of nobility, her clichéd theater morals for virtue, and therefore he offered this absurd creature his hand, which she snatched with both of hers, since she didn't dare hope to continue her deception much longer, even with her wealth of talent in coquetry. (234)

The novel thus presents us with a final, teasing paradox: the actress who justified immoral behavior by invoking a philosophy of naturalness is also the character through which the narrative takes a parting shot at reigning notions of "Ideal Womanhood," by clearly situating femininity as a projection of masculine desire, fantasy, and mystification. Yet of course, it makes perfect sense: for who might better understand what men want in a woman than the woman who makes a living personating their fantasies on stage? In this final, ironic commentary on the essential fictionality of femininity—that it is, fundamentally, a projection of masculine fantasy and patriarchal wish-fulfillment—Unger shows herself keenly attuned to the ways in which female identity was shaped and pressured by a complex and dynamic relationship between available social scripts, a woman's ability and willingness to enact them, and the expectations and desires of her audience.

What links the two texts discussed in this chapter is their interest in teasing out the role of the eye of the beholder in pressuring and policing female subjectivity. They share a suspicion of the trustworthiness of the audience and challenge the notion that, in the absence of a performance of self, a woman's "truth" is transparently readable. Read together, moreover, these two stories reveal the contradictory and essentially unresolvable position into which the social audience placed women, in particular women who felt that their "natural" self met the criteria for the ideal, but then felt pressured (against their own moral principles) to perform that self, or risk being misread. In *Melanie* these contradictions get played out not only on the narrative level but also in the novel's internal inconsistencies; in "Aglaja" those pressures also seem to reflect Bürger's own life experience. In both narratives, then, the performance of ideal femininity is figured as a response to audience coercion: it as a role that *must* be performed, and performed in a specific way, in order to avoid undesirable social consequences.

6. Play's the Thing

Sophie Mereau's "Marie" and "Flight to the City"

The works analyzed in the previous chapters of this book all walk a fine line between accepting reigning ideas about what constitutes "ideal femininity" and using notions of theatricality and performance to challenge those ideas. In this, all to a certain extent adopt and work within the categories and oppositions set up by eighteenth-century discourse—they attempt to craft an image of ideal femininity that both accords with social definitions and at the same time carves out some space for female public activity, self-definition, and self-fulfillment. The two short stories by Sophie Mereau that I consider in this chapter take a radically different approach: they mobilize theatricality and performance as a means of jettisoning the limitations placed on women by dominant discourse, and, in so doing, parodically—and fundamentally—undermine eighteenth-century notions of proper identity and gender role.

Both of these stories are about a woman who becomes an actress, and both figure the theater as a site of freedom and self-fulfillment for the female protagonist. In "Marie" (1798), Mereau interrogates eighteenth-century assumptions about the natural, naive woman and uses her heroine's life-journey from innocent country girl to happy fulfilled actress to demonstrate that not all women are destined by nature to be fulfilled by domestic duties. "Flight to the City" ("Die Flucht nach der Hauptstadt," 1796/1806),[1] with its utter superficiality of character and action, puts at stake the concept of a fixed and stable identity, and, with it, notions about naturalized or proper social and gender roles. The ease and fluidity with which the narrator of "Flight to the City" performs her "self," and the matter-of-factness with which she accepts the performativity of "self" in others, challenge the rigid definition of identity that threatens to severely narrow the range of roles a woman can play.

During the years in which she wrote these stories, Mereau herself felt trapped in an unhappy marriage and fantasized about leaving her husband and supporting herself through acting and writing. In a letter to Johann Heinrich Kipp, a young student with whom she had been having an affair, she wrote,

> I must have money—my child must come with me—[Mereau] cannot learn of this. . . . I will go to a distant place, where I am unknown, become—an actress, in order to be something, and also write of course. (Cited in Gersdorff 81)

Mereau never did work in the theater professionally, but as both audience member and as lay participant she took great pleasure in the theater. She was a frequent visitor to the Weimar Court Theater (which was, at the time, under Goethe's direction) and also acted in private amateur theater performances organized by friends (Fleischmann 40–44; Hammerstein, " 'Das uns allein' " 257–59). Her lack of professional theater experience leads her to idealize the actress's life in her stories, and consequently they can be read as a utopian projection of her own fantasies and yearnings for freedom and independence. But, at the same time, in these texts the theater is not merely a site of escape for the protagonists, or a temporary refuge during times of financial insecurity; instead, Mereau fantasizes the theater as a place in which a woman's natural creative energies can be fully and properly expressed. In the process, she both reconfigures the relationship between naturalness and performance and radically reconceptualizes female subjectivity. While both stories place a woman in the theater, in style and in content they are quite different, and provoke different insights into what constitutes female "nature."

Mereau herself hardly fit the eighteenth-century definition of the "ideal woman." A beautiful and charming woman, she was the center of both adoration and scandal. In his memoirs the diplomat

Johann Georg Rist recalls that

> where she appeared, people crowded around her and almost only around her, a thick swarm of admirers who angled for a word or smile from her, and all around her the gawkers formed an impenetrable circle. (Cited in Gersdorff 13)

Too vivacious for her dull, humorless husband, Mereau fell in love with other men, most notably the law student Johann Heinrich Kipp and the medical student Georg Philipp Schmidt; she caused quite a stir when she traveled alone with the latter to Berlin in 1796. Mereau was notorious for her other displays of independence too: she was the only female student to audit Fichte's philosophical lectures in Jena; she was one of the first women in Germany to make a profession out of writing; and she divorced her husband in 1801 in order to live independently.

She had no desire to remarry—her distaste for the institution of marriage is evident in many of her writings—but she lived according to the principle that love was the most important aspect of life.[2] In 1803, her tempestuous love affair with Clemens Brentano resulted in pregnancy, and she reluctantly married him. The next three years were largely unhappy ones. Brentano was unsupportive of her artistic aspirations and disappointed with her fulfillment of her domestic duties; Mereau was once again trapped in marriage and nearly constantly pregnant. She had four pregnancies in three years: she lost the first two babies when they were barely a month old, the third pregnancy resulted in a miscarriage, and neither she nor the baby survived the fourth. Sophie Mereau died in childbirth on October 31, 1806.[3]

Mereau's work has been the subject of an increasing body of scholarship in the last twenty years, helped enormously by Katharina von Hammerstein's reissue of her works, which spans three volumes and includes previously unpublished journal entries and fragments, along with Mereau's published poetry and prose texts.[4] Many of Mereau's works have received a good deal of attention from modern scholars, in particular her two novels—*The Blossoming of Sensibility (Das Blütenalter der Empfindung*, 1794) and *Amanda and Eduard* (1803)—and her biographical sketch, "Ninon de Lenclos" (1802).[5]

Her short stories have received far less critical treatment. "Marie" has, to my knowledge, been the subject of only two critical essays: Hammerstein's afterword to her volume and a brief treatment by Gersdorff. "Flight to the City" has fared only a bit better: it is the subject of analyses by Gersdorff, Bürger, Hammerstein, and Kontje.[6] Critics seem divided on how to assess Mereau's writing. While most agree that Mereau steadily challenged the eighteenth century's limited and limiting definition of proper gender roles and behavior for women, several dismiss her work for lacking depth and direction, or for being too eclectic and dilettantish (cf. C. Bürger, *LebenSchreiben* 171; Schmidt 25, 29–30). Others, most notably Purdy, Hammerstein, and Kontje, argue that the formal unconventionality of her work reflects its unconventional politics: Kontje, for example, sees Mereau as an experimental writer, and Hammerstein argues that Mereau employs a theory of aesthetics that is ahead of her time, and that her writing should be understood as a form of indirect political engagement that "contains . . . a definitive element of subversion" (Hammerstein, " 'Ein magisches Gemisch' " 115–16; Kontje 76).

My analyses of these two stories takes as a given that Mereau's writing directly and purposefully confronts the restrictions on women's behavior, and often does so by creating literary figures who defied conventional expectations, acted in ways that were completely counter to social codes and mores, and yet developed into happy, satisfied women in the process. My focus in this chapter will be to investigate the ways in which Mereau uses the theater and performance as part of that challenge.

* * *

"MARIE"

"Marie" tells the story of a young woman who has been raised in an isolated village and kept from knowledge of the world by her father, a former court musician. She is the embodiment of innocence, a child of nature. A carriage accident brings two aristocrats into her life: Antonie, the beautiful daughter of well-known landed gentry, and Brandem, a young virtuoso musician employed as tutor and chaperone to Antonie. Marie's father reluctantly agrees to let Marie return to court with Antonie and Brandem, under condition that Brandem keep watch over her and protect her. Secretly in love with Marie, Brandem looks on in dismay as she falls in love with Seeberg, Antonie's fiancé. Circumstances call Brandem away from court; during his absence, Marie's father dies and Seeberg convinces her to flee with him to his remote country house. They live together as happy lovers for a short while until Antonie arrives and revives Seeberg's interest in her. When Marie realizes that Seeberg is torn between herself and Antonie, she decides to release him from any obligation to her. She goes to a nearby town, joins a theater troupe, becomes a successful actress, and lives a happy, independent, and fulfilled life, with little remorse about her decision to leave Seeberg. Brandem, in the meanwhile, searches everywhere for Marie and finally happens to be at the theater when she is playing Miranda in *The Tempest*. They reunite and live together—unmarried—in a "lasting bond of respect, trust, and friendship" ("Marie" 83).

From the plot outline above, it is clear that "Marie" offers a revision of Sophie Sternheim's fate. Like La Roche, Mereau puts a naive girl into contact with an aristocratic world of masks and intrigue, but the results of that encounter are very different: Marie's innocence does not make her a victim. In reworking this familiar material, Mereau offers a different definition of, and perspective on, what it might mean to be a "natural" woman. Marie is repeatedly described in the story as natural, open, and transparent—her upbringing has not only given her close ties to the natural world, but also lent her its innocent characteristics:

> Healthy air, freedom of movement, beautiful nature, and inner and outer peace worked upon Marie, and shaped her into a creature who was serenely in harmony with herself. Her life was a clear stream. . . . (50)

This natural transparency makes Marie attractive to the courtiers—both Antonie and Brandem are instantly charmed by "her inexperience, her openness," and her "absolute ingenuousness" (52, 53). Mereau repeatedly uses the word *Unbefangenheit*—which translates as ingenousness, openness, candidness, unselfconsciousness—to describe Marie as her admirers see her, and it is this characteristic that makes both Brandem and Seeberg view her as the ideal woman of their dreams (57–58, 62–64).

But while Marie seems to embody an eighteenth-century ideal of femininity—totally honest, open, and transparent, even to the extent of confessing "with the greatest exactness" all of the details of her feelings for Seeberg to Brandem (65)—Mereau takes such naturalness to its logical conclusion and creates a figure who, in acting according to her nature, ends up defying social (and literary) expectations. So, for example, when the story sets up the usual opposition between the manipulative courtier—in this case, Antonie—and the innocent girl, the consequences are wholly unexpected. Antonie uses a clever ruse to reawaken Seeberg's interest in her: she arrives at the country house where he and Marie are living in illicit bliss and announces to him that she has realized that he no longer loves her and decided to release him from their engagement. In so doing, Antonie demonstrates the kind of other-directed performance at which Derby also excelled: she understands Seeberg's character well enough to realize that such a rejection will rope him back in. This betrayal ought to destroy Marie, but Mereau's heroine is too "serenely in harmony with herself" to be ruined by a lover's sudden disinterest: she decisively leaves him, "not without disquietude, but also not without self-confidence" (77).

The story thus proposes a very different image of the natural Ideal Woman: she is not only transparent, open, and candid, but also self-assured, capable, sharp-witted, and independent. In addition, she understands intuitively that there are many roles to be played in life. When Marie decides to elope with Seeberg—a decision that would have seemed shocking to eighteenth-century readers—she is clear-eyed about the choice, seeing it as "necessary to make a firm decision, step onto the stage of life, and take on one of those roles that she had up until then only seen played by others in true or made-up performances" (72). But at the same time, her decision is based on being who she is, naturally—she tells Seeberg, "it is my only happiness, to be your beloved. I am, what I must be, and am satisfied" (73). Mereau does not seem to view "natural being" and the performance of role here as mutually exclusive: on the contrary, for Marie they are linked. Her faith and trust in nature translates into a self-assurance and self-possession that empower her to choose from among many roles, even those considered scandalous, precisely because "she is, what she must be, and is satisfied."

Mereau has, in other words, dismissed the social audience and robbed it of its power to define proper gendered subjectivity. In this, Mereau's attitude toward antitheatrical being is markedly different from that of the other authors considered in this book. Where the other authors discussed are concerned with revealing the unreliability of audience response, and hence the impossibility of guaranteeing that a woman's virtuous self is properly read in the absence of performance, Mereau fantasizes a woman whose cardinal "natural" virtues—sincerity, openness, and unselfconsciousness—render her immune to others' opinions. Marie acts according to natural impulse and an inner drive to be satisfied; her performance of self is for herself alone, and she is the only audience she needs to please. Her self-realization stands in direct contrast to eighteenth-century assumptions about female weakness, dependency, and need for domesticity. When Brandem (upon hearing about her involvement with Seeberg) worries that "the peace of that beautiful soul is perhaps lost forever," he voices those assumptions, imagining her as another Sophie Sternheim (81). But Mereau makes sure that her reader is in a position to recognize that assumption as a false one: we already know that Marie has become a happy and successful actress. Mereau thus exposes eighteenth-century definitions of what constitutes a "natural" woman as nothing more than a discursive construct: what comes "naturally" to Mereau's heroine is not, as Brandem fears, victimhood or marriage, but an artistic career.

Additionally, the fact that Marie chooses to become an actress because that is what she wants to do with her life not only challenges ideas about what a woman's "natural" destiny might be, but also represents a fundamental reconceptualization of the decision to become an actress. While many of the women writers considered in this study want to present the profession of acting as a viable choice for survival for a woman, none of them see becoming an actress as a life goal in and of itself; with the exception of Mereau, all of them—and especially those who had worked professionally in the theater—present acting as something that must be excused, justified, and escaped from (through marriage) at the first opportunity.[7] In "Marie" (and, as we shall see, in "Flight to the City" as well), Mereau presents the choice to become an actress in the most glowing terms:

> [A] favorable fate had in the meantime taken control of Marie's life. . . .[S]he soon found herself in an independent and secure situation. In this self-attained free existence she felt, if not happier, at least more peaceful than she had ever been.—Nearly everyone dreams in his youth of a situation in which he might best like to live. If his friendly fate grants him this situation, he will probably still have desires, still have sad moments, but a secret satisfaction will still attest to the fulfillment of his dearest wish. Marie now found herself in this condition. . . . She was now completely what she wanted to be. (79–80)

While Mereau's vision of the life of the actress is clearly utopian, such an image of the artistically fulfilled, independent woman is both compelling and unprecedented. By imagining into existence female characters who feel empowered, by their "nature," to choose artistic careers that allow for an independent and rewarding existence, Mereau discursively counters those culturally constructed restrictions that prevented women from making such choices.

However, while for the most part Marie is presented as a woman who is fundamentally antitheatrical—that is, as someone who is consistently transparent and readable—it does not do justice to this story to read it as simply creating an alternative, and more progressive, image of the "natural" woman. For "Marie" is also concerned with interrogating the notion of "naturalness" and revealing it as something that is always already an effect of aesthetic representation—that is, as a social fiction. In particular, the end of the story, with its intertextual reference to *The Tempest*, functions to reconfigure fundamentally the relationship between naturalness and performance. When Brandem rediscovers Marie performing the role of Miranda, we are, of course, expected to recognize immediately the parallels between Miranda's story and Marie's: both girls were raised in isolation by genius/artist fathers; both have first contact with the world due to an "accident"; both charm others through their innocence and inexperience; both fall in love with worldly aristocrats; and each is decisive about her desire for her lover—in *The Tempest*, Miranda tells Ferdinand "I am your wife, if you will marry me; / If not, I'll die your maid" (III.i.83–84). An effect of this paralleling is a conflation of the two characters that calls attention to the fictionality of their "naturalness": that is, it highlights the status of *both* Miranda and Marie as characters in fictional narratives, and reminds us that both women are the products of textual construction, and not "real" or "natural" at all.

But Mereau goes further, turning the scene into a commentary on aesthetic transparency and its ideological aims. Her depiction of Brandem's response to Marie's performance reads at first like a testament to the power of antitheatrical acting. Marie is so convincing and perfect as Miranda that at first Brandem does not recognize her:

> Miranda entered the scene, and his heart stopped. Her inexperience, the lovely confusion of first love, everything reminded him, seized him with sweet violence. He relived the sudden rapture of that beautiful hour when he had seen, heard, and observed Marie in her lovely innocence. What set his feelings aflame was not the actress, who gave satisfaction to the faculty of reason through her beautiful performance, but this living, charming creature of divine imagination, Miranda herself. Gradually she disappeared, and Marie stepped into her place. With each passing moment this seemed more real for him, with each movement even more so—and it really was her! (82)

The conflation of character and actor here seems a dream come true not only for Brandem, but also for the theorist of aesthetic transparency, as the depiction of a "natural" woman on stage by a "natural" woman produces the wished-for reality. Mereau quite explicitly describes the scene in terms of a displacement of illusion by reality, as Miranda turns into Marie (for Brandem, at least) mid-performance, thus giving the impression of the kind of absorption of character into actress, and vice versa, that was at the root of many theories of realistic acting.

But, at the same time, the scene also acts as a parodic rebuke of both the effects of aesthetic transparency on an audience and of the idea of a "natural" woman. For, on the one hand, it satirizes the audience's state of mind: Brandem is so taken up by an illusionistic performance of natural womanhood that he cannot recognize the "real" natural woman behind the performance. He is, in effect, too willing to map fiction onto reality (and vice versa). On the other hand, we can also read this scene as a recognition, on Mereau's part, of the ways in which male fantasy and desire produce ideal femininity. For Brandem's desire to read Marie *as* Miranda mirrors the process by which discourse polices female subjectivity—that is, by mapping reality onto preexisting fictional models. Mereau's depiction of this moment of aesthetic transparency in the theater can thus be read as a critique of its aims, as she reveals the power of illusionism to efface the difference between fiction and reality and, in the process, produce a social consensus of what constitutes the "real" and the "natural."

This scene also points to a connection between Marie's activity, as an actress, in producing an image of "natural" femininity for her audience, and Mereau's activity, as a writer, in producing a counter-image of "natural" femininity for her readership. For in highlighting the fact that Marie's ability to represent Miranda fictionally is grounded in both her own "naturalness" and in her biography, the text also calls attention to the fact that Mereau's creation of Marie is connected to *her* own "naturalness" and biography. Marie stands in much the same relationship to Mereau as Miranda does to Marie: both are projections of a female artist's creative impulses. Marie, the character, and "Marie," the story, can thus be read as Mereau's own performance of ideal femininity—a performance that calls into being a radical redefinition of woman's nature along lines that could accommodate women who, like Mereau, had aspirations beyond what society deemed "natural" for them.

* * *

"FLIGHT TO THE CITY"

In "Flight to the City," a young woman tells the story of her adventurous life. In the course of acting in her father's amateur theatrical productions, the narrator falls in love with a young man named Albino. But her father, in his quest to establish himself as an aristocrat, arranges for her to marry a grotesque and disgusting local nobleman. She and Albino decide to flee: Albino steals money and a horse from his father, and they escape to B. Once in B., they lead a happy and carefree life together, filled with freedom and pleasure. They make the acquaintance of a young man named Felix, who seems to take them under his wing. But, he betrays them: he invents a ruse to separate them and then establishes himself in Albino's place as the narrator's lover. Felix and the narrator then travel to D., where they launch their theatrical careers. But Felix soon becomes tyrannical, and so the narrator breaks with him, joins a new troupe, finds a new lover, and continues on her theatrical journey. She and her lover establish a harmonious and egalitarian relationship, and they live together in freedom and happiness until his sudden death. Alone again, she continues her acting career, until she is spotted on stage one evening by Albino, who, in the meantime, has become rich speculating on merchant ships. They are joyfully reunited and resolve to return to their hometown. Shortly before the journey, however, one last adventure awaits them: Albino confronts Felix with his betrayal and fatally wounds him in a duel. The narrator and Albino flee across the border, are warmly received at home, and give up the adventurous life for the stability and peace of bourgeois domesticity.

Dagmar von Gersdorff has noted that there is nothing like this story in the contemporary literature, and, indeed, the narrator's picaresque journey is unusual (249). It is unusual not only because it features a woman who has a series of adventures and affairs without being punished for it, but also because of its "superficiality." From the moment of its first appearance, "Flight to the City" has been criticised for the lack of deep subjectivity and moral grounding in its characters. While some modern critics see this as a flaw in the work, I argue that it is precisely the surface, performative nature of its characterizations that gives "Flight to the City" the opportunity to make a radical critique of eighteenth-century conceptions of ideal femininity. By forsaking self-reflexivity and self-understanding, and by refusing to present the narrator's "self" as an expression of her inner thoughts and motives, Mereau's story puts at stake the concept of a fixed and stable identity, and, with it, notions about natural gender roles. But even more importantly, in creating a character who does not reflect on her own actions and intentions, Mereau also once again refuses to grant the social audience power to define and control the character. By freeing her heroine from self-reflection, Mereau also frees her from the need to consider how others perceive her and subject herself to their scrutiny and judgment. Mereau forecloses the possibility of the social audience policing her character and effecting an internalization of its norms and standards by creating a character who seemingly has no interior and is, as a result, immune to the penetrating glance of the virtuous. Mereau's narrator's extraordinary freedom depends upon the latter's wholehearted embrace and exploitation of the performative possibilities of life.

At the same time, the fact that Mereau presents the story from the point of view of an unnamed first-person narrator suggests that she is purposefully playing with her own audience's expectations and response. Where first-person narration might be expected to provide a fuller and deeper understanding of the narrating character's state of mind, true feelings, motivations, et cetera (as in the case of the epistolary novel), Mereau presents the opposite. Her narrator tells her story as if it had happened to someone else. Consequently, the text encourages us to read the narrative "I" as the author's voice ventriloquized: that is, as Mereau performing a fictional "I" for her reader/audience (rather than trying to present her fictional character as a real person).[8] But additionally, the use of an unnamed "I" also involves that audience by provoking an internalization of the narrator's story and an identification between reader and narrator—and, by extension, author. Consequently, the "lack of depth" in Mereau's narrative also represents a sophisticated and complex engagement with the performer–audience dynamic.

Sophie Mereau's "I" begins both her narrative and her journey in the theater, the site of the genesis of her love affair with Albino. She describes their love as, *quite* literally, an effect of cumulative theatrical performances:

> I was barely fifteen years old when I first performed all the lead roles to great acclaim in this temple consecrated to the arts. A young man from the neighborhood, whom I will call Albino, played the First Lover, and

> as such he told me so often that he loved me that he himself finally felt it and I believed it. Our imagination was kindled ever higher, and soon we were only playing ourselves in the most fervent roles. ("Flight" 381/ "Flucht" 204)[9]

There is a self-conscious irony in her admission that the repetition of a romantic scene causes their love—that, in effect, they become "real" lovers by playing the role of lovers. But despite the fact that their love originates in and as performance, she sees it as a "truth" that operates both in opposition to and in enhancement of deception:

> The audience's most ardent applause gave our talents the praise that was actually due to our hearts: they thought that the deception had been heightened to truth, while we were actually giving them truth as deception. ("Flight" 381/"Flucht" 204)

The pretending or playacting of love on the stage produces a real love between the two actors that, when inserted back into the context of a stage performance, is perceived once again as an illusion—"heightened to truth." The opposition between deception and truth, and between the theater and life, is thus parodically destabilized at the very beginning of Mereau's story. Mereau's lack of concern about policing the boundaries between the stage and real life is in marked contrast to bourgeois moral theorists who wanted to keep performance contained on the stage: she is not only comfortable with imagining those boundaries as permeable, but also sees that permeability as decidedly positive.

The casual crossover of performance into real life (and vice versa) is a recurrent trope in the narrative. Later in the story, after Felix has separated her from Albino, the narrator allows herself to be seduced by Felix through a similar act of performance:

> When I entered my room, the man who had enchanted me so much on the stage jumped toward me with a mask over his face, gesturing to me playfully. . . . Automatically, I assumed the role of his beloved; we surrendered to the whims of the moment and improvised a number of amusing scenes, which had probably never been performed in such a lively manner on stage. ("Flight" 389/"Flucht" 214)

The wall between performance and reality is rendered literally immaterial in this text. The narrator carries the "enchantment" of Felix's theatrical performance, which had made her "heart beat faster," out of the playhouse and into her room, where their friendship is transformed into sexual intimacy through playacting.

The nonchalant tone with which she reports this scene demonstrates the narrator's (and, perhaps, Mereau's own) lack of anxiety about the moral dimensions of *Verstellung*. Unlike *Sternheim*, which was deeply concerned with the perils of a deceptive performance of identity, "Flight to the City" takes the performed self at face value and mobilizes performance as a means of liberating its heroine from societal constraints on behavior and morality. To this end, Mereau literalizes and exploits two contemporary conceptions about the power of the theater. First, both scenes of seduction-through-performance represent an ironic reconfiguration of Kant and Lessing's theories of acting as a means of behavior modification. Where Kant and Lessing wished to press performance into the service of morality (and where Sophie Sternheim uses it as a tool for disciplining the bourgeois subject), the "I" of Mereau's story uses performance as a way of opening up the limited range of potential roles available to her as a woman. The heroine's decision to become an actress is, in fact, consciously framed in these terms. Felix's glowing description of the actor's life—"We live in all times, run about in all walks of life, from beggar to king, and that is why we stay forever young"—has irresistible appeal to the narrator, who responds, "All right!. . . I shall follow your call! One day queen, the next shepherdess, the next a heroine, and in all forms beautiful, beloved, and exalted—who would not gladly choose this way of life?" ("Flight" 89/"Flucht" 214–15).

Second, these scenes of seduction are also comic turns on the stereotype of theater as a dangerous and immoral site for young women. Both life in the theater and the theatrical spectacle itself were suspected of having deleterious effects on young women's morality. Actresses' notorious reputation for easy virtue was based in part on the theory that playing love scenes on stage made them more susceptible to seduction off stage; and comedies were thought to put romantic notions into a girl's head and soften her ability to resist attempts on her virtue.[10] The narrator experiences both these effects of the theater: her offstage love for Albino derives directly from their onstage romances, and her "enchantment" with Felix's performance predisposes her to a post-show tryst. But instead of having disastrous consequences, her encounter with the theater brings her a life of happiness, fulfillment, and adventure.

In addition, unlike in Kant and Lessing, there is no evidence in "Flight to the City" of a belief that performance has either a negative or positive impact on the inner life or self—indeed, as noted at the beginning of this section, the lack of reflection on the characters' inner lives and motives is one of the most striking features of the narrative. Mereau's characters have no deep sense of self and identity. The story's commitment to the play of performance across the boundary separating the theater from life stands as a parodic reproach to the obsession with locating identity in self-reflexivity and self-examination found in *Sternheim*, or in *Bildungsromane* like Moritz's *Anton Reiser* or Goethe's *Wilhelm Meister*. In a radical subversion of modernist conventions of identity, the text matter-of-factly proposes that identity is both produced and read solely through the performance of self.

Thus, not only does performance impact the narrator's reality, but also her "real life" is repeatedly misread as performance. For example, in a moment of grief over her separation from Albino, she begins to "bemoan [her] fate with bitter tears" in Felix's presence. He reads her sadness not as an expression of real emotion, however, but as a sign of her potential talent: "Truly, my dear, nature destined you to be an actress" ("Flight" 388/"Flucht" 213). She is at once surprised and calmed by this remark. Both Felix's assumption that her tears were a manifestation of her performance ability and her odd response demonstrate a lack of concern about the extent to which outward behavior faithfully reflects the inner self: although her tears appear to have been motivated by real emotion, her tacit acceptance of Felix's compliment (and her later choice to pursue an acting career) works to undermine that appearance. "Destined . . . to be an actress," the narrator's elusive subjectivity can only be located in the play of performances that make up her journey.

Still later in the story, in a scene reminiscent of the effect her love for Albino had on her ability to effectively play his lover on stage, the narrator describes how the audience mistakes her real emotional state for talent:

> I first performed the role of the maiden from Marienburg. My heart pounded fiercely when I threw a glance at the assembled crowd. But my fearful timidity itself brought me an advantage because it gave my acting a girl-like shyness and my expression an uncommon warmth. The audience, which is always sympathetic to a tolerable figure, encouraged me . . . with its lively applause. ("Flight" 392/"Flucht" 217–18)[11]

The "truth" of her performance here derives from "real" emotions—her feelings of fear and shyness—which, although they would seem to be at odds with a successful performance, serve paradoxically to heighten it. The "real" inner self is not expressed through performance, but exploited to enable it.

A few lines later, however, she produces the mirror image of this performance by cynically deploying her theatrical talents in real life as a mask for her inner feelings. After the show, she consciously displays the proper deference to her admirers to achieve her desired ends:

> [A]fter the play was over, I found myself surrounded by a crowd. . . . I was unaccustomed to such fragrant offerings and unpracticed in the divine art of pleasing everyone, but innate tact soon let me find the way. Meaningful glances, flattering replies, polite nonsense absentmindedly spoken, a loud laugh honoring an inanity—were sufficient to make everyone perfectly satisfied with me.
>
> How many invitations did I receive after this day! How many splendid festivities were planned with me as their queen! ("Flight" 392/"Flucht" 218)

Although her language implies that this is a deceptive performance, we are given few clues about the narrator's "real" feelings and attitudes, and there is a decided lack of engagement with the moral implications of what appears to be a consciously "false" representation of the self. Mereau's narrator's attitude toward her fans here is in pointed contrast to that of Karoline Schulze-Kummerfeld, who insists that she would rather be silent than utter meaningless, flattering replies. In fact, concerns about the morality of deception are entirely absent from the narrator's tale: she does not worry about whether or not an action is good or evil, but whether or not it brings her pleasure.

Our intrepid actress has, in other words, adopted the code of the rake. Like the evil Derby of *Sternheim*, she is self-consciously deceptive and deploys performance in the single-minded pursuit of pleasure. But unlike Derby, she does not use deceit to harm another person or to purchase her pleasure at anyone else's expense. She is the rake stripped of evil intentions, traveling through Germany in search of love and pleasure. Although other writers of the eighteenth century would define the woman who adopted this code in strictly negative terms (for example, Lady Marwood in *Miss Sara Sampson* or the Countess Orsina in *Emilia Galotti)*, in what Hammerstein calls the "Mereaudian thought system" independence and a desire to control her own destiny and love life are positive attributes of the female protagonist. Mereau establishes her own system of morality throughout her work, and that morality differs significantly from the ideals promoted by male writers of the period. In Mereau's writings, negative qualities in a woman include selfishness, a lack of sensitivity and social sympathy, narrowmindedness, and infidelity in love; but the chief crime in the "Mereaudian thought system" is a life without true love (Hammerstein, *Freiheit, Liebe, Weiblichkeit* 170–77).

The heroine of "Flight to the City," while she takes advantage of whatever pleasure life brings her way, never compromises her happiness or integrity for money, and she lives for love. Although she may employ the tactics of the rake, she maintains a core sense of right and wrong consistent with the Mereaudian hierarchy of values. In addition, the narrator's "rakishness" combines a charming innocence and naiveté with a striking sophistication about the liberatory and empowering potential of performance for a woman. When Felix shows himself to be a tyrannical companion, she decides to break with him, explaining,

> I . . . held pleasure and freedom to be the sole requisites of life. They had led me into the arms of love and consoled me when love was gone. In order to be their worthy priestess I had chosen my present station, and it was natural that now I had to sacrifice everything else to them. For some time I concealed my aversion for Felix, but since he did not change his

> conduct, I decided to take revenge. On the occasion of a new argument, which arose because of some gifts I had received, I broke with him forever. ("Flight" 393/"Flucht" 219)

Mereau's narrator is only interested in playing the roles that allow her to lead the life she desires. Tragedy is not in her repertoire.

Her commitment to playing comedy becomes clear in the parodic ending to the story. The heroine is unexpectedly reunited with Albino, who has literally had his ship come in and can purchase their way back into their parents' graces. They decide to get married and forsake the life of abandonment and adventure they have both led. But their marriage and reentrance into bourgeois domesticity seem no more "real" or fixed than any other scene in the story. In fact, the narrator implies with her use of a theatrical metaphor to describe the event that it is merely one more (comic) role to play:

> Thus ended unexpectedly in comedy what had started out as sure tragedy. Nothing seemed funnier to us than to remember how we had once left our country as heroes, full of pathos, and now returned, imperceptibly transformed into married bourgeois. ("Flight" 399/"Flucht" 227)

Mereau here posits a possibility of marital bliss that eluded her in her own life: she herself experienced marriage and domesticity as a form of stifling captivity, not as an extension of a life of freedom and happiness.[12] Mereau solves the marriage problem by keeping her characters squarely in front of the curtain, always performing, always ready to play a new role. The fantasy-parody of marriage that is implied at the end of the story is perhaps, as Hammerstein notes, "a flight from the given reality" (Hammerstein, *Freiheit, Liebe, Weiblichkeit* 279). But it is also an expression of Mereau's deep suspicion of and dissatisfaction with the confining expectations of a societal system that locked women out of virtually every possible role except that of housewife and mother. By suggesting that marriage and bourgeois life might merely be seen as another act of performance, Mereau pointedly undermines the institution of marriage and the role it plays in anchoring bourgeois mores and values.[13]

Performance is, however, not unequivocally valorized in "Flight to the City" any more than it is uniformly condemned in *Sternheim*.

The central plot of Mereau's story involves a series of a deceptions and betrayals similar in scope to Derby's seduction of Sophie. But in "Flight to the City," the staging of fictions to influence a character's "real" life has comic rather than tragic consequences. Mereau's parody of the dangers of *Verstellung* specifically satirizes the categories of "comic" and "tragic" love and demonstrates that one woman's tragedy is another woman's picaresque adventure. There are several places in the story in which the narrator is the (potentially tragic) victim of deception or performance: her father's attempts to "stage [her] fate" by arranging for her marriage to a grotesque and boorish local nobleman ("Flight," 381/"Flucht," 205); Felix's devious separation of her and Albino ("Flight," 386, 397/"Flucht," 209, 224); the landlady's attempt to prostitute her to a nobleman ("Flight," 389–90/"Flucht," 215–16); and the deceit Felix practices on her to blind her to his tyrannical nature ("Flight," 392/"Flucht," 218–19). But each of these events is quickly pressed into the service of comedy: the narrator's lack of concern about the morality of performance frees her from any experience of shame or self-pity at being a victim of deception, and she quickly bounces from one role to the next, from adventure to adventure.

By positing a heroine who survives *Verstellung* through the deployment of *Verstellung*, "Flight to the City" ironically calls the bourgeois commitment to antitheatricality into question, and suggests the emancipatory possibilities that an embrace of the performative in life might offer. It also reveals a deep suspicion of the singular role (as privatized, domesticated housewife and mother) that women were given to play. Although "Flight to the City's" rather frivolous tone and outrageous plot work against its being taken seriously as a challenge to received notions of ideal femininity—the narrator embodies everything bourgeois moralists hated and feared about actresses—it is, like "Marie," a work that uses the theater to break free of the limitations that impinged on what Mereau saw as women's natural creativity and desire for self-determination and self-fulfillment. Both works represent a challenge to received notions about female nature, and of the two "Flight to the City" is perhaps the more radical work. For where "Marie" proposes an alternative vision of who the natural woman might be—and in the process reveals the essential fictionality of ideas about women's nature—"Flight to the City" suggests that true freedom lies in understanding all being as an effect and instance of performance. For Sophie Mereau, "Theater" represents much more than a temporary (and somewhat disreputable) occupation for the unmarried woman—it is a site in and through which she fundamentally challenges restrictive ideas about female subjectivity by jettisoning the baby of "female nature" with the bathwater of antitheatrical subjectivity.

Conclusion

This book has presented an exploration of the ways in which eighteenth-century German women writers used an engagement with the theater and performance to reveal ideal femininity as an impossible act. Because many of the paradoxes exposed by these women's narratives can also be traced in their own engagement with social pressures to "not perform," I conclude with an investigation of their own untidy and contradictory performances of femininity, on the stage, in their lives, and via their texts.

* * *

The Scene: Braunschweig, Germany, 1763. A command performance for the duke and his court of G. E. Lessing's *Miss Sara Sampson* by Ackermann's Hamburg troupe, with eighteen-year-old Karoline Schulze in the title role. For two days, the young actress has been ill with a respiratory disease, coughing violently and on occasion spitting up blood. But the show must go on. Schulze manages to make it through most of the play, but at the end of the fourth act, at the moment in which she, as Sara, recognizes the villainess Lady Marwood and rushes from the stage, she begins coughing up blood. She is carried to the dressing room by a fellow actor, where word comes that the nobility in the audience would prefer not to see the rest of the play if it would endanger her health. But as grateful as she is for their concern, she decides to play the role to the end. I give the rest of the story in her words:

> I played my fifth act—the dying act—without white makeup, but certainly was never so natural. The play ended. Mr. Doebbelin helped me up and said: "How do you feel, poor Miss Schulze?" I: "Bad, very bad."

> He: "We can see that." I: "It is after all just performance (*Verstellung*)." He: "Ha, it's abominable!"
>
> This was the first time I felt hatred for life in the theater, and felt the desire stir in me: oh, if only you could leave it! (*KSK* I: 171)

This anecdote from Karoline Schulze-Kummerfeld's memoirs crystallizes and encapsulates many of the concerns and issues that have animated this book. First, her conflation of her very real illness with her successful creation of the illusion of dying on stage reflects the late eighteenth-century theater's shift in the direction of antitheatricality: Schulze-Kummerfeld's boast that her acting was made more "natural" and illusionistic by her actual physical condition indicates both the increased premium placed on realism on stage and the uncertainty over how such realism might best be achieved (i.e., externally, via the use of "realistic" white makeup, or internally, by somehow inducing the "feeling" of the role). At the same time, her claim that her real illness made her performance of Sara's death scene seem more natural exposes one of the central dilemmas facing eighteenth-century proponents of antitheatrical subjectivity, namely, discerning where "naturalness" stops and performance begins. The slippage between the "real" and the "performed" in this moment on stage reveals just one of the many ways an expression of a person's "true" self can be misread as performance—and vice versa.

The fact that the role Schulze-Kummerfeld was playing that evening was Sara from *Miss Sara Sampson* illuminates a second set of concerns that have been central to this book, namely, the connections between the eighteenth-century valorization of an antitheatrical subjectivity, the aesthetically transparent modes of discourse that both constructed and reflected such a mode of being, and the particular burdens the demand for antitheatricality placed on women of the era. Lessing's play naturalistically depicted, in Sara, the virtuous, naive, antitheatrical femininity that was the model for Ideal Womanhood in late eighteenth-century Germany. At the same time, his play also revealed the dangers and difficulties of conforming to such a model, for not only is Sara's demise directly related to her overinvestment in a discourse of authenticity (through her inability to recognize Marwood's dissimulation as such), but also she stands as an example of the extent to which women's claims to authenticity were purchased at the cost of mobility and publicity. Sara's predicament in the play is emblematic of the contradiction posed by the discourse of antitheatricality for women of the era: unlike men, women did not have public activities in which they could authentically "be" themselves, and were as a result immediately suspect of a theatricalized performance of self the moment they entered the public sphere. Having left the confines of her father's home, Sara has no means of making visible her continued commitment to virtue without raising the suspicion that she too is engaging in dissimulation.

As this book demonstrates, for women of the eighteenth century, this was a particularly vexing problem. The definition of ideal femininity in terms of innocence, sincerity, and naiveté put women in a curious and contradictory position: by precluding a performance of self, it left women vulnerable to being perpetually misread, or having their sincere actions misframed as performance, particularly if they ventured out of the private sphere, where they "naturally" belonged. Karoline Schulze's performance of self in this context—and by this I mean both her own performance as a stage professional in finishing out the show and her performance of the role of Sara within the play—emblematically troubles the distinction between acting and being that late eighteenth-century theorists were anxious to establish and maintain, especially for women, who were always already under suspicion of theatricality and deceit.

Schulze-Kummerfeld's strange dismissal of Mr. Doebbelin's concerned gaze by calling what he sees "just performance" evokes yet another set of issues raised by women's engagement with the theater and performance. Her comment can be read several ways. If we read it the way she seems to have intended—that is, the whole incident is "just" performance, play, theater—it is clearly a sarcastic commentary on the cheapness of life in the theater, and a jab at a theater management that not only insisted that she perform in the play that night, but also had intended for her to dance as well. It is, then, a commentary on how difficult and potentially dangerous it was for a woman to work in the theater, and it functions as an antidote of realism to the many fictional works that imagined the theater as a utopic site of freedom and carefree living. The comment also seems to give tacit support to the bourgeois prejudice against the theater, an impression reinforced by her final comment that this incident engendered her first feelings of hatred for life in the theater. Clearly, the theater, as described by Schulze-Kummerfeld—with its harsh working conditions and its obligations to perform under even the most extreme conditions of distress—was *not* a proper place for the "naturally" weak, soft, demure woman imagined by eighteenth-century discourse.

But her statement also provokes a different reading: by calling her experience on stage "just performance," Schulze-Kummerfeld calls attention to the potential performability of all human conditions and behavior and to the difficulty of discerning where "being" stops and "acting" begins. This is reinforced by Mr. Doebbelin's puzzling response to her jest, which begs the question of what, precisely, is "abominable" in this scenario: Is it the fact that the young actress felt obliged to perform while ill? Or is he commenting on the quality of her performance itself, or, perhaps, on the bad taste of her comment? In light of the argument presented throughout this book, I suggest that perhaps what is most "abominable" here may be the implication that in the face of an illusionistic performance of female weakness even a seasoned actor like Mr. Doebbelin cannot trust what he sees. A similar suspicion and distrust is played out in many of the works discussed in this book, in their depiction, on the one hand, of the gap between a heroine's attempts to "be" antitheatrically virtuous in accord with social demands, and on the other, of the social reception of her being as somehow always already performed—or, at the very least, not performed "well."

But despite Schulze-Kummerfeld's comment that "it is after all just performance," her anecdote also serves as a stark reminder that there *is indeed* a difference between the "real" and the "performed." Mr. Doebbelin, the nobles in the audience, and, presumably, her readers, know that the blood she coughed up, her paleness, and her weakness were all *real* physical events for her, however much they might have aided her in dissimulating Sara's dying moments. Schulze-Kummerfeld's story thus both calls attention to the distinction between the "truth" of a subject and the social framing and reception of that truth, and points to the power of audience response in determining how a given event is read and interpreted. Indeed, her flippant mislabeling of real physical distress as *Verstellung* reminds us that a great deal can be at stake when the real is misread as "performance." Schulze-Kummerfeld's anecdote thus shares with the other works discussed in this study concerns about audience receptivity, framing, and the potentially dire consequences for a woman of doing what that audience expected: that is, not performing ideal femininity.

Moreover, Schulze-Kummerfeld's story is of interest not only because it evokes many of the concerns addressed in this book; but also because it speaks to, and reminds us of, the position of the female creative artist/writer herself. That is, like Schulze-Kummerfeld, each of the writers discussed felt compelled—through a complex combination of internal and external factors—to produce the image of Ideal Womanhood expected by *her* audience, both in her writing and, to varying degrees, in her life. In making this analogy, I want to reemphasize that the performance of femininity, as it plays out not just *in*, but also *via* these women's writings, is ultimately an untidy and contradictory affair. In what follows I consider the kinds of slippages and contradictions that emerge if we consider each of these writers as performers themselves, producing performances that were often subject to the same pressures and paradoxes that confronted their fictional heroines.

The first of these slippages has to do with female identity and identification, as mobilized by the authors themselves. When we look at the conventions of naming and self-identification employed by the writers discussed in this book, it is difficult to escape the impression that at times they were quite consciously using literature as masquerade. For example, Sophie La Roche's use of the name Sophie for her heroine is simultaneously a self-reference and an intertextual reference to Rousseau's heroine. The fact that she calls the character her "paper girl" further encourages a reading of the character as a mask for La Roche herself, a mask that functions to replace her own public image with one that more closely matches that Rousseauian ideal. In that sense, both Sophie Sternheim the character and the book in which she appears can be read as performative interventions in the public sphere that both effect a proper identity for La Roche and affect the social reception of, and understanding of, her nonideal public activity as a writer.

Marianne Ehrmann's adoption of the name "Sternheim" as both her stage name and as the pseudonym under which she published her first book represents a similar use of masquerade: Germany's fictional model for ideal femininity served as her cover for unideal public activities like writing and acting. Ehrmann then published under a series of intertextually referential pseudonyms until, in 1790, she attached her name to the editorship of her journal, *Amalie's Leisure Hours*—at which point readers could trace her literary production backward (Madland, *Marianne Ehrmann* 27). As a result, her adoption of her own nickname, "Amalie," as the name of the main character in her novel and as the title for her journals represents an even more complex performance of identity through writing and publishing, as she gradually crafted a fictional persona that both stood for herself, as a writer and woman, and was at the same time a distancing from herself.

We see a different use of masquerade in the narratives of Elise Bürger and Sophie Mereau. Both of these authors published the texts I consider under their own names, and in these stories they create a first-person narrator who remains anonymous, a move which encourages the reader to assume that the author and narrator are the same person and also sets up a process of identification between reader, narrator, and author. The anonymous "I" in their stories thus has a performative effect on both author and reader, creating a potent image of the author in the reader's mind, and simultaneously creating a sympathetic bond between reader and author/narrator through the first-person voice. The fact that the fictional first-person narrators resist discursive definitions of ideal femininity further encourages a reading of these texts as an authorial masquerade, as the stories also serve partly to justify and explain the unconventional lives led by their authors.

Friederike Helene Unger's intertextual references represent yet another kind of slippage. Her adoption and reworking of characters from the dominant writers of her age (most notably Goethe) is both a means by which she establishes her own identity as a writer through differentiation, and a strategy for combating the power of images of femininity created by men and imposed on women.[1] The fact that she published anonymously adds another layer of masquerade, since her gender as a writer was not always patently obvious to her readers. Thus, for example, when Goethe reviewed two of her novels in a single article, he attributed the first to a male author and the second, *Melanie*, to a female (Goethe, "Rev. of *Bekenntnisse*" 627). At the same time, within the novel *Melanie* the character of Mme. Leerheim can be read as satirically self-referential—a portrait of the female artist as she feels perceived by her public. Such a performance of "self"—one that not only plays into every savage stereotype of the learned woman but also rehearses all of the social opprobrium heaped upon women writers like Unger—parodically and effectively preempts and coopts negative audience response. Unger's strategy here can be read as the diametric opposite of La Roche's and Ehrmann's: where they adopt the masquerade of the feminine ideal, Unger masquerades as its opposite, and in the process robs the stereotype of its power to define her.

These authors' use of textual performance as a means of masquerading identity has everything to do with the negative connotations that pertained to women who entered the public sphere by dint of writing—anonymous or pseudonymous publication was the norm among early women writers.[2] It also serves as evidence of their awareness of their own status vis-à-vis a social audience that had power to define them, just as the social audiences in their books define their heroines. Consequently another slippage that occurs when we consider these writings as a form of performance has to do with the writers' engagement with the public sphere, and the ways in which both their texts and their lives were subject to the pressures and vagaries of audience reception.

Just as the social audience functions, in the texts considered, to pressure a performance of a femininity that it paradoxically defines as unperformable (and, likewise, just as the audience can be seen, in Schulze-Kummerfeld's anecdote, to pressure her performance as an actress, both through her own reading of their expectations, and through the representation of "the audience's" ideas about what constitutes a proper woman in the canonical text she performs on stage) so the women writers discussed in this book were pressured by *their* social audiences, both in ways that they were aware of and could attempt to respond to, and in ways that they were not. If we consider their writing as performance, the "audience" factors that come into play can be grouped into four rough and interrelated categories. First, the audience can be seen to play a role in what each author had to do in order to find a market for her work: that is, her writing had to meet audience expectations and desires in order to sell on the marketplace (cf. Brandes, "Der Frauenroman"). For most of the writers discussed in this book, this was not a negligible consideration: La Roche, Bürger, Ehrmann, Unger, and Mereau all depended to a greater or lesser extent upon the income their writing provided for their survival, in much the same way that Schulze-Kummerfeld depended upon acting for hers. As a result, marketplace considerations exerted pressure on these writers to conform to social norms regarding appropriate activities and modes of being for women, not only within the narratives themselves, but also in each author's own presentation of herself *as* an author, much the same way that we see the market pressuring actors and actresses to modify their behavior in order to "sell" their product—which likewise consisted of both their performance and their public persona—to *their* audience.

Along similar lines, since what each of these women had to "sell" was not merely a story, but also her own public face and reputation, the second way in which the audience impacted these writings as performance is in the text's function, within society, as a performance of the author's identity. Here, the identity slippage just mentioned comes into play—one of the strategies employed by these writers was to use their texts as masquerade, often quite successfully. For example, Sophie La Roche's novel helped to engender and shape her public image in positive ways: readers imagined her as the properly virtuous mother to her ideal paper daughter, despite the fact that La Roche herself was more like the courtiers in her tale than like her heroine (Becker-Cantarino, "Nachwort" 391–92). But the fact that many of these works were published anonymously or pseudonymously attests to their authors' awareness of how perilous it was to put themselves into the public sphere in textual form, and suggests that, for most of these authors, it was important that their texts in fact *not* function as a public performance of their "self." Indeed, rather than reading anonymous or pseudonymous publication as an act of self-effacement or escape, we can read it as a response to discursive definitions of ideal femininity in terms of antitheatricality: anonymous publication enabled women writers to perform ideal femininity in the public sphere (both in and via their writings) and simultaneously produce the illusion that they were *not performing*.

But Goethe's mistake in his review of Unger's works also points to one of the hazards of publishing anonymously: the possibility that the writer's "self," as interpreted by her public via her text, could be egregiously misread.[3] Indeed, whether women published anonymously, pseudonymously, under a chain of mutually referential names, or under their own names, their texts "performed" in the public sphere in ways that at times went beyond the author's control. In some cases, this meant that the public imposed their judgment of the author's character onto her writing: Elise Bürger's reputation was so besmirched by scandal that even almost a century after her death Touiallon dismissed her writing on the basis of her personality. In other cases, the fact that her text functioned as a "performance of self" in the public sphere compelled an author to proactively police her identity, in ways reminiscent of those employed by Schulze-Kummerfeld. For the public often regarded women writers with the same ambivalent mixture of admiration and suspicion with which they received actresses, and writers had to employ similar strategies to manage their reputation and image. Thus, Marianne Ehrmann had to work hard to gain acceptance in bourgeois circles and overcome the stigma of having been an actress: she justified her editorship of her journals by insisting that her efficient fulfillment of her domestic duties left her plenty of free time to write, and she carefully and deliberately crafted and maintained an image of herself as open, natural, and authentic—an image that is belied by the fact that it was crafted and not "natural" at all.[4] In still other cases, the text produced an image of its author that substituted for her "real self" to such an extent that it precluded any true knowledge of the author or her intentions. The extrapolation of a virtuous La Roche from her novel falls into this category, as do the multiple "authors" that emerge in reviews of Unger's various works.

But it was not simply the authors themselves who could be misframed or misread—their texts themselves were of course also subject to audience interpretation and critical response. Thus the third way in which these texts can be understood as performance vis-à-vis an audience is in their performative effect as moral tales and as models for ideal femininity—or, conversely, as potentially subversive interventions in the discursive construction of such models. Judging how any of these works might have "performed" for its public gets particularly tricky, given (1) the paucity of reviews of these works, (2) the fact that the intended readership was usually female but the majority of reviewers male, (3) that often reviewers did not know the identity of the author but made assumptions about gender and social position that affected their interpretation of the work, (4) that authorial intent is often not clear, and (5) that, in addition, many of these works seem to contain challenges that may not have been intended by their authors and/or may not have been evident to all readers. As a result, my comments here are necessarily speculative; in the following, I want to point to the range of responses these works could and might have provoked in their readership.

Many of these works seem to have had the kind of performative effect that their authors intended, insofar as conformity to convention functioned to sell their work in the marketplace—that is, they seem to have been read by eighteenth-century readers as appropriately replicating and promoting prevailing mores and values. The reception of *Sternheim* as a model for Germany's girls has already been noted; Ehrmann's *Amalie* obtained a similar reception. The reviewer of the *Allgemeine Literatur-Zeitung* noted that the novel's "fine sentiments, honorable principles, [and] frank punishment of follies, vices and prejudices are linked to successful imitations of nature and lively descriptions, all of which make this book of value to the moralist."[5] Reviews of Unger's *Melanie* also took it at face value as a depiction of ideal femininity. The *Neue Allgemeine Deutsche Bibliothek* pulls a quote from Unger's novel in which she claims that it is her "intention to show you . . . a young woman who . . . feels enough strength in herself . . . to submit to duty and necessity, and so make herself worthy of the love of the best man by showing she has the strength and courage to renounce him" (*Melanie* 185) and then proceeds to comment that Unger's depiction is "done so skillfully . . . that it deserves a place among the better class of original texts of this type" (Sm. 296). Reviews of Bürger's and Mereau's texts also indicate that contemporary readers took them as a reaffirmation of eighteenth-century ideas about proper roles and attitudes for women, despite their clear distancing from those norms. So, for example, Ebeling took Bürger's *Labyrinths* as a text that helped women "recognize their true vocation" (198); the *Neue Allgemeine Deutsche Bibliothek* panned it for being "ordinary, . . . mawkish and sentimental" ("Bürger, Elise" 102). Reviews of Mereau's work tended to emphasize her attention to feeling and sentiment (areas of interest that belonged to the feminine sphere) at the expense of mentioning aspects of her work that were outspokenly political (Hammerstein, " 'In Freiheit der Liebe' " 277).

But as Susanne Zantop has noted, many works by women writers of the eighteenth century functioned as literary "trojan horses" that cloaked challenges to convention under seemingly conservative exteriors.[6] Thus, the eighteenth-century reception of each of these works in terms of its replication of dominant values depends at one and the same time on an act of misreading or misframing: they require *not* seeing, for example, the critique embedded in *Sternheim*, the double standard exposed by *Amalie*, and the satire pervading *Melanie*—and, in the case of Bürger and Mereau, they require a willful and wishful imposition of conformity, ordinariness, and sentimentality onto writers whose work was clearly moving in new directions. What is difficult to discern, of course, is whether, and to what extent, eighteenth-century readers saw past or through the authors' claims that they were presenting models of female virtue, and detected the ways the works challenged or subverted the norms they seemed to reproduce. We might, then, draw an analogy between these texts' performance of their social or moral message and the (non)performance of femininity on the part of their heroines, as both exist in a mutually determining relationship with their audience's interpretation.

Finally, the fourth way in which audience response pressures the performance of ideal femininity in these women's writings is, of course, in the resuscitation, rereading, reframing, and possible misreading of these works through interpretive efforts like this book. By focusing an interpretive lens on these texts, we ensure that they continue to "perform" long beyond their immediate social relevance or usefulness, both as artifacts and as potentially powerful commentary on our own ideas about gendered subjectivity. Indeed, given that the late eighteenth century "invented . . . the gender characteristics that have had psychosocial validity well into our century," texts like these, which reveal femininity as a performative construct at the historical moment in which it was being defined as a natural attribute, demonstrate that their authors were quite savvy about the consequences of that definition of femininity and did not meet it without resistance (Hoffman 80). As a result, one of the functions that these texts continue to "perform" is to challenge us to rethink our understanding of the historical processes and discourses that produced ideas about gendered subjectivity: that is, by standing as evidence of the historical use of the idea of performance to combat the cementing of gender on to sex nearly two centuries before Butler's conceptualization of gender as performatively constituted, they reveal current debates as part of a longer, deeper, and bumpier historical process than is usually imagined.

It is the project of another book to trace out the genealogy of notions of femininity as performance from the late eighteenth century through the nineteenth century and on to Riviere's notion of female masquerade and Butler's ideas about gender as a performative act. Instead, I would like to end this book by pointing forward toward the nineteenth century and looking at a work that begins to raise new challenges to the image of the antitheatrical, domestic, ideal woman and to reconfigure ideal femininity and performance in ways that are recognizably modern: Elise Bürger's play *The Antique Statue from Florence* (*Die Antike Statue aus Florenz*, 1814), which picks up several of the issues seen in the other works discussed in this book—in particular, the implication, at the end of Unger's novel, that femininity is fundamentally a projection of masculine desire—and pulls them in a very different direction.

The Antique Statue from Florence is a short one-act play about a marriage in trouble. Laura's husband, Ludwig, has lost interest in her—he spends all of his time in the attic with pictures and busts from Greek antiquity. With the help of her sister, Rosaura, Laura eavesdrops on him and discovers that she has been displaced in her husband's affections by images of beautiful women, a displacement that began when he saw an actress represent Greek figures in a *tableau vivant*. Ludwig is eagerly awaiting the arrival of a statue of a vestal virgin from Florence, which he anticipates will satisfy his desire for beauty. He retires to his attic to gaze at his pictures; Laura and her sister intercept a letter with news that the statue has been destroyed in shipping. Laura veils herself, poses on a pedestal, and presents herself to Ludwig as the long-awaited statue. Duped at first, Ludwig is then so enchanted by Laura's "trick" that he reaffirms his love for her and promises "to seek strange forms no more" (*Antike Statue* 27).[7]

In this play, Bürger introduces instability into the notion of the Ideal Woman, by revealing that the discursive definition of ideal femininity is not necessarily what men really want. One of the first things to be noted about this play is that it begins where most domestic fiction ends: this is a story about what happens to "Sophie" *after* she marries. Laura is safely ensconced in the domestic sphere, where she belongs, and Ludwig describes her in terms that would qualify her as an ideal wife and mother.

> For my Laura has a gentle and good heart;
> But she has no feeling for music, society,
> Lighthearted jests and the splendor of art.
> . . . .
> She is sufficient for counting our household pennies
> And she lives quietly with moral propriety,
> And, I must admit, I believe she loves me deeply. (7)

But Ludwig no longer finds Laura attractive; the innocence and virtue that made her seem ideal before their marriage has lost its appeal:

> Back then, to be sure, ach, it's been six years now——
> I loved in her the charm of virtue, but that is long past,
> Now my eye is accustomed to a more noble desire. (8)

The feminine ideal is no longer enough: in her depiction of a common dilemma (the seven-year, or, in this case, six-year itch) Bürger focuses attention on the fact that what the husband desires is in fact a performance of femininity, and that what he wants to have performed is the projection of his desire—a desire that has been shaped and inflected not by nature, but by artistic representations and, above all, *performances*. Laura's sister Rosaura makes the connection explicit:

> He also recently saw the lady,
> The one who is a practitioner of the thespian arts, it was truly beautiful.
> I was also there and—oh, how it's coming to me in a flash!
> Yes. Yes, that's it! His ideas have been altered by her.

> There he saw groups, Greek figures
> And his love of art wanted to dwell in them.
> As a result he cannot hear or see. (12)

Laura then decides to produce a performance of femininity that matches his desire—she takes the place of the broken statue. There is clearly more than a hint here of what Riviere will later term femininity as masquerade: Laura adopts the mask of femininity defined by the audience who matters most to her—her husband—and her performance is compulsory insofar as it is necessary for her happiness and the survival of her marriage, which is, of course, still the only socially viable option for a woman of her day. As a result, Bürger's play suggests that antitheatrical femininity may be an impossible act not only in the public sphere but also in the private sphere: she ironically demonstrates that the pressure to enact a culturally defined ideal of femininity does not cease once a woman takes up her "natural" role as wife and mother.

At the same time, Laura's performance of femininity for her husband is also a performance staged for a theatrical audience, which is called upon directly to take note of and imitate Laura's example. Rosaura turns to the audience and exhorts:

> You ladies! Take an example from this woman
> Always show yourselves to your men in new forms
> The charm of newness, even if it is sometimes borrowed,
> Is the one and only fairy that men's senses obey. (19)

Remarkable here is Bürger's use of the theater to do what the theater does best—to show the effectiveness, usefulness, and above all delightfulness of audience-oriented performance, and to encourage the women in her audience to adopt theatrical strategies as a means of controlling men's minds and behavior.

Bürger's satirical understanding of the dynamic that produces the "right" performance of gender is simultaneously behind and ahead of its time, hearkening back as it does to the kind of flirtatious ostentation of femininity that piqued Rousseau, and looking forward to an understanding of gender as a performative act, as something that acquires naturalness and interiority by dint of repeated, socially compelled performances. Moreover, as a work that is already influenced by social and cultural changes of the nineteenth century, it reveals that the eighteenth century's impossible act might have undergone even more challenges and permutations in the century that followed, as the pressures to conform to ever more rigid definitions of femininity collided with women's dreams, desires, and expectations.

Notes

INTRODUCTION

Notes to pages 3–6

1. For a discussion of the pressures of performance in such situations, see Pin and Turndorf.
2. An early example of theory that sees the performance of self as liberatory can be found in Hegel's *Phenomenology of Mind*: "The content uttered by Spirit and uttered about itself is . . . a universal deception of itself and others. . . . The shamelessness manifested in stating this deceit is just on that account the greatest truth" (543). See also Trilling's commentary on this section of Hegel in *Sincerity and Authenticity* 33–52. More recently, queer theory has taken up the liberating potential of the "performance of self" and translated it into a form of political action; the fact that such action remains *oppositional* speaks to the lingering force of the ideology of authenticity. See, for example, Butler, "Performative Acts." On the history of the association of acting with hypocrisy, see Barish, Wikander, and Wild.
3. Cf. Geitner, *Die Sprache der Verstellung* esp. Ch. 1.
4. See Bausinger; Blackbourn; Kocka, "Bürgertum und Bürgerlichkeit"; Lepsius; and chapter 1 of this book.
5. The issue was framed in many different—sometimes conservative, sometimes progressive—ways. See, for example, Campe; Curtius; Fichte; Hippel; Humboldt. For recent commentary see Frevert, *Women in German History*; Hausen, "Family and Role-division"; "Überlegungen"; Hochstrasser; Honegger; Kuhn; Leierseder; Olenhusen; P. Schmid; Sharpe; Steinbrügge, "Aufteilung"; *The Moral Sex*; Stephan; and Toppe.
6. This is an observation that crops up repeatedly in scholarship on eighteenth-century German women's writing. See, for example, Dawson, *The Contested Quill* 16; Dietrick; Kirstein 18, 34; Krimmer, "A Spaniard in the Attic" 215; Meise, *Die Unschuld und die Schrift* 175; S. Schmid 27–28; Weigel, "Der schielende Blick"; and Zantop, "Aus der Not" 134–35.

7. Bovenschen 193–94.
8. Catherine Burroughs, *Closet Stages*; Judith Pascoe, *Romantic Theatricality*; and Ellen Donkin, *Getting into the Act*. Scholars of nineteenth-century English literature have also employed a similar approach. See, for example, Allen; Auerbach; and Voskuil.
9. Cheryl Wanko, "The Eighteenth-Century Actress"; Matthew Wikander, *Fangs of Malice*; Lisa Freeman, *Character's Theatre*; Tracy Davis, "Theatricality and Civil Society." Christopher Wild's excellent study *Theater der Keuschheit* is another work that intersects closely with my own in its analysis of both the antitheatrical debate in the eighteenth century and its impact on configurations of ideal femininity; unfortunately, Wild's book came to my attention just as I was finalizing this book for publication and could not, as a result, be taken into fuller consideration here.
10. Susanne Kord, *Sich einen Namen machen*; Elisabeth Krimmer, *In the Company of Men*. Other scholars in the field of German studies who investigate the idea of the performance of self in eighteenth-century women's writing include Emde; Fleig; Geitner; and Niethammer.
11. See also D. Goodman; Maza; Vickery.
12. Cf. Kammler 65. Charlotte von Stein has a play, *Leichtsinn und gutes Herz*, that features two actresses as characters, but because the play does not describe an actress's life in any detail, it has not been included among the works analyzed.
13. Schulze-Kummerfeld's memoirs have been published, but always in heavily redacted form. See chapter 3 of this study.

CHAPTER 1 "SOPHIE" AND THE "THEATER"

1. For related perspectives on the antitheatrical prejudice in the eighteenth century see Barish; Wikander; and Wild.
2. In my use of the term "bourgeois" I follow social historians who define the class less on the basis of socioeconomic status and more in terms of its cultural effects. As Wierlacher notes, the German terms "Bürger" and "bürgerlich" referred less to social class than as "synonyms for human/humane, civis/civilis and private man/private (domestic)" (77). For historical/sociological analysis of the German "bourgeoisie" see Bausinger; Blackbourn; Bruford 227; Engelbrecht 137; Frevert, *Women in German History* 31–33; Kaschuba; Kocka, "Bürgertum und Bürgerlichkeit"; "European Pattern"; "Middle Classes"; Koopmann esp. 13–14; Lepsius; and Nipperdey.

3. Von Mücke refers to the illusionist aesthetic which marked eighteenth-century European literature as the "Project of *Anschaulichkeit*"; my interpretation of the ideological function of this shift here and below is indebted to her reading. See esp. 40–60.
4. Most thoroughly, in Bovenschen. See also: Becher; Dülmen; Frevert, *Bürgerinnen und Bürger*; Hausen, "Family and Role-division"; Joeres and Maynes; Leierseder; and Bronfen.
5. Hausen argues that the modern bipolar gender system stems from the late eighteenth-century fixing of gender roles on to sex; Frevert refines her argument, noting that where earlier periods had legitimized gendered divisions of labor on social or religious grounds, the late eighteenth century justified them on the basis of nature—and thus gave the bipolar gender system its "modern" form. See Hausen, "Family and Role-division"; Frevert, "Einleitung" 40; and Frevert, *Women in German History* 18. Rang offers a response to and critique of Hausen in "Zur Geschichte."
6. Rousseau's influence is evident in a number of German pedagogical manuals of the late eighteenth century, including Campe and L'Escun. For a detailed discussion of Rousseau's image of women and his profound influence on female writers in the Enlightenment, see Mary Trouille's *Sexual Politics in the Enlightenment*. For discussions of Rousseau's impact on German writers and philosophers throughout the eighteenth century see Blochmann 26–45; Fleischmann; Hammerstein, *Freiheit, Liebe, Weiblichkeit* esp. 33–37; Kammler 86; Plath; Winkle Ch. 2; and Bovenschen 158–81. For a reading of Rousseau which downplays his misogyny, see Garbe.
7. For a more detailed discussion of naiveté in this context, see Geitner, *Die Sprache der Verstellung* 293–301.
8. Even Rousseau admits having arrived at his ideas about the naive, transparent self through a series of self-observations in his *Confessions*, and he is careful to educate "Émile" to be conscious of his public self. See Rousseau, *Confessions*; Starobinski Ch. 3; and Wikander 70–78.
9. For example, see the *First and Second Discourses* 37, 155.
10. Knigge, *Über den Umgang* 57–58.
11. Cf. Geitner, *Die Sprache der Verstellung* 36; and Rousseau, *First and Second Discourses* esp. 38.
12. As is evident, for example, in Rousseau's concern for Émile's maintenance of his reputation, and in particular in Rousseau's *Confessions*, which stands as a complex engagement with the problem of shaping the "presentation" of an "authentic" self (cf. Herbold; Starobinski).

13. The concern with the man's presentation of self in everyday life is also evident in Knigge's recommendation of different forms of behavior in dealing with different classes of people (i.e., he devotes separate chapters to proper social intercourse with the nobility, with the lower classes, and with doctors, lawyers, priests, etc.).
14. The infantilization of woman's "character" in this text points to very real similarities between women and children in terms of their social and legal status: both were disenfranchised and excluded from the public sphere, and both were materially dependent on the household patriarch. Cf. Ariès 241; Langeveld 56.
15. On perceptions of the actress in late eighteenth-century Europe see the following: Becker-Cantarino, "Von der Prinzipalin zur Künstlerin"; Berlantstein; Blair; I. Buck; Davis "Private Women"; Emde, "Manuskripte und Memoiren"; *Schauspielerinnen im Europa*; Geitner, *Schauspielerinnen*; Gutjahr; Harris; Kord, *Ein Blick*; "Tugend im Rampenlicht"; Laermann; Möhrmann; Schwanbeck; Straub; Wanko; and Wetzels.
16. Cf. Mücke 60 and Wikander 74–76.
17. See the collection of essays in Frevert, *Bürgerinnen und Bürger*; Landes makes a similar argument.
18. Cf. Roulston xvi; Mücke 66; Baudry 6–12; and Hahn 66. On the status of the letter, and the *Briefroman*, as an expression of "naturalness" and thus the form considered most suited to female writing, see S. Schmid 12–15.
19. Cf. Burger 87; Elias 104–11; A. Buck; and Geitner, *Die Sprache der Verstellung*. Many Elizabethan scholars argue that the *theatrum mundi* which we now take to be a metaphor was in fact the organizing principle of both social life and subjectivity, for example: Barker; Belsey; and Dollimore.
20. As Michael Fried has observed, such a reorientation in the arts in general, and in the theater in particular, fundamentally altered the spectator's attitude toward representation—no longer seen as an aesthetic object in and of itself, representation took on a new "truth" value as the spectator became convinced of his or her own absence from the scene (104).
21. Cf. Graf 282–85; Maurer-Schmoock 149–201.
22. Cf. Haider-Pregler, III.1, esp. 155–70; and Wierlacher.
23. Translations in the following section are from Lessing, *Sara*, trans. Bell.
24. See Ziolkowski.
25. See also Kosenina, *Anthropologie und Schauspielkunst* 81.

26. Wolff, *Vernünfftige Gedancken von der Menschen thun und lassen* 139, note 65 (§215); Gottsched 100, §46 and 101, §47.
27. Recent scholarship in eighteenth-century studies has mapped out in some detail the intersections of acting theory with anthropology (Kosenina, *Anthropologie und Schauspielkunst* and Geitner, *Die Sprache der Verstellung*); with biological science (Roach, *The Player's Passion*); and with pedagogy and ideology (Graf, *Das Theater im Literaturstaat* and Haider-Pregler, *Des sittlichen Bürgers Abendschule*). Among the (seventeenth and) eighteenth century writers whose ideas about acting are investigated in detail in these studies: from Germany—Wolff, Gellert, Mendelssohn, Kant, Lichtenberg, Lavater, Lessing, Goethe, Schlegel, Schiller, Sulzer, Mylius, Engel, Dyck; from England—Bacon, Smith, A. Hill, J. Hill, Hartley, Home, Hume, Garrick, Battie, Addison, Steele, Johnson; from France—Descartes, Du Bos, Condillac, Diderot, Rousseau, Sainte-Albine, Riccoboni.
28. See Fischer-Lichte, *Kurze Geschichte* Ch. 2 and Cole and Chinoy 255 for descriptions of the structural changes that occurred in German theater during the eighteenth century; for history of the Ackermann, Schröder, Eckhof, and Schönemann troupes see Litzmann; Maurer-Schmoock; H. Fetting; and H. Devrient.
29. On acting theory in eighteenth-century Germany see: Baldyga; Barnett; Bender, " 'Mit Feuer und Kälte' "; *Schauspielkunst im 18. Jahrhundert*; Downer; Duerr; Fischer-Lichte, "Entwicklung"; Flaherty; Käuser; Mercier; Oberländer; Veltrusky; and Williams.
30. The phrase "enlightened *Kardiognostik*" is Kosenina's, and refers to a system for reading another's heart (*Anthropologie und Schauspielkunst* 77). Both Kosenina and Geitner present detailed accounts of the eighteenth-century debate on decoding *Verstellung* in: Kosenina, *Anthropologie und Schauspielkunst*, esp. chapters 2 and 3; "Anthropologie und Verstellungskunst"; and Geitner, *Die Sprache der Verstellung*, esp. chapters 3 and 4.

CHAPTER 2 PERFORMANCE AS POWER

1. A poet, novelist, editor, and the first translator of Shakespeare's plays into English, Wieland was an influential figure in eighteenth-century literary circles. For discussions of Wieland's editorial and ideological influence on *Sternheim* and its reception, see Loster-Schneider 48–88 and Baldwin 105–12. Additional discussions of the relationship

between Wieland and La Roche can be found in Assing; Baldwin; Becker-Cantarino, "Nachwort"; " 'Muse' und 'Kunstrichter' "; *Der Lange Weg* 285–88; Bovenschen 196; Lynn xv–xvii; Ridderhoff, *La Roche und Wieland*; Sachs; Winkle 58–60.

2. For analyses of the function and development of domestic fiction and discussions of its pedagogical/moral purposes in general in the eighteenth century, and particularly in Germany, see: Armstrong; Backscheider; Brinker-Gabler; Burkhard; Cook; Halperin; Jirku; Kontje; Mandelkow; Meise, *Die Unschuld und die Schrift*; "Frauenroman"; Roulston; Runge; Schieth; Touaillon; Turner; Voßkamp; Watt; Weigel, "Der schielende Blick." For summaries of eighteenth-century responses to La Roche's novel, see Bovenschen 192–93; Heidenreich 64–66; Touaillon 121–23 and Becker-Cantarino, *Der Lange Weg* 282–89. Becker-Cantarino also includes contemporary reviews and reactions in her edition of the novel on 363–76.
3. This review has often been attributed to Goethe, but Haenelt has fairly conclusively established Merck's authorship (376–78). The review is reprinted by Becker-Cantarino in her edition of *Sternheim* on 367–68. Cf. Swanson 147–52 and S. Schmid 45–49 for an analysis of the relationship between the novel's formal transparency and its interest in subjective transparency that accords with my own interpretation.
4. Lynn vii. La Roche's influence on male writers is also discussed in Spickernagel; Touaillon 107–08, 74–79; Zantop, "Trivial Pursuits?" 34 and Kastinger Riley 27–52.
5. For interpretations and analyses of La Roche's novel not specifically treated in my discussion here, see the following: Baldwin; Becker-Cantarino, "Zur Theorie"; Brown; Brüggemann; Dawson, "Emerging Feminist Consciousness"; *The Contested Quill*; Heidenreich; Hyner; Joeres; Kammler; Kastinger Riley; Langner; Loster-Schneider; Maier; M. Maurer; Nerl-Steckelberg and Pott; Petschauer; Russo; S. Schmid; Spickernagel; Spies; Swanson; Umbach, "Anglophilia"; Wellbery; Wiede-Behrendt.
6. On Richardson and Rousseau's influence, see Arnds; Kontje 18–40; Northcutt; Ridderhoff, *Schülerin*; Umbach, "Case Study"; and Wiede-Behrendt 159–61. On the divergence between La Roche's ideas of education and Rousseau's see S. Schmid 55.
7. Kastinger-Riley is the exception here; she interprets the novel as a thinly veiled critique of the bourgeois value system and reads Sophie as primarily a negative example (27–54).
8. Collyer's translation has her attending the opera, but in La Roche's original she specifically attends a *Komödie*.

9. Translations from the text are my own; however, for ease of reference I have also included the citation for the English translation. Henceforward the German text will be referred to by the abbreviation *GS*, and the English translation by *HS*.
10. See Graf 287f. and Haider-Pregler passim on the pedagogical function of the illusionistic theater.
11. This is, of course, a common problem for bourgeois heroines of the domestic novel; similar plot lines, and a similar theme that theatricality is always both immoral and aristocratic, can be found in Richardson's *Clarissa*, Burney's *Evelina*, Edgeworth's *Belinda*, Laclos' *Les Liaisons Dangereuses*, Goldsmith's *The Vicar of Wakefield*, Defoe's *Roxana*, and Hardy's *Tess of the D'Urbervilles*.
12. The example from Gellert has been noted in chapter 1; in *Émile* Rousseau writes that the tutor should give his pupil the impression that he is not under observation, in order to best observe the pupil's "true" character and progress (*Émile* 99, 149, 81); and Knigge advises "observe others at those moments in which they believe they are not being watched by you!" (*Über den Umgang* 36).
13. This is a clear example of courtly "improvisation" as defined by Greenblatt (227).
14. Seymour's remarks about the actress he once loved do not appear in the translation.
15. See Alewyn; Geitner, *Die Sprache der Verstellung*; and Kosenina, *Anthropologie und Schauspielkunst*.

CHAPTER 3 THE PERFORMANCE OF A LIFETIME

Chapter 3 of this book previously appeared in slightly altered form under the title " 'Laß mich sein, was ich bin': Karoline Schulze-Kummerfeld's Performance of a Lifetime," *The German Quarterly* 76.1 (2003): 68–85; permission to reprint granted by the American Association of Teachers of German.

1. See, for example, Becher; Coleman; Emde, *Schauspielerinnen im Europa*; Gilmore; K. Goodman; Madland, "Women's Journals"; Molloy; Niethammer; Niggl; Nussbaum; Postlewait; Runge; Spacks.
2. Cf. Wanko 75–76.
3. The first manuscript is currently housed at the Staats- und Universitätsbibliothek Hamburg, indexed as cod. hist. 383 d. Schulze-Kummerfeld apparently wrote three different versions of her second

memoirs, but only one survives. It is located at the Thüringisches Haupstaatsarchiv Weimar, indexed as HA A XXII Nr. 425. Cf. Niethammer, 147–152, esp. ftnte. 140 on 149. Microfiche copies of both manuscripts are in the collection of the Hesburgh Library, University of Notre Dame.

4. Reichard 255; Schulze-Kummerfeld wrote a letter to Reichard protesting his depiction of her, which he printed in his *Theater-Kalender 1793* on 297–99 along with a dismissive response on 299–303; her letter also comprised some of the missing opening pages from the Weimar manuscript (the letter's end corresponds with the first extant page of the ms.) Schulze-Kummerfeld also felt insulted by Schink's unfavorable comparison of her to Sophie and Charlotte Ackermann, the wife and daughter of the director of the Ackermann troupe (and Schulze-Kummerfeld's perceived rivals), in his *Theaterzeitung* of 29 September 1792. See also Niethammer 148–60.
5. The letter is reprinted in Niethammer 155–57.
6. For a summary of material left out of published editions, see Niethammer, ftnte. 140 on 149.
7. Scholars who have drawn on these memoirs for evidence in writing the history of German theater and acting include Eduard Devrient, Heinrich Laube, Berthold Litzmann, Anne Fleig, Susanne Kord (*Ein Blick*; "Tugend im Rampenlicht"), Sybille Maurer-Schmoock and Gisela Schwanbeck. In addition, Walter Wetzels mines these memoirs for evidence of the reality of an actress's life and compares that reality to Goethe's fictional depiction of the actress in *Wilhelm Meister* in "Schauspielerinnen im 18. Jahrhundert."
8. Emde, *Schauspielerinnen im Europa* 15–25, 331–36 and Gutjahr 91–98. See also Geitner, *Schauspielerinnen*.
9. Critical responses to and assessments of her performances on stage can be found in Jacobs; Pasquè I: 36, I: 88–89, and II: 96; Peiba 85; Schrickel 80, 146; and Schütze. Schulze-Kummerfeld's performances are also remarked upon by Lessing and Goethe. See Lessing, *Sämtliche Schriften* XX: 50–53 and XXIX: 248–53 and Goethe, *Gedenkausgabe* II: 206, XII: 606–08 and XXIII: 531.
10. The trope of being "driven" to the theater out of necessity becomes a stereotype in eighteenth-century (auto)biography and fiction, its truth value mediated by its usefulness in justifying and/or excusing the pursuit of a nonconforming lifestyle. For example, the parallel between Schulze-Kummerfeld's mother's story and the opening to Mereau's short story "Flight to the City" is rather remarkable: both women are

driven to professional acting by the threat of being mated to a horrid nobleman.

11. Schulze-Kummerfeld provides many fascinating anecdotes about her childhood in the theater, many of which tax credibility. For example, at the tender age of five she had her first major stage accident: she dropped a real knife, which she was using as a prop, through her foot while waiting to make an entrance on stage. She carried on with her role despite the pain and bleeding, she tells us, and never told her parents about the injury, even though she nearly lost her foot to gangrene. An adult neighbor, noticing her limping up the stairs, took her in, found a doctor to take care of the foot, and helped her keep the injury a secret from her parents (*KSK* I: 29–30).
12. Cf. Gutjahr 91–98.
13. Many historians attribute the founding of the Hamburg National Theater at least in part to the competition between these two actresses, and to Hensel's machinations to establish herself as the leading actress in Ackermann's company. See, for example, Kord, "Tugend im Rampenlicht" 2; and Fleig 55–56. In "Zur Situation," Buck argues that Schulze-Kummerfeld's departure was motivated by her discomfort with the new, naturalistic playing style introduced by Lessing and Eckhof (321–22).
14. Among her admirers was Goethe, who attended her performances again and again. Johanna Schopenhauer writes: "Goethe told me, that at the time she created quite a sensation, and that as a student he was madly in love with her and clapped so hard in the parterre in Leipzig that his hands nearly bled . . ."Goethe, *Gedenkausgabe* XXIII: 531. Goethe himself praises Schulze-Kummerfeld's acting twice in his writings (Goethe, *Gedenkausgabe* XII: 606–08 and II: 206).
15. Although I do not discuss them in detail in this chapter, Schulze-Kummerfeld's letters to Kummerfeld outlining the conditions under which she would agree to marry provide fascinating insight into her deep and complex awareness of her standing in society. The letters appear in *KSK* I: 272–75 and are also discussed by Niethammer, 171.
16. The nature of Kummerfeld's disease is never made completely clear: he seems to have suffered from depression, but the precise cause of his death is a mystery.
17. Caroline Großman in a letter to her husband, 11 November 1783. Reprinted in D. Maurer and Maurer 165.
18. For example, in "Die Kummerfelden"; see also "Damengärtchen"; "Handelt von der alten Kummerfelden" and "Kuriose Geschichte."

19. Benezé refers to her invention, "Kummerfeldsches Waschwasser gegen Sommersprossen und Flechten," in his introduction to her memoirs (*KSK*, I:xxxi). In addition, Böhlau notes that it was available throughout Europe: she calls Schulze-Kummerfeld "the inventor of Kummerfeld's Washing and Beauty Water, which even today is still available in every apothecary in Germany and many other lands besides" ("Handelt von der alten Kummerfelden" 77–78).
20. Such a strategy was not unusual for eighteenth-century self-writing: Spacks points out that many eighteenth-century female autobiographers similarly "sketch a drama of self-defense" (73), and, in *Sexual Suspects*, Straub notes that "players and managers who brought their cases before the public eye were consciously struggling for control over the spectacle they made, both of themselves and of others" (15).
21. This is, of course, true of much autobiography, particularly in the eighteenth century; Rousseau's *Confessions* famously engage in a similar move. Cf. Starobinski 180–200.
22. See Becker-Cantarino and Mauser for discussions of eighteenth-century conceptions of friendship.
23. Schulze-Kummerfeld often refers to herself in terms of literary figures from contemporary women's fiction, and her allusion to the world of fiction serves both to heighten the glamour of her life as an actress and to legitimate her portrait of herself as a "good" bourgeois woman. See p. 99 below.
24. Jürgen Habermas notes that in the bourgeois public sphere, "Subjectivity, as the innermost core of the private, was always already oriented to an audience (Publikum)" and draws connections between that audience-oriented interiority and the development of the genres of domestic novel and autobiography (49–50).
25. For discussions of the kinds of social negotiations actresses in the eighteenth century engaged in, and the literary representations which to an extent determined their reputations, see: Becker-Cantarino, "Von der Prinzipalin zur Künstlerin"; Berlantstein; Dawson, "Frauen und Theater: Vom Stegreifspiel zum bürgerlichen Rührstück."; Emde, *Schauspielerinnen im Europa*; Gutjahr; Kord, "Tugend im Rampenlicht"; Laermann; Lohn-Siegel; Möhrmann; Schwanbeck; Straub; Wanko.
26. Rousseau, *Letter* 88: "[A] woman outside of her home loses her greatest luster, and despoiled of her real ornaments, she displays herself indecently. If she has a husband, what is she seeking among men? If she does not, how can she expose herself to putting off, by an immodest

bearing, he who might be tempted to become her husband? Whatever she may do, one feels that in public she is not in her place. . . ."

27. Geitner reproduces a 1784 article out of the *Theater-Journal für Deutschland* which makes a similar attempt to cast the actress as virtuous in *Schauspielerinnen* 53–56. See also Fleig's description of Maria Teutscher's reputation as "blameless" in *Handlungs-Spiel-Räume* 56.
28. This appears to have been a typical workload. For example, the year previously she reports that the troupe performed 172 times. The repertory consisted of 16 tragedies, 81 dramas and comedies, and 32 "after-plays." Schulze-Kummerfeld claims she performed 123 times (not including ballet) in 84 roles, of which 56 were new (*KSK* II: 114).
29. For a fuller account of Schulze-Kummerfeld's description of her working conditions and life, see Buck, "Zur Situation"; for a vivid description of life behind the curtain for women in the eighteenth century drawn from this and other sources see Kord, *Ein Blick* esp. Ch. 2.
30. See Harris 183; Gutjahr 83–84.
31. *GS* 193–99; *HS* 107–10.
32. Cf. Niethammer 173–74.
33. Cf. Nussbaum 134: "Women's self-writing in Restoration and eighteenth-century England ventriloquizes dominant ideologies of gender and class while it allows alternative discourses of 'experience' to erupt in the gaps between subject positions."
34. If we *do* take Schulze-Kummerfeld's story about recognizing the "sham marriage" to be a truthful account of an incident from her youth, then this episode could provide evidence that when young eighteenth-century girls read novels like *Sternheim* they looked beyond the modeling of naive female virtue and learned important lessons about the costs of such naiveté. For while such novels clearly valorize an antitheatrical mode of being for both women and men, their depiction of the dissimulating villain may have served to make naive girls a little less naive about the ways of the world.
35. Rousseau, *Letter* 81–89. See also Geitner, *Die Sprache der Verstellung* esp. 293–94.
36. Niethammer also sees a shift in Schulze-Kummerfeld's prose when she is describing life postmarriage (169).
37. Schulze-Kummerfeld's motives for writing her memoirs seem to come into play in a particularly complex manner in her description of her marriage. She left acting at the height of her career to marry—full of expectation for happiness and stability—and her marriage was clearly a

terrible disappointment. The suspicious reader might wonder about the extent to which she has retroactively depicted her marriage as a "bourgeois tragedy" in which she gives herself the role of a martyred victim.

38. For a discussion of the duties and responsibilities of married women, see Frevert, *Women in German History* 38–49.
39. Böhlau depicts Schulze-Kummerfeld advising her young students against marriage, especially when "one is a resolute woman and knows what one wants" ("Handelt von der alten Kummerfelden" 82).
40. I am grateful to Susanne Kord for calling my attention to this allusion, and to its connections with my own argument.

CHAPTER 4 ANTITHEATRICALITY AND THE PUBLIC WOMAN

1. On these works, see Brandes, "Frauenzimmer-Journal"; Dawson, "Women Communicating"; "Emerging Feminist Consciousness"; Kammler 87–91; Kirstein; Kord, "Discursive Dissociations"; Madland, "Women's Journals."
2. Details of Ehrmann's biography—at times conflicting—can be found in Dawson, *The Contested Quill* 236–40; Gerig; Madland, "Introduction"; *Marianne Ehrmann*; Stump 481–98 and in Theophil Ehrmann, *Denkmal.*
3. In the prologue to *Leisure Hours of a Gentlewoman*, which contains the beginning letter to *Amalie*, Ehrmann writes: ". . . for I am certainly Amalie." (Widmer, "Amalie—eine wahre Geschichte?" 500).
4. Widmer reads the novel along these lines in " 'Mit spitzer Feder,' " as does Gerig 27–35. Other critics who have paid close attention to *Amalie*, and in particular its use of the theater to investigate women's social position, include Dawson, *The Contested Quill* 240–58; Madland, *Marianne Ehrmann* 107–34.
5. See Dawson, "Women Communicating" 106–09; *The Contested Quill*; Gerig esp. Ch. 4; Kammler 86–91; Kirstein 12–13; 50–53; Madland, *Marianne Ehrmann* 107–34; Widmer, "Mit spitzer Feder" 56–60; "Amalie—eine wahre Geschichte?" 502–15.
6. See also Gerig 36–37.
7. Cf. Rousseau, *Émile* 392.
8. She also dissociates female intellect from its negative association with book knowledge; see Böhmel-Fischera.

9. Christoph Ludwig Seipp (1747–93) was an actor and playwright who managed a theater company in Vienna from 1780–93.

CHAPTER 5 THE EYE OF THE BEHOLDER

1. Gottfried August Bürger (1747–97) gained fame for being the first German writer to adopt the folk ballad as a literary form; he was also the first significant political poet in German literature. He was far better known in the late eighteenth and early nineteenth centuries than he is today; he is most remembered as the author of the ballad *Lenore* (1774) and the prose work *Adventures of the Baron von Münchhausen* (1786/1789). Despite the fact that his work was generally esteemed during his lifetime, he struggled financially and died in poverty.
2. The poem was published on September 8 1789 and is reprinted in Kinder 9–13.
3. Biographical information on Elise Bürger has been drawn from Ebeling; Geiger; Kinder; Laddey; Petlick; Pfister; Weckel.
4. Toward the end of her life, Elise Bürger emphatically denied that she had written the poem with the intention of getting G. A. Bürger's attention, claiming that she had written it on the spur of the moment as a joke (Laddey 127–28). For contesting interpretations of the Bürgers' marriage and courtship, see: *Gottfried August Bürger's Ehestands-Geschichte*; Ebeling; Geiger; Gerhard; Kinder; Laddey; Madland, *Marianne Ehrmann* 44–50; Mentzel; Petlick; Pfister; Schiefer; Weckel.
5. The attacks appeared primarily in an anonymous pamphlet entitled *Schicksale einer theatralischen Abentheurerin bei der Hannöverschen Bühne*. It is believed the Reinhards, a married couple who were her rivals in the theater company in Hannover, wrote the pamphlet. Bürger tried to defend herself in writing, in a pamphlet entitled *Ueber meinen Aufenthalt in Hannover* but it was an effort that largely backfired, only giving more fuel to her critics. See Ebeling 170ff.
6. Bürger's dramatic writing has been less neglected. See Hoff; Petlick; Wurst, "Negotiations of Containment"; "Spurensicherung."
7. Lange also refers to the unresolvability characteristic of Unger's work, noting that in *Bekenntnisse einer schönen Seele* the "spiraling of shifting references from reality to text seems to lead to infinity" (Lange 73).
8. Cf. Bailet; Brewer; Giesler; Heuser; Kontje; Krimmer, "A Spaniard in the Attic"; *In the Company of Men*; Lange; Meise, *Die Unschuld und die Schrift*; S. Schmid; Touaillon; Zantop, "Aus der Not"; "Nachwort";

"The Beautiful Soul." In addition, there are two contemporary reviews of *Melanie*, both largely positive: see Goethe, "Rev. of Melanie" and Sm., "Melanie, das Findelkind."

9. Cf. Heuser; Zantop, "The Beautiful Soul"; Brewer; and especially Giesler.
10. See, for example, Brewer; Giesler; Heuser; Krimmer, "A Spaniard in the Attic"; Zantop, "Nachwort"; "The Beautiful Soul."
11. Unger pointedly leaves out the details of this encounter. The original reads: "Bei einem Hofballe sey sie in ein unrechtes Zimmer gerathen, und da—und da—Kurz, Melanie, von Vaterswegen sind wir Schwestern" (203).
12. The German *Urheber* can also refer to God, which adds another layer of meaning onto the text—it hints at an equation between authorial and divine creation.
13. Celebrated "naturalistic" French actress of the eighteenth century (1723–1803) whose *Mémoires d'Hyppolite Clairon* were published 1798–99 and translated almost immediately into both German and English. The first volume of the German version appeared in 1799 under the title *Betrachtungen über sich selbst.*
14. Riccoboni and Schröder 77–78.
15. Giesler notes that in general "the most remarkable formal quality of Unger's prose is its pronounced intertextuality" (10). While she notes Unger's reference to Lessing in passing, like Zantop she places emphasis on reading *Melanie* as a response to Goethe's *Wilhelm Meister* (69; see also Zantop, "The Beautiful Soul" 38).

CHAPTER 6 PLAY'S THE THING

1. The publication date of "Flight to the City" is 1806; Mereau seems to have written it in 1796 and suppressed it after Schiller criticised: "I have serious objections to the story, and I want to advise you not to make use of it at the present. . . . The characters are too little defined; the maxims, according to which they behave, are difficult to condone. . . ." (Cited in Mereau-Brentano, *Ein Glück* 276). Hammerstein surmises that since Schiller does not mention the title of the story to which he refers in this criticism, he could be referring either to "Flight" or to "Marie" (Mereau-Brentano, *Ein Glück* 276, 293). Given Schiller's criticism, however, it seems more likely that he is referring to "Flight": the characters in "Marie" are very well defined, and their thoughts, motivations and objectives are explored with depth and detail. See also Hammerstein, *Freiheit, Liebe, Weiblichkeit* 50 and Gersdorff 117, 251.
2. See Mereau-Brentano, *Wie sehn' ich mich* 110; Harper 335.

3. Biographical information on Mereau can be found in: F. Fetting; Fleischmann; Gersdorff; Hammerstein, *Freiheit, Liebe, Weiblichkeit*; " 'Das uns allein' "; Harper; Horn; Richter; Schwarz; Touaillon 523–54; Weigel, "Sophie Mereau."
4. The three volumes are: Mereau-Brentano, *Blütenalter der Empfindung; Ein Glück, das keine Wirklichkeit umspannt*; and *Wie sehn' ich mich hinaus in die freie Welt.*
5. Her novels are treated in depth in: C. Bürger, " 'Die mittlere Sphäre' "; F. Fetting 118–27; Fleischmann; Hammerstein, " 'In Freiheit der Liebe' "; Kastinger Riley; Kontje 76–79, 82–93; Lange; Richter; Touaillon 523–54; Treder. Discussions of "Ninon de Lenclos" can be found in: Kontje 79–82; Purdy; Richter.
6. Gersdorff discusses "Marie" on 248–50 and "Flight" on 250–52; Hammerstein treats both stories in " 'Schaffen wir uns neue Welten' " 245–51 and also mentions both in " 'Ein magisches Gemisch' " 104; Bürger's comments on "Flight" can be found in C. Bürger, " 'Die mittlere Sphäre' " 383–85; Kontje discusses "Flight" on 79–80.
7. Kammler notes that it is, in fact, rare to find a female protagonist in women's literature who becomes an artist for the sake of becoming an artist (67–68).
8. On Mereau's use of first person as authorial masquerade in her other texts, see Weigel, "Der schielende Blick" 93–96 and Purdy.
9. Translations are from Mereau-Brentano, "Flight to the City"; citations from the German refer to Mereau-Brentano, "Die Flucht nach der Hauptstadt."
10. Cf. Laermann 140–47. Because actresses were very limited in the scenarios they played on stage, they spent most of their time imitating love scenes, and since imitation was believed to be able to affect the actor's character, actresses in particular were thought to be morally compromised by their roles. Goethe exploits this association of actresses with "easy virtue" in his depiction of the actress Marianne in the opening chapter of *Wilhelm Meister's Apprenticeship.*
11. Franz Kratter's *Das Mädchen von Marienburg* (*The Maid of Marienburg*) premiered in 1793 and was published in 1795; it was a highly popular play in which the Emperor of Russia falls in love with, and in the end marries, a village maid that his soldiers have taken prisoner.
12. See Fleischmann; Gersdorff; and Hammerstein, *Freiheit, Liebe, Weiblichkeit.*
13. Cf. Hammerstein, *Freiheit, Liebe, Weiblichkeit* 285.

CONCLUSION

1. Cf. Brewer; Giesler; Zantop, "The Beautiful Soul."
2. See in particular Kord, *Sich einen Namen machen.*
3. Although, as Kord notes, being taken for a male author by Goethe would have been a high compliment to Unger (*Sich einen Namen machen* 157–58). Kord observes that, in the eighteenth century, anonymous and pseudonymous publication aimed primarily at hiding the author's *identity*, whereas in the nineteenth century it was mobilized to hide an author's *gender* (55). Unger mainly published anonymously, but did not, for the most part, try to hide her gender: other works by her are attributed to "the female author (*Verfasserin*) of Julchen Grünthal." In fact, the work that Goethe assumed had male authorship was *Confessions of a Beautiful Soul, written by herself*: Goethe was clearly second-guessing Unger's own self-identification in his review.
4. Kirstein 49; Madland, *Marianne Ehrmann* 179–81; Stump 494.
5. A later review, in the *Allgemeine Deutsche Bibliothek*, criticises the work for being too conformist, an assessment which also confirms that it was read as conventional and moralistic.
6. Zantop, "Aus der Not"; Weigel makes a similar argument in "Der schielende Blick."
7. The play has been reprinted in Wurst, "Spurensicherung." Page numbers refer to the play's original pagination, as indicated in Wurst's reprint.

Bibliography

Allgemeine Literatur-Zeitung Sept. 1788: 604.

Allgemeine Deutsche Bibliothek 90.1 (1794): 124–25.

Alewyn, Richard. *Das große Welttheater: Die Epoche der höfischen Feste.* Munich: Beck, 1989.

Allen, Emily. *Theater Figures: The Production of the Nineteenth-Century Novel.* Columbus: Ohio State Univ. Press, 2003.

Anderson, Benedict. *Imagined Communities: Reflections on the Origin and Spread of Nationalism.* London: Verso, 1983.

Anon. *Schicksale einer theatralischen Abentheurerin bei der Hannöverschen Bühne.* Hannover, 1801.

Ariès, Philippe. *Geschichte der Kindheit.* Munich, Hanser: 1979.

Armstrong, Nancy. *Desire and Domestic Fiction: A Political History of the Novel.* New York: Oxford Univ. Press, 1987.

Arnds, Peter. "Sophie von La Roche's *Geschichte des Fräuleins von Sternheim* as an Answer to Samuel Richardson's *Clarissa.*" *Lessing Yearbook* 29 (1997): 87–105.

Arons, Wendy. " 'Laß mich sein, was ich bin': Karoline Schulze-Kummerfeld's Performance of a Lifetime." *The German Quarterly* 76.1 (2003): 68–85.

Assing, Ludmilla. *Sophie von La Roche, die Freundin Wielands.* Berlin: Janke, 1859. UMI, 1984.

Auerbach, Nina. *Private Theatricals: The Lives of the Victorians.* Cambridge, MA: Harvard Univ. Press, 1990.

Backscheider, Paula, ed. *Revising Women: Eighteenth-Century "Women's Fiction" and Social Engagement.* Baltimore: Johns Hopkins Univ. Press, 2000.

Bailet, Dietlinde S. *Die Frau als Verführte und als Verführerin in der deutschen und französischen Literatur des 18. Jahrhunderts.* Bern: Lang, 1981.

Baldwin, Claire. *The Emergence of the Modern German Novel: Christoph Martin Wieland, Sophie von La Roche, and Maria Anna Sagar.* Rochester: Camden House, 2002.

Baldyga, Natalya. "Political Bodies and Bodies Politic: Cultural Identity and the Actor in G. E. Lessing's *Hamburg Dramaturgy.*" *The Eighteenth Century* 43.3 (2002): 253–67.

Barish, Jonas. *The Anti-Theatrical Prejudice*. Berkeley: University of California Press, 1981.

Barker, Francis. *The Tremulous Private Body: Essays on Subjection*. Ann Arbor: University of Michigan Press, 1995.

Barkhoff, Jürgen and Eda Sagarra, eds. *Anthropologie und Literatur um 1800*. Munich: Iudicium, 1992.

Barnett, Dene. *The Art of Gesture: The Practices and Principles of Eighteenth-Century Acting*. Heidelberg: Winter, 1987.

Baudry, Leo. "The Form of the Sentimental Novel." *Novel* 7 (1973): 5–13.

Bausinger, Hermann. "Bürgerlichkeit und Kultur." Kocka, *Bürger und Bürgerlichkeit* 121–42.

Becher, Ursula A. J. "Weibliches Selbstverständnis in Selbstzeugnissen des 18. Jahrhunderts." *Weiblichkeit in geschichtlicher Perspektive: Fallstudien und Reflexionen zu Grundproblemen der historischen Frauenforschung*. Ed. Ursula A. J. Becher and Jörn Rüsen. Frankfurt aM: Suhrkamp, 1988. 217–33.

Becker-Cantarino, Barbara. *Der Lange Weg zur Mündigkeit: Frau und Literatur (1500–1800)*. Stuttgart: Metzler, 1987.

———. " 'Muse und 'Kunstrichter': Sophie La Roche und Wieland." *MLN* 99.3 (1984): 571–88.

———. "Nachwort." La Roche, *Geschichte des Fräuleins von Sternheim* 381–415.

———. "Von der Prinzipalin zur Künstlerin und Mätresse: Die Schauspielerin im 18. Jahrhundert in Deutschland." Möhrmann, *Schauspielerin* 88–113.

———. "Zur Theorie der literarischen Freundschaft im 18. Jahrhundert am Beispiel der Sophie La Roche." Becker-Cantarino and Mauser 47–74.

Becker-Cantarino, Barbara, and Wolfram Mauser, eds. *Frauenfreundschaft-Männerfreundschaft: Literarische Diskurse im 18. Jahrhundert*. Tübingen: Niemeyer, 1991.

Belsey, Catherine. *The Subject of Tragedy: Identity and Difference in Renaissance Drama*. London: Methuen, 1985.

Bender, Wolfgang F. " 'Mit Feuer und Kälte' und–'Für die Augen symbolisch': Zur Ästhetik der Schauspielkunst von Lessing bis Goethe." *Deutsche Vierteljahresschrift für Literaturwissenschaft und Geistesgeschichte* 62 (1988): 60–98.

Bender, Wolfgang F. ed. *Schauspielkunst im 18. Jahrhundert: Grundlagen, Praxis, Autoren*. Stuttgart: Steiner, 1992.

Berlantstein, Lenard R. "Women and Power in Eighteenth-Century France: Actresses at the Comédie-Française." *Feminist Studies* 20.3 (1994): 475–506.

Blackbourn, David. "The German Bourgeoisie: An Introduction." *The German Bourgeoisie: Essays on the Social History of the German Middle Class from the Late Eighteenth to the Early Twentieth Century*. Ed. David Blackbourn and Richard Evans. London: Routledge, 1991. 1–45.

Blackwell, Jeannine, and Susanne Zantop, eds. *Bitter Healing: German Women Writers, 1700–1830*. Lincoln: University of Nebraska Press, 1990.

Blair, Juliet. "Private Parts in Public Spheres: The Case of Actresses." *Women and Space: Ground Rules and Social Maps*. Ed. Shirley Ardener. Oxford: Berg, 201–21.

Blochmann, Elisabeth. *Das "Frauenzimmer" und die Gelehrsamkeit*. Heidelberg: Quelle & Meyer, 1966.

Böhlau, Helene. "Das Damengärtchen." *Gesammelte Werke* I: 101–33.

———. "Die Kummerfelden zieht mit ihrer Nähschule durch Alt-Weimar." *Gesammelte Werke* II: 457–71.

———. "Eine kuriose Geschichte." *Altweimarische Liebes– und Ehegeschichten*. Stuttgart: Engelhorn, 1897. 119–58.

———. *Gesammelte Werke*. 2 vols. Berlin: Ullstein, 1915.

———. "Handelt von der alten Kummerfelden." *Gesammelte Werke* I: 75–92.

Böhmel-Fischera, Ulrike. " 'Keine eigentliche Schulgelehrsamkeit': Marianne Ehrmanns Begriff der 'Denkerin.' " *Querelles: Jahrbuch für Frauenforschung* (1996): 142–57.

Bovenschen, Silvia. *Die imaginierte Weiblichkeit: Exemplarische Untersuchungen zu kulturgeschichtlichen und literarischen Präsentationsformen des Weiblichen*. Frankfurt: Suhrkamp, 1979.

Brandes, Helga. "Das Frauenzimmer-Journal: Zur Herausbildung einer journalistischen Gattung im 18. Jahrhundert." Brinker-Gabler 452–68.

———. "Der Frauenroman und die literarisch-publizistische Öffentlichkeit im 18. Jahrhundert." Gallas and Heuser 41–51.

Brehmer, Ilse, ed. *"Wissen heisst leben . . .": Beiträge zur Bildungsgeschichte von Frauen im 18. und 19. Jahrhundert*. Düsseldorf: Schwann, 1983.

Brewer, Cindy Patey. "The Seduction of the Beautiful Soul: Anxiety of Influence in Friederike Unger's *Bekenntnisse einer schönen Seele von ihr selbst geschrieben.*" *Monatshefte* 98.1 (2006): 45–67.

Brinker-Gabler, Gisela, ed. *Deutsche Literatur von Frauen: Vom Mittelalter bis zum Ende des 18. Jahrhunderts*. Vol. 1. Munich: Beck, 1988.

Bronfen, Elisabeth, ed. *Die schöne Seele oder Die Entdeckung der Weiblichkeit*. Munich: Goldmann, 1996.

Brown, Hilary. "Sarah Scott, Sophie von La Roche, and the Female Utopian Tradition." *Journal of English and Germanic Philology* 100.4 (2001): 469–81.

Bruford, W. H. *Germany in the Eighteenth Century: The Social Background of the Literary Revival.* Cambridge (England): Cambridge Univ. Press, 1959.

Brüggemann, Fritz. *Sophie von la Roche:* Geschichte des Fräuleins von Sternheim. Darmstadt: Wissenschaftliche Buchgesellschaft, 1964.

Buck, August. "Die Kunst der Verstellung im Zeitalter des Barocks." *Festschrift der wissenschaftlichen Gesellschaft an der Johann Wolfgang Goethe-Universität Frankfurt am Main.* Wiesbaden: Steiner, 1981. 85–103.

Buck, Inge. "Zur Situation der Frauen am Theater im 18. Jahrhundert am Beispiel von Karoline Schulze-Kummerfeld (1745–1815)." *Lessing und die Toleranz.* Ed. Peter Freimark, Franklin Kopitzsch and Helga Slessarev. Detroit: Wayne State Univ. Press, 1985. 313–24.

Bürger, Christa. " 'Die mittlere Sphäre': Sophie Mereau—Schriftstellerin im klassischen Weimar." Brinker-Gabler 366–89.

———. *LebenSchreiben: Die Klassik, die Romantik und der Ort der Frauen.* Stuttgart: Metzler, 1990.

Bürger, Elise. "Aglaja." *Irrgaenge des weiblichen Herzens.* Hamburg: Buchhandlung der neuen Verlagsgesellschaft, 1799.

———. *Die antike Statue aus Florenz.* 1814. Frankfurt aM: Schäfer, 1929. Rpt. in Wurst, Karin A. "Spurensicherung: Elise Bürgers Einakter *Die antike Statue aus Florenz* (1814) als Beispiel dramatischer Experimente an der Jahrhundertwende." *Goethe Yearbook.* Ed. Thomas P. Saine. Vol. 8. Columbia, SC: Camden House, 1996. 210–37.

———. *Ueber meinen Aufenthalt in Hannover gegen den ungenannten Verfasser der Schicksale einer theatralischen Abentheurerin.* Altona, 1801.

"Bürger, Elise, Irrgänge des weiblichen Herzens." Rev. of *Irrgaenge des Weiblichen Herzens,* by Elise Bürger. *Neue Allgemeine Deutsche Bibliothek* 1.66 (1801): 101–03.

Burger, Heinz Otto. *"Dasein heisst eine Rolle spielen": Studien zur deutschen Literaturgeschichte.* Munich: Hanser, 1963.

Burkhard, Marianne, ed. *Gestaltet und Gestaltend: Frauen in der Deutschen Literatur.* Amsterdam: Rodopi, 1980.

Burney, Fanny. *Evelina.* Oxford: Oxford Univ. Press, 2002.

Burroughs, Catherine B. *Closet Stages: Joanna Baillie and the Theater Theory of British Romantic Women Writers.* Philadelphia: University of Pennsylvania Press, 1997.

Butler, Judith. *Gender Trouble: Feminism and the Subversion of Identity.* New York: Routledge, 1990.

———. "Performative Acts and Gender Constitution: An Essay in Phenomenology and Feminist Theory." *Performing Feminisms: Feminist Critical Theory and Theatre*. Ed. Sue-Ellen Case. Baltimore: Johns Hopkins Univ. Press, 1990. 270–83.

Campe, Joachim Heinrich. *Vaeterlicher Rath für meine Tochter. Ein Gegenstück zum Theophron*. Braunschweig, 1791.

Castle, Terry. *Masquerade and Civilization: The Carnivalesque in Eighteenth-Century English Culture and Fiction*. Stanford: Stanford Univ. Press, 1986.

Clairon, Hyppolite. *Betrachtungen über sich selbst: und über die dramatische Kunst*. Zürich: Füssli, 1830.

———. *Mémoires d'Hyppolite Clairon, et réflexions sur l'art dramatique*. Paris: F. Buisson, 1799.

———. *Memoirs of Hyppolite Clairon, the celebrated French actress: with reflections upon the dramatic art, written by herself*. London: Robinson, 1800.

Cole, Toby, and Helen Krich Chinoy. *Actors on Acting*. New York: Crown, 1978.

Coleman, Linda S., ed. *Women's Life-Writing: Finding Voice/Building Community*. Bowling Green: Bowling Green State Univ. Press, 1997.

Cook, Elizabeth Heckendorn. *Epistolary Bodies: Gender and Genre in the Eighteenth-Century Republic of Letters*. Stanford: Stanford Univ. Press, 1996.

Curtius, Michael Conrad. *Von der Erziehung des weiblichen Geschlechts*. Marburg, 1777.

Davis, Tracy. "Theatricality and Civil Society." *Theatricality*. Ed. Tracy Davis and Thomas Postlewait. Cambridge: Cambridge Univ. Press, 2003. 127–55.

———. "Private Women and the Public Realm." *Theatre Survey* 35.1 (1994): 65–71.

Dawson, Ruth. " 'And this Shield Is Called—Self Reliance': Emerging Feminist Consciousness in the Late Eighteenth Century." Joeres and Maynes 157–75.

———. *The Contested Quill*. Newark: University of Delaware Press, 2001.

———. "Frauen und Theater: Vom Stegreifspiel zum bürgerlichen Rührstück." Brinker-Gabler 421–34.

———. "Women Communicating: Eighteenth-Century German Journals Edited by Women." *Archives et Bibliotheques de Belgique* 54.1–4 (1983): 95–111.

Defoe, Daniel. *Roxana*. Thorndike, ME: Hall, 2000.

Devrient, Eduard. *Geschichte der Deutschen Schauspielkunst*. Ed. Rolf Kabel and Christoph Trilse. 2 vols. Berlin: Henschel, 1967.

Devrient, Hans. *Johann Friedrich Schönemann und seine Schauspielergesellschaft. Ein Beitrag zur Theatergeschichte des 18. Jahrhunderts*. Hamburg: L. Voss, 1895.

Dietrick, Linda. "Women Writers and the Authorization of Literary Practice." *Unwrapping Goethe's Weimar: Essays in Cultural Studies and Local Knowledge*. Ed. Burkhart Henke, Susanne Kord and Simon Richter. Rochester: Camden House, 2000. 213–32.

Dollimore, Jonathan. *Radical Tragedy: Religion, Ideology and Power in the Drama of Shakespeare and his Contemporaries*. Chicago: University of Chicago Press, 1984.

Donkin, Ellen. *Getting into the Act: Women Playwrights in London, 1776–1829*. New York: Routledge, 1995.

Downer, Alan S. "Nature to Advantage Dressed: Eighteenth-Century Acting." *PMLA* 58 (1943): 1002–37.

Duerr, Edwin. *The Length and Depth of Acting*. New York: Holt, 1962.

Dülmen, Andrea von, ed. *Frauenleben im 18. Jahrhundert*. Munich: Beck, 1992.

Ebeling, Friedrich W. *Gottfried August Bürger und Elise Hahn. Ein Ehe-, Kunst und Literaturleben*. Leipzig: Wartig, 1868.

Edgeworth, Maria. *Belinda*. Oxford: Oxford Univ. Press, 1999.

Ehrmann, Marianne. *Amalie. Eine wahre Geschichte in Briefen. Von der Verfasserin der Philosophie eines Weibs*. Bern: Hortin, 1788. Ed. Maya Widmer and Doris Stump. 2 vols. Bern: Haupt, 1995.

———. *Amaliens Erholungsstunden. Teutschlands Töchtern geweiht*. 4 vols. Tübingen, 1790.

———. "Brief vom 29. September 1789, an Johann Caspar Lavater." Rpt. in Ehrmann, *Amalie* 525–27.

———. *Kleine Fragmente für Denkerinnen. Von der Verfasserin der Philosophie eines Weibes*. Isny, 1789.

———. *Philosophie eines Weibs. Von einer Beobachterin*. Kempten, 1784.

Ehrmann, Theophil. *Denkmal der Freundschaft und Liebe der verewigten Frau Marianne Ehrmann errichtet, und allen ihren Gönnerin, Freundinnen und Leserinnen geweiht*. Leipzig: Gräff, 1796.

Elias, Norbert. *The Court Society*. Trans. Edmund Jephcott. Oxford: Blackwell, 1983.

Emde, Ruth B. "Manuskripte und Memoiren von Schauspielerinnen des 18. Jahrhunderts: Ein Leben mit Texten, durch Texte, für Texte, in Texte." *Das achtzehnte Jahrhundert* 20.2 (1996): 181–96.

———. *Schauspielerinnen im Europa des 18. Jahrhunderts: Ihr Leben, ihre Schriften und ihr Publikum*. Amsterdam: Rodopi, 1997.

Engelbrecht, Johann Andreas. "Von dem bürgerlichen Trauerspiel." *Willhelm Cooke: Grundsätze der dramatischen Kritik. Aus dem Englischen übersetzt, mit Zusätzen und Anmerkungen [von Johann Andreas Engelbrecht]*. Lübeck, 1777. 132–38.

Fetting, Friederike. *"Ich fand in mir eine Welt": eine sozial– und literaturgeschichtliche Untersuchung zur deutschen Romanschriftstellerin um 1800: Charlotte von Kalb, Caroline von Wolzogen, Sophie Mereau-Brentano, Johanna Schopenhauer*. Munich: Fink, 1992.

Fetting, Hugo. *Conrad Ekhof, ein Schauspieler des achtzehnten Jahrhunderts*. Berlin: Henschel, 1954.

Fichte, Johann Gottlieb. "Grundriß des Familienrechts." Lange, *Ob die Weiber Menschen sind* 362–410.

Fischer-Lichte, Erika. "Entwicklung einer neuen Schauspielkunst." Bender, *Schauspielkunst* 51–70.

———. *Kurze Geschichte des deutschen Theaters*. Tübingen: Francke, 1993.

Flaherty, Gloria. "The Dangers of the New Sensibilities in Eighteenth-Century German Acting." *Theatre Research International* 8.2 (1983): 95–110.

Fleig, Anne. *Handlungs-Spiel-Räume: Dramen von Autorinnen im Theater des ausgehenden 18. Jahrhunderts*. Würzburg: Königshausen & Neumann, 1999.

Fleischmann, Uta. *Zwischen Aufbruch und Anpassung: Untersuchungen zu Werk und Leben der Sophie Mereau*. Frankfurt aM: Lang, 1989.

Frankfurter Gelehrte Anzeigen. Frankfurt, 1772. Rpt. Ed.: *Frankfurter Gelehrte Anzeigen*. Ed. Bernhard Seuffert. Deutsche Literaturdenkmale des 18. Jahrhunderts, Vol. 7/8. Heilbronn, 1882.

Freeman, Lisa. *Character's Theatre: Genre and Identity on the Eighteenth-Century English Stage*. Philadelphia: University of Pennsylvania Press, 2002.

Frevert, Ute. "Bürgerliche Meisterdenker und das Geschlechterverhältnis. Konzepte, Erfahrungen, Visionen an der Wende vom 18. zum 19. Jahrhundert." Frevert, *Bürgerinnen und Bürger* 17–48.

———. "Einleitung." Frevert, *Bürgerinnen und Bürger* 11–16.

———, ed. *Bürgerinnen und Bürger: Geschlechterverhältnisse im 19. Jahrhundert*. Göttingen: Vandenhoeck & Ruprecht, 1988.

———. *Women in German History: From Bourgeois Emancipation to Sexual Liberation*. Trans. Stuart McKinnon-Evans. Oxford: Berg, 1989.

Fried, Michael. *Absorption and Theatricality: Painting and Beholder in the Age of Diderot*. Berkeley: University of California Press, 1980.

Gallas, Helga, and Magdalene Heuser, eds. *Untersuchungen zum Roman von Frauen um 1800*. Tübingen: Niemeyer, 1990.

Garbe, Christine. "Sophie oder die heimliche Macht der Frauen: Zur Konzeption des Weiblichen bei J.-J. Rousseau." Brehmer 65–87.

Geiger, Ludwig. "Eine Ausgestoßene. Elise Bürger." *Die Insel* 3 (1902): 156–65.

Geitner, Ursula. *Schauspielerinnen: Der theatralische Eintritt der Frau in der Moderne*. Bielefeld: Haux, 1988.

———. *Die Sprache der Verstellung. Studien zum rhetorischen und anthropologischen Wissen im 17. und 18. Jahrhundert*. Tübingen: Niemeyer, 1992.

Gellert, Christian Fürchtegott. *Gesammelte Schriften*. Ed. Sibylle Späth. Vol. VI: Moralische Vorlesungen. Moralische Charaktere. New York: de Gruyter, 1992.

Gerhard, C. "Bürger's dritte Gattin. Skizze zur Erinnerungen an seinen 150 Geburtstag am 31. Dezember." *Didaskalia* 306 (1897): 1223.

Gerig, Maya. " 'Ein Weib ein Wort': Marianne Ehrmanns Literarischer Beitrag zur Mündigkeit der Frau in der Aufklärung." MA Thesis. University of North Carolina, 2002.

Gersdorff, Dagmar von. *Dich zu lieben kann ich nicht verlernen: Das Leben der Sophie Brentano-Mereau*. Frankfurt aM: Insel, 1984.

Giesler, Birte. *Literatursprünge*. Göttingen: Wallstein, 2003.

Gilmore, Leigh. *Autobiographics: A Feminist Theory of Women's Self-Representation*. Ithaca: Cornell Univ. Press, 1994.

Goethe, Johann Wolfgang von. "Berlin, b. Unger: *Bekenntnisse einer schönen Seele*, von ihr selbst geschrieben. 1806." Rev. of *Bekenntnisse einer schönen Seele*, von ihr selbst geschrieben, by F. H. Unger. *Jenaische Allgemeine Literatur-Zeitung* 167 (1806). Rpt. in Goethe, *Sämtliche Werke* 6.2: 626–32.

———. "Berlin, b. Unger: *Melanie das Findelkind*. 1804." Rev. of Melanie das Findelkind, by F. H. Unger. *Jenaische Allgemeine Literatur-Zeitung* 167 (1806). Rpt. in Goethe, *Sämtliche Werke* 6.2: 632–33.

———. *Gedenkausgabe der Werke, Briefe, und Gespräche*. Ed. Ernst Beutler. 24 vols. Zürich: Artemis, 1950.

———. *Wilhelm Meister's Apprenticeship*. Trans. Thomas Carlyle. New York: Collier, 1962.

———. *Sämtliche Werke nach Epochen seines Schaffens*. Ed. Karl Richter. 21 vols. Munich: Hanser, 1988.

Goffman, Erving. *The Presentation of Self in Everyday Life*. Woodstock, NY: Overlook, 1973.

Goldsmith, Oliver. *The Vicar of Wakefield*. Ware: Wordsworth, 1998.

Goodman, Dena. "Introduction: The Public and the Nation." *Eighteenth-Century Studies* 29.1 (1996): 1–4.

Goodman, Katherine. *Dis/Closures: Women's Autobiography in Germany between 1790 and 1914*. New York: Lang, 1986.
Gottfried August Bürger's Ehestands-Geschichte. Berlin, 1812.
Gottsched, J. C. *Erste Gründe der gesamten Weltweisheit, darinn alle Philosophische Wissenschaften in ihrer natürlichen Verknüpfung abgehandelt werden, zum Gebrauche academischer Lectionen entworfen*. Leipzig: Breitkopf, 1734. Frankfurt, 1965.
Graf, Ruedi. *Das Theater im Literaturstaat: Literarisches Theater auf dem Weg zur Bildungsmacht*. Tübingen: Niemeyer, 1992.
Greenblatt, Stephen. *Renaissance Self-Fashioning: From More to Shakespeare*. Chicago: University of Chicago Press, 1980.
Gutjahr, Ortrud. "Gesellschaftsfähigkeit und gesellige Rolle der Schauspielerin im 18. Jahrhundert." Gutjahr, Kühlmann and Wucherpfennig 83–110.
Gutjahr, Ortrud, Wilhelm Kühlmann and Wolf Wucherpfennig, eds. *Gesellige Vernunft: Zur Kultur der literarischen Aufklärung*. Würzburg: Königshausen & Neumann, 1993.
Habermas, Jürgen. *The Structural Transformation of the Public Sphere: An Inquiry into a Category of Bourgeois Society*. Trans. Thomas Burger. Cambridge, MA: MIT Press, 1989.
Haenelt, Karin. "Die Verfasser der Frankfurter Gelehrten Anzeigen von 1772: Ermittlung von Kriterien zu ihrer Unterscheidung durch maschinelle Stilanalyse." *Euphorion* 78.4 (1984): 368–82.
Hahn, Aloïs. "Contribution à la sociologie de la confession et autres formes institutionnalisées d'aveu: Autothématisations et processus de civilisation." *Actes de la recherche en sciences sociales* 62/63 (1986): 54–68.
Haider-Pregler, Hilde. *Des sittlichen Bürgers Abendschule. Bildungsanspruch und Bildungsauftrag des Berufstheaters im 18. Jahrhundert*. Vienna: Jugend und Volk, 1980.
Halperin, Natalie. "Die deutschen Schriftstellerinnen in der zweiten Hälfte des 18. Jahrhunderts. Versuch einer soziologischen Analyse." Diss. Frankfurt aM, 1935.
Hammerstein, Katharina von. " 'Das uns allein zu freien Wesen gründet, woran allein sich unsre Würde bindet, dies höchste Gut, es heißt—Selbständigkeit.' Ein Nachwort zu Sophie Mereau-Brentanos Leben." Mereau-Brentano, *Wie sehn' ich mich* 249–78.
———. " 'Ein magisches Gemisch aus Wahn und Wirklichkeit': Sophie Mereaus verborgene Poetologie und die politische Asthetik des posttorthodoxen Marxismus." *Colloquia Germanica* 35.2 (2002): 97–124.
———. " 'In Freiheit der Liebe und dem Glück zu leben.' Ein Nachwort zu Sophie Mereaus Romanen." Mereau-Brentano, *Blütenalter* 263–86.

Hammerstein, Katharina von. " 'Schaffen wir uns neue Welten.' Ein Nachwort zu Schreibspuren in Sophie Mereau-Brentanos Lyrik und Erzählungen." Mereau-Brentano, *Ein Glück* 231–59.

———. *Sophie Mereau-Brentano: Freiheit, Liebe, Weiblichkeit. Trikolore sozialer und individueller Selbstbestimmung um 1800.* Heidelberg: Winter, 1994.

Hardenberg, Friedrich von. *Novalis' Schriften: Die Werke Friedrich von Hardenbergs.* Ed. Paul Kluckhorn and Richard Samuel. Stuttgart: Kohlhammer, 1960.

Hardy, Thomas. *Tess of the d'Urbervilles.* London: Penguin, 2002.

Harper, Anthony J. "Sophie Mereau (1770–1806)." *Sappho in the Shadows: Essays on the Work of German Women Poets of the Age of Goethe (1749–1832).* Ed. Anthony J. Harper and Margaret C. Ives. Oxford: Lang, 2000. 113–44.

Harris, Edward P. "From Outcast to Ideal: The Image of the Actress in Eighteenth-Century Germany." *The German Quarterly* 54.2 (1981): 177–87.

Hausen, Karin. "Family and Role-Division: The Polarisation of Sexual Stereotypes in the Nineteenth Century—An Aspect of the Dissociation of Work and Family Life." *The German Family: Essays on the Social History of the Family in Nineteenth and Twentieth Century Germany.* Ed. Richard J. Evans and W.R. Lee. Totowa, NJ: Croom Helm, 1981. 51–83.

———. "Überlegungen zum geschlechtsspezifischen Strukturwandel der Öffentlichkeit." *Differenz und Gleichheit: Menschenrechte haben (k)ein Geschlecht.* Ed. Ute Gerhard. Frankfurt aM: Helmer, 1990. 268–82.

Hegel, G. W. F. *The Phenomenology of Mind.* Trans. J. B. Baillie. Second ed. London: Allen and Unwin, 1931.

Heidenreich, Bernd. *Sophie von La Roche—eine Werkbiographie.* Frankfurt aM: Lang, 1986.

Herbold, Sarah. "Rousseau's Dance of Veils: The *Confessions* and the Imagined Woman Reader." *Eighteenth-Century Studies* 32.3 (1999): 333–53.

Heuser, Magdalene. " 'Spuren trauriger Selbstvergessenheit': Möglichkeit eines weiblichen Bildungsromans um 1800: Friederike Unger." *Frauensprache-Frauenliteratur? Für und Wider einer Psychoanalyse literarischer Werke.* Ed. Inge Stephan and Carl Pietzcker. Tübingen: Niemeyer, 1986. 30–42.

Hill, John. *The Actor: A Treatise on the Art of Playing. Interspersed with Theatrical Anecdotes, Critical Remarks on Plays, and Occasional Observations on Audiences.* 1750. New York: Bloom, 1971.

Hippel, Theodor Gottlieb von. *Über die bürgerliche Verbesserung der Weiber.* Berlin, 1792.

Hochstrasser, Olivia. "Armut und Liederlichkeit. Aufklärerische Sozialpolitik als Disziplinierung des weiblichen Geschlechts—das Beispiel Karlsruhe." Weckel et al. 323–44.

Hoff, Dagmar von. "Zwischen Einschluß und Befreiung: Das weibliche Drama um 1800 am Beispiel der Dramatikerin und Schauspielerin Elise Bürger (1769–1833)." *Der Menschheit Hälfte blieb noch ohne Recht: Frauen und die Französische Revolution.* Ed. Helga Brandes. Wiesbaden: Deutscher Universitätsverlag, 1991. 74–87.

Hoffman, Volker. "Elisa und Robert oder das Weib und der Mann, wie sie sein sollten: Anmerkungen zur Geschlechtercharakteristik der Goethezeit." *Die Weimarer Klassik als historisches Ereignis und Herausforderung im kulturgeschichtlichen Prozeß.* Ed. Karl Richter and Jorg Schönert. Stuttgart: Metzler, 1983. 80–97.

Home, Henry, Lord Kames. *Elements of Criticism.* 1761. Eleventh ed. London: B. Blake, 1763.

Honegger, Claudia. *Die Ordnung der Geschlechter. Die Wissenschaften vom Menschen und das Weib 1750–1850.* Frankfurt: Campus, 1991.

Horn, Gisela. *Romantische Frauen: Caroline Michaelis-Böhmer-Schlegel-Schelling, Dorothea Mendelssohn-Veit-Schlegel, Sophie Schubart-Mereau-Brentano.* Rudolstadt: Hain, 1996.

Humboldt, Wilhelm von. "Über den Geschlechtsunterschied und dessen Einfluß auf die organische Natur." Lange, *Ob die Weiber Menschen sind* 284–308.

Hyner, Bernadette H. "Exploring 'I's: Relocation and the Self in Works by Sophie von La Roche and Elisabeth von der Recke." Diss. Vanderbilt University, 2001.

Jacobs, Monty. *Deutsche Schauspielkunst: Zeugnisse zur Bühnengeschichte klassischer Rollen.* Leipzig: Insel, 1913.

Jirku, Brigitte E. *"Wollen Sie mit Nichts . . . ihre Zeit versplittern?": Ich-Erzählerin und Erzählstruktur in von Frauen verfassten Romanen des 18. Jahrhunderts.* Frankfurt aM: Lang, 1994.

Joeres, Ruth-Ellen. " 'That Girl Is an Entirely Different Character!' Yes, but is she a Feminist?: Observations on Sophie von La Roche's *Geschichte des Fräuleins von Sternheim.*" Joeres and Maynes 137–57.

Joeres, Ruth-Ellen, and Mary Jo Maynes, eds. *German Women in the Eighteenth and Nineteenth Centuries.* Bloomington: Indiana Univ. Press, 1986.

Kammler, Eva. *Zwischen Professionalisierung und Dilettantismus: Romane und ihre Autorinnen um 1800.* Opladen: Westdeutscher, 1992.

Kant, Immanuel. *Anthropology from a Pragmatic Point of View.* Trans. Victor Lyle Dowdell. Carbondale: Southern Illinois Univ. Press, 1978.

Kaschuba, Wolfgang. "German Bürgerlichkeit after 1800: Culture as Symbolic Practice." Kocka and Mitchell 392–422.

Kastinger Riley, Helene M. *Die weibliche Muse: sechs Essays über künstlerisch schaffende Frauen der Goethezeit.* Columbia, SC: Camden House, 1986.

Käuser, Andreas. "Körperzeichentheorie und Körperausdruckstheorie." *Theater im Kulturwandel des 18. Jahrhunderts: Inszenierung und Wahrnehmung von Körper, Musik, Sprache.* Ed. Erika Fischer-Lichte and Jorg Schönert. Göttingen: Wallstein, 1999. 39–51.

Kinder, Hermann, ed. *Bürgers Liebe: Dokumente zu Elise Hahns und G. A. Bürgers unglücklichem Versuch, eine Ehe zu führen: mit zeitgenössischen Illustrationen.* Frankfurt aM: Insel, 1981.

Kindermann, Heinz. *Conrad Ekhofs Schauspielerakademie.* Vienna: Rohrer, 1956.

Kirstein, Britt Angela. *Marianne Ehrmann: Publizistin und Herausgeberin im ausgehenden 18. Jahrhundert.* Wiesbaden: Deutscher Universitätsverlag, 1997.

Kittler, Friedrich A. *Discourse Networks 1800/1900.* Trans. Michael Metteer and Chris Cullens. Stanford: Stanford Univ. Press, 1990.

Klein, Lawrence E. "Gender and the Public/Private Distinction in the Eighteenth Century: Some Questions about Evidence and Analytic Procedure." *Eighteenth-Century Studies* 29.1 (1996): 97–109.

Klopstock, Friedrich Gottlieb. "Von der heiligen Poesie [1755]." *Der Messias, Gesang I-III, Studienausgabe.* Ed. Elisabeth Höpker-Herberg. Stuttgart: Reclam, 1986. 114–27.

Knigge, Adolph Freiherr von. *Über den Umgang mit Menschen.* 1790. Ed. Irving Fetscher. Frankfurt: Fischer, 1962.

———. "Von dramatischen Schriftstellern und solchen, die über andere schöne Künste schreiben." *Ueber Schriftsteller und Schriftstellerey.* Ed. Adolph Freiherr von Knigge. Hannover, 1793. 205–55.

Kocka, Jürgen, ed. *Bürger und Bürgerlichkeit im 19. Jahrhundert.* Göttingen: Vandenhoeck & Ruprecht, 1987.

———. "Bürgertum und Bürgerlichkeit als Probleme der deutschen Geschichte vom späten 18. zum frühen 20. Jahrhundert." Kocka, *Bürger und Bürgerlichkeit* 21–63.

———. "The European Pattern and the German Case." Kocka and Mitchell 3–39.

———. "The Middle Classes in Europe." *The Journal of Modern History* 67.4 (1995): 783–806.

Kocka, Jürgen, and Allan Mitchell, eds. *Bourgeois Society in Nineteenth-Century Europe.* Oxford: Berg, 1993.

Kontje, Todd. *Women, the Novel, and the German Nation 1771–1871: Domestic Fiction in the Fatherland.* Cambridge: Cambridge Univ. Press, 1998.

Koopmann, Helmut. "Der bessere Bürger: Ideal und Wirklichkeit der bürgerlichen Welt im Spiegel der Literatur des 18. Jahrhunderts." *Der bessere Bürger. Schaubühne und Drama 1750–1800 im Spiegel der Oettingen-Wallersteinschen Bibliothek. Katalog zur Ausstellung des Lehrstuhls für Neuere Deutsche Literaturwissenschaft und der Universitätsbibliothek Augsburg, 9. Juli–29. August 1992.* Ed. Helmut Koopmann and Rudolf Frankenberger. Augsburg: Universitätsbibliothek Augsburg, 1992. 11–17.

Kord, Susanne. "Discursive Dissociations: Women Playwrights as Observers of the Sturm und Drang." *Literature of the Sturm und Drang.* Ed. David Hill. Rochester: Camden House, 2003. 241–73.

———. *Ein Blick hinter die Kulissen.* Stuttgart: Metzler, 1992.

———. *Sich einen Namen machen: Anonymität und weibliche Autorschaft 1700–1900.* Stuttgart: Metzler, 1996.

———. "Tugend im Rampenlicht: Friederike Sophie Hensel als Schauspielerin und Dramatikerin." *The German Quarterly* 66.1 (1993): 1–19.

Kosenina, Alexander. *Anthropologie und Schauspielkunst: Studien zur "eloquentia corporis" im 18. Jahrhundert.* Tübingen: Niemeyer, 1995.

———. "Wie die 'Kunst von der Natur überrumpelt' werden kann: Anthropologie und Verstellungskunst." Barkhoff and Sagarra 53–71.

Kratter, Franz. *Das Mädchen von Marienburg: ein fürstliches Familiengemälde in fünf Akte.* Frankfurt, 1795.

Krimmer, Elisabeth. *In the Company of Men: Cross-Dressed Women around 1800.* Detroit: Wayne State Univ. Press, 2004.

———. "A Spaniard in the Attic: The Texture of Gender in Friederike Helene Unger's Rosalie und Nettchen." *Journal of Popular Culture* 34.3 (2000): 209–27.

Kuhn, Annette. "Das Geschlecht—eine historische Kategorie?" Brehmer 29–50.

L'Escun, Marie Josephine de. *Sophie, oder von Erziehung der Töchter.* Berlin: Leipzig, 1777.

La Roche, Sophie von. *Geschichte des Fräuleins von Sternheim.* Ed. Barbara Becker-Cantarino. Stuttgart: Reclam, 1983.

———. *The History of Lady Sophia Sternheim.* Trans. Joseph Collyer. Ed. James Lynn. London: Pickering & Chatto, 1991.

La Roche, Sophie von. *Melusinens Sommerabende*. Ed. C. M. Wieland. Halle: Societäts- Buch- und Kunsthandlung, 1806.

Laclos, Choderlos de. *Les Liaisons Dangereuses*. Trans. Ernest Christopher Dowson. New York: Doubleday, 1998.

Laddey, E. "Aus den letzten Tagen einer Vielgenannten, Elise Bürger." *Gartenlaube* (1872): 126–28.

Laermann, Klaus. "Die riskante Person in der moralischen Anstalt: Zur Darstellung der Schauspielerin in deutschen Theaterschriften des späten 18. Jahrhunderts." Möhrmann, *Schauspielerin* 127–53.

Landes, Joan B. *Women and the Public Sphere in the Age of the French Revolution*. Ithaca: Cornell Univ. Press, 1988.

Lange, Sigrid, ed. *Ob die Weiber Menschen sind: Geschlechterdebatten um 1800*. Leipzig: Reclam, 1992.

———. *Spiegelgeschichten: Geschlechter und Poetiken in der Frauenliteratur um 1800*. Frankfurt aM: Helmer, 1995.

Langeveld, M. J. *Studien zur Anthropologie des Kindes*. Tübingen: Niemeyer 1968.

Langner, Margrit. *Sophie von La Roche—die empfindsame Realistin*. Heidelberg: Winter, 1995.

Laube, Heinrich. *Das norddeutsche Theater: Ein neuer Beitrag zur deutschen Theatergeschichte*. Leipzig: Weber, 1872.

Leierseder, Brigitte. *Das Weib nach den Ansichten der Natur*. Munich: Ludwig-Maximilians-Universität, 1981.

Lepsius, M. Rainer. "Zur Soziologie des Bürgertums und der Bürgerlichkeit." Kocka, *Bürger und Bürgerlichkeit* 79–100.

Lessing, Gotthold Ephraim. "Auszug aus dem Schauspieler." Lessing, *Sämtliche Schriften* VI: 120–52.

———. *Emilia Galotti, a Tragedy in Five Acts*. New York: Ungar, 1962.

———. *Hamburgische Dramaturgie*. Stuttgart: Kröner, 1963.

———. *Sämtliche Schriften*. Ed. Karl Lachmann and Franz Muncker. 23 vols. Stuttgart: Göschen'sche Verlagshandlung, 1890.

———. *Sara*. Trans. Ernest Bell. Bath: Absolute, 1990.

Litzmann, Berthold. *Friedrich Ludwig Schröder. Ein Beitrag zur deutschen Litteratur und Theatergeschichte*. 2 vols. Hamburg and Leipzig: Voß, 1890/1894.

Lohn-Siegel, Anna. *Wie ich Schauspielerin wurde*. Berlin: Gerschel, 1880.

Loster-Schneider, Gudrun. *Sophie La Roche: Paradoxien weiblichen Schreibens im 18. Jahrhundert*. Tübingen: Narr, 1995.

Lynn, James. "Introduction." La Roche, *The History of Lady Sophia Sternheim*. vii–xxxi.

Madland, Helga Stipa. "An Introduction to the Works and Life of Marianne Ehrmann (1755–95): Writer, Editor, Journalist." *Lessing Yearbook* 21 (1989): 171–96.

———. *Marianne Ehrmann: Reason and Emotion in her Life and Works.* New York: Lang, 1998.

———. "Three Late Eighteenth-Century Women's Journals: Their Role in Shaping Women's Lives." *Women in German* 4 (1988): 167–86.

Maier, Hans-Joachim. *Zwischen Bestimmung und Autonomie: Erziehung, Bildung und Liebe im Frauenroman des 18. Jahrhunderts: eine literatursoziologische Studie von Christian F. Gellerts* Leben der schwedischen Gräfin von G*** *und Sophie von La Roches* Geschichte des Fräuleins von Sternheim. Hildesheim: Olms-Weidmann, 2001.

Mandelkow, Karl Robert. "Der deutsche Briefroman. Zum Problem der Polyperspektive im Epischen." *Neophilologus* 44 (1960): 200–08.

Maurer, Doris, and Arnold E. Maurer, eds. *Dokumente zur Bonner Theatergeschichte 1778–1784: Hoftheater unter Gustav Friedrich Wilhelm Großmann und Karoline Großmann.* Bonn: Bouvier, 1990.

Maurer, Michael. "Das Gute und das Schöne: Sophie von La Roche (1730–1807) wiederentdecken?" *Euphorion* 79.2 (1985): 111–38.

Maurer-Schmoock, Sybille. *Deutsches Theater im 18. Jahrhundert.* Tübingen: Niemeyer, 1982.

Maza, Sarah. "Women, the Bourgeoisie, and the Public Sphere: Responses to David Bell and Daniel Gordon." *French Historical Studies* 17 (1992): 935–50.

Meise, Helga. "Der Frauenroman: Erprobungen der 'Weiblichkeit.' " Brinker-Gabler 434–52.

———. *Die Unschuld und die Schrift. Deutsche Frauenromane im 18. Jahrhundert.* Berlin: Helmer, 1983.

Mentzel, Elizabeth. "Neues über Elise Bürger." *Bühne und Welt: Monatsschrift für das deutsche Kunst- und Geistesleben* 1 (1912–13): 371–78.

Mercier, Louis Sébastian. *Neuer Versuch über die Schauspielkunst.* Heidelberg: Schneider, 1967. Facsimile reprint of 1776 edition.

Mereau-Brentano, Sophie. *Das Blütenalter der Empfindung; Amanda und Eduard: Romane.* Ed. Katharina von Hammerstein. Munich: DTV, 1997.

———. "Die Flucht nach der Hauptstadt." Mereau-Brentano, *Ein Glück* 203–27.

———. *Ein Glück, das keine Wirklichkeit umspannt: Gedichte und Erzählungen.* Ed. Katharina von Hammerstein. Munich: DTV, 1997.

———. "Flight to the City." Trans. Jacqueline Vansant. Blackwell and Zantop 380–99.

Mereau-Brentano, "Marie." Mereau-Brentano, *Ein Glück* 49–83.

———. *Wie sehn' ich mich hinaus in die freie Welt: Tagebuch, Betrachtungen und vermischte Prosa*. Munich: DTV, 1997.

Möhrmann, Renate, ed. *Die Schauspielerin: Zur Kulturgeschichte der weiblichen Bühnenkunst*. Frankfurt aM: Insel, 1989.

———. "Die Schauspielerin als literarische Fiktion." Möhrmann *Schauspielerin* 154–74.

Molloy, Sylvia. *At Face Value: Autobiographical Writing in Spanish America*. Cambridge: Cambridge Univ. Press, 1991.

Moritz, Karl Philipp. *Anton Reiser: ein psychologischer Roman*. 1785/1790. Köln: Könemann, 1997.

Mücke, Dorothea von. *Virtue and the Veil of Illusion*. Stanford: Stanford Univ. Press, 1991.

Nenon, Monika. *Autorschaft und Frauenbildung: Das Beispiel Sophie von La Roche*. Würzburg: Königshausen & Neumann, 1988.

Nerl-Steckelberg, Charlotte, and Klaus Pott. *Das wahre Glück ist in der Seele des Rechtschaffenen: Sophie von La Roche (1730–1807), eine bemerkenswerte Frau im Zeitalter von Aufklärung und Empfindsamkeit*. Katalog zur Ausstellung. Bönnigheim: Museum Sophie La Roche, 2000.

Nicolai, Friedrich. "Abhandlung vom Trauerspiele." *Lessings Briefwechsel mit Mendelssohn und Nicolai über das Trauerspiel*. Ed. Robert Petsch. Leipzig, 1910. 2–42.

Niethammer, Ortrun. *Autobiographien von Frauen im 18. Jahrhundert*. Tübingen: Francke, 2000.

Niggl, Günter. *Geschichte der deutschen Autobiographie im 18. Jahrhundert: Theoretische Grundlegung und literarische Entfaltung*. Stuttgart: Metzler, 1977.

Nipperdey, Thomas. "Kommentar: 'Bürgerlich' als Kultur." Kocka, *Bürger und Bürgerlichkeit* 143–48.

Northcutt, Rose-Marie. "Female Protagonists in the Eighteenth-Century Epistolary Novel: a Study of Richardson, La Roche, and Burney." Diss. University of California Riverside, 1990.

Nussbaum, Felicity. *The Autobiographical Subject: Gender and Ideology in Eighteenth-Century England*. Baltimore: Johns Hopkins Univ. Press, 1989.

Oberländer, Hans. *Die geistige Entwicklung der deutschen Schauspielkunst im 18. Jahrhundert*. Hamburg: Voß, 1898.

Olenhusen, Irmtraud Götz von. "Das Ende männlicher Zeugungsmythen im Zeitalter der Aufklärung. Zur Wissenschafts- und Geschlechtergeschichte des 17. und 18. Jahrhunderts." Weckel et al. 259–84.

Pascoe, Judith. *Romantic Theatricality*. Ithaca: Cornell Univ. Press, 1997.
Pasquè, Ernst. *Goethes Theaterleitung in Weimar*. 2 vols. Leipzig, 1863.
Paul, Jean. "Levana oder Erziehlehre (1807)." *Werke*. Ed. Norbert Miller. Vol. 5. Munich: Hanser, 1963.
Peiba, Abraham. *Galerie von deutschen Schauspielern und Schauspielerinnen*. Berlin, 1910.
Petlick, Jennifer Ann. "Shattered Images: Breaking the Tradition of Enforced Domesticity in the Life and Works of Elise Bürger." MA Thesis. Michigan State University, 1992.
Petschauer, Peter. "Sophie von La Roche, Novelist between Reason and Emotion." *The Germanic Review* 57.2 (1982): 70–78.
Pfister, Kurt. "Drei Frauen um Gottfried August Bürger." *Frauenschicksale aus Acht Jahrhunderten*. Ed. Kurt Pfister. Munich: Nymphenburg, 1949. 230–36.
Pin, Emile J., and Jamie Turndorf. "Staging One's Ideal Self." *Life as Theater: a Dramaturgical Sourcebook*. Ed. Dennis Brissett and Charles Edgley. New York: de Gruyter, 1990. 163–81.
Plath, Hermann. *An welchen Punkten kann Jean Pauls "Levana" von Rousseau beeinflusst erscheinen*. Diesdorf bei Gäbersdorf: Schreiberhau-Diesdorfer Rettungsanstalten, 1903.
Pockels, Carl Friedrich. *Versuch einer Charakteristik des weiblichen Geschlechts. Ein Sittengemählde des Menschen, des Zeitalters und des geselligen Lebens*. 5 vols. Hannover: Ritscher, 1797–1802.
Postlewait, Thomas. "Autobiography and Theatre History." *Interpreting the Theatrical Past: Essays in the Historiography of Performance*. Ed. Thomas Postlewait and Bruce A. McConachie. Iowa City: University of Iowa Press, 248–72.
Purdy, Daniel. "Sophie Mereau's Authorial Masquerades and the Subversion of Romantic Poesie." *Women in German Yearbook* 13 (1997): 29–48.
Rang, Brita. "Zur Geschichte des dualistischen Denkens über Mann und Frau. Kritische Anmerkungen zu den Thesen von Karin Hausen zur Herausbildung der Geschlechtscharaktere im 18. und 19. Jahrhundert." *Frauenmacht in der Geschichte*. Ed. Jutta Dalhoff et al. Düsseldorf: Schwann, 1986. 194–204.
Reichard, Heinrich August Ottokar. *Theater-Kalender auf das Jahr 1793*. Gotha: Ettinger, 1793.
Riccoboni, Anton Franz [Francesco], and Friedrich Ludwig Schröder. *Vorschriften über die Schauspielkunst*. Leipzig: Hartmann, 1821.
Richardson, Samuel. *Clarissa, or, The history of a young lady*. Harmondsworth: Penguin, 1985.

Richter, Simon. "Sophie Mereau (1770–1806)." *Women Writers in German-Speaking Countries: A Bio-Bibliographical Critical Sourcebook*. Ed. Elke Frederiksen and Elizabeth Ametsbichler. Westport, CT: Greenwood, 1998. 333–40.

Ridderhoff, Kuno. *Sophie von La Roche und Wieland*. Hamburg: Lütcke & Wulff, 1907.

———. *Sophie von La Roche, die Schülerin Richardsons und Rousseaus*. Einbeck: Schroedter, 1895.

Riviere, Joan. "Womanliness as Masquerade." *The International Journal of Psycho-analysis* 10 (1929): 303–13.

Roach, Joseph R. *The Player's Passion: Studies in the Science of Acting*. Newark: University of Delaware Press, 1985.

Roulston, Christine. *Virtue, Gender and The Authentic Self in Eighteenth-Century Fiction: Richardson, Rousseau, and Laclos*. Gainesville: Univ. Press of Florida, 1998.

Rousseau, Jean Jacques. *The Confessions and Correspondence, Including the Letters to Malesherbes*. Trans. Christopher Kelly. *The Collected Writings of Rousseau*. Ed. Christopher Kelly, Roger D. Masters and Peter G. Stillman. Vol. 5. Hanover, NH: Dartmouth College and Univ. Press of New England, 1990.

———. *Émile*. Trans. Barbara Foxley. London: Everyman, 1993.

———. *The First and Second Discourses*. Trans. Roger D. and Judith R. Masters. Ed. Roger D. Masters. New York: St. Martin's, 1964.

———. *Politics and the Arts: Letter to M. d'Alembert on the Theater*. Trans. Allan Bloom. Glencoe, IL: The Free Press, 1960.

Runge, Anita. *Literarische Praxis von Frauen um 1800: Briefroman, Autobiographie, Märchen*. Hildesheim: Olms-Weidmann, 1997.

Rüppel, Michael. " 'Was sagen Sie von Mme. Bürger?' Elise Bürger (1769–1833) als Schauspielerin und das Theater zur Zeit der 'Weimarer Klassik.' " *G.A. Bürger und J. W. L. Gleim*. Ed. Hans-Joachim Kertscher. Tübingen: Niemeyer, 1996. 224–38.

Russo, Eva-Maria. " 'Auf keinen Teufel gefasst': the Discourse of Seduction and Rape in Eighteenth-Century German Literature." Diss. University of California Los Angeles, 2000.

Sachs, Jetta. *Sophie La Roche: Jugendliebe Wielands und erste Frau, die einen deutschen Roman schrieb*. Heilbronn: Salzer, 1985.

Sainte-Albine, Pierre Rémond de. *Le Comédien*. 1749. Geneva: Slatkine Reprints, 1971.

Schauer, Hans, ed. *Herders Briefwechsel mit Caroline Flachsland*. 2 vols. Weimar: Schriften der Goethe-Gesellschaft, 1926.

Schiefer, Karl. "Elise Bürger. Ein Beitrag zur deutschen Literatur- und Theatergeschichte." Diss. Frankfurt am Main, 1921.

Schieth, Lydia. *Die Entwicklung des deutschen Frauenromans im ausgehenden 18. Jahrhundert: ein Beitrag zur Gattungsgeschichte.* Frankfurt aM: Lang, 1987.

Schiller, Friedrich von. *Naive and Sentimental Poetry and On the Sublime.* Trans. Julius A. Elias. New York: Ungar, 1966.

Schink, Johann Friedrich. *Dramaturgische Monate.* Schwerin, 1790.

———. *Theaterzeitung* September 29 1792.

Schmid, Pia. "Weib oder Mensch, Wesen oder Wissen? Bürgerliche Theorien zur weiblichen Bildung um 1800." *Geschichte der Mädchen- und Frauenbildung: Vom Mittelalter bis zur Aufklärung.* Ed. Elke Kleinau and Claudia Opitz. Frankfurt: Campus, 1996. 327–45.

Schmid, Sigrun. *Der "selbstverschuldeten Unmündigkeit" entkommen. Perspektiven bürgerlicher Frauenliteratur. Dargestellt an Romanbeispielen Sophie von La Roches, Therese Hubers, Friederike Helene Ungers, Caroline Auguste Fischers, Johanna Schopenhauers und Sophie Bernhardis.* Würzburg: Königshausen & Neumann, 1999.

Schmidt, Peter. "Nachwort." *Kalathiskos.* By Sophie Mereau. Ed. Peter Schmidt. Heidelberg: Lambert Schneider, 1968. 3–43.

Schrickel, Leonhard. *Geschichte des Weimarer Theaters von seinen Anfängen bis heute.* Weimar: Panses, 1928.

Schulze-Kummerfeld, Karoline. *Ein fahrendes Frauenzimmer: die Lebenserinnerungen der Komödiantin Karoline Schulze-Kummerfeld 1745–1815.* Ed. Inge Buck. Berlin: Orlanda, 1988.

———. "Hamburg Manuscript [1782]: 'Die Ganze Geschichte meines Lebens.' " Cod. hist. 383 d. Staats- und Universitätsbibliothek Hamburg.

———. *Lebenserinnerungen der Komödiantin Karoline Schulze-Kummerfeld.* Ed. Emil Benezé. 2 vols. Berlin: Gesellschaft für Theatergeschichte, 1915.

———. "Letter to Friedrich Nicolai, 8. August 1793." Preußischer Kulturbesitz, Nachlaß Nicolai: 42 Kummerfeld. Staatsbibliothek zu Berlin.

———. "Weimar Manuscript [1793]: 'Wahre Geschichte meines theatralischen Lebens.' " HA A XXII Nr. 425. Thüringisches Haupstaatsarchiv Weimar.

Schütze, Johann Friedrich. *Hamburgische Theatergeschichte.* Hamburg: Treder, 1794.

Schwanbeck, Gisela. *Sozialprobleme der Schauspielerin im Ablauf dreier Jahrhunderte.* Berlin-Dahlem: Hess, 1957.

Schwarz, Gisela. *Literarisches Leben und Sozialstrukturen um 1800: zur Situation von Schriftstellerinnen am Beispiel von Sophie Brentano-Mereau geb. Schubart.* Frankfurt aM: Lang, 1991.

Shakespeare, William. *The Tempest.* Ed. David Lindley. Cambridge: Cambridge Univ. Press, 2002.

Sharpe, Lesley. "Über den Zusammenhang der tierischen Natur der Frau mit ihrer geistigen: Zur Anthropologie der Frau um 1800." Barkhof and Sagarra 213–25.

Sm. "Melanie, das Findelkind. Mit einem Kupfer. Berlin, bey Unger. 1804." Rev. of *Melanie, das Findelkind*, by F. H. Unger. *Neue Allgemeine Deutsche Bibliothek* 103 (1805): 295–96.

Spacks, Patricia Meyer. *Imagining a Self: Autobiography and Novel in Eighteenth-Century England.* Cambridge, MA: Harvard Univ. Press, 1976.

Spickernagel, Wilhelm. *Die* Geschichte des Fräuleins von Sternheim *von Sophie von La Roche und Goethes* Werther. Greifswald: Adler, 1911.

Spies, Bernard. "Sophie von La Roches *Geschichte des Fräuleins von Sternheim* und die moderne Trivialliteratur: das moralische Vorbild als psychologische Kompensation." *Literatur für Leser* 2 (1991): 80–89.

Starobinski, Jean. *Jean-Jacques Rousseau: Transparency and Obstruction.* Trans. Arthur Goldhammer. Chicago: University of Chicago Press, 1988.

Steinbrügge, Lieselotte. "Die Aufteilung des Menschen. Zur anthropologischen Bestimmung der Frau in Diderots Encyclopedie." Brehmer 51–64.

———. *The Moral Sex: Woman's Nature in the French Enlightenment.* Trans. Pamela E. Selwyn. New York: Oxford Univ. Press, 1995.

Stephan, Inge. *Inszenierte Weiblichkeit: Codierung der Geschlechter in der Literatur des 18. Jahrhunderts.* Köln: Böhlau, 2004.

———. " 'So ist die Tugend ein Gespenst': Frauenbild und Tugendbegriff im bürgerlichen Trauerspiel bei Lessing und Schiller." *Lessing Yearbook* 17 (1985): 1–20.

Straub, Kristina. *Sexual Suspects: Eighteenth-Century Players and Sexual Ideology.* Princeton: Princeton Univ. Press, 1992.

Stump, Doris. "Eine Frau 'von Verstand, Witz, Gefühl, Fantasie und Feuer': Zu Leben und Werk Marianne Ehrmanns." Ehrmann, *Amalie* 481–98.

Swanson, Christina. "Textual Transgression in the Epistolary Mode: Sophie von La Roche's *Geschichte des Frauleins von Sternheim.*" *Michigan Germanic Studies* 22.2 (1996): 144–61.

Toppe, Sabine. " 'Polizey' und Mutterschaft: Aufklärerischer Diskurs und weibliche Lebensrealitäten in der zweiten Hälfte des 18. Jahrhunderts." Weckel et al. 303–22.

Touaillon, Christine. *Der Deutsche Frauenroman des 18. Jahrhunderts.* Leipzig: Braumüller, 1919.

Treder, Uta. "Sophie Mereau: Montage und Demontage einer Liebe." Gallas and Heuser 172–83.

Trilling, Lionel. *Sincerity and Authenticity*. Cambridge, MA: Harvard Univ. Press, 1972.

Trouille, Mary Seidman. *Sexual Politics in the Enlightenment: Women Writers Read Rousseau*. Albany: SUNY Press, 1997.

Turner, Cheryl. *Living by the Pen: Women Writers in the Eighteenth Century*. London: Routledge, 1992.

Uden, Konrad Friedrich. *Über die Erziehung der Töchter des Mittelstandes*. Stendhal: Franzen and Grosse, 1783.

Umbach, Regina. "The Role of Anglophilia in Sophie von La Roche's *Geschichte des Frauleins von Sternheim* (1771)." *German Life and Letters* 52.1 (1999): 1–13.

———. "Sophie von La Roche's *Geschichte des Fräuleins von Sternheim* and Richardson's *Clarissa*: a Case Study in Eighteenth-Century Anglo-German Literary Relations." Diss. University of Oxford, 1999.

Unger, Friederike Helene. *Melanie, das Findelkind*. Berlin: Unger, 1804.

Valdastri, Abbé I. "Welche Vorzüge hat das bürgerliche Trauerspiel vor dem heroischen Trauerspiele und dem Lustspiel? Warum steht es dem letztern nach? Und welches sind die ihm ausschliesslich zukommenden Eigenschaften?" *Neue Bibliothek der schönen Wissenschaften und freyen Künste*. Ed. Christian Felix Weisse and Johann Gottfried Dyk. Vol. 52. Leipzig, 1794. 26–116.

Veltrusky, Jarmila. "Engel's Ideas for a Theory of Acting." *The Drama Review* 24.4 (1980): 71–80.

Vickery, Amanda. "Golden Age to Separate Spheres? A Review of the Categories and Chronology of English Women's History." *The Historical Journal* 2 (1993): 383–414.

Voskuil, Lynn. *Acting Naturally: Victorian Theatricality and Authenticity*. Charlottesville: University of Virginia Press, 2004.

Voßkamp, Wilhelm. "Erzählte Subjektivität: Zur Geschichte des empfindsamen Romans im 18. Jahrhundert in Deutschland." Gutjahr, Kühlmann and Wucherpfennig 339–52.

Wanko, Cheryl. "The Eighteenth-Century Actress and the Construction of Gender: Lavinia Fenton and Charlotte Charke." *Eighteenth-Century Life* 18 (1994): 75–90.

Watt, Ian P. *The Rise of the Novel: Studies in Defoe, Richardson, and Fielding*. Harmondsworth: Penguin, 1963.

Weckel, Ulrike. "Bürgerliche Raffinesse. Zur wohlinszenierten Eheanbahnung von Elise Hahn und Gottfried August Bürger." Weckel et al. 143–66.

Weckel, Ulrike et al., eds. *Ordnung, Politik und Geselligkeit der Geschlechter im 18. Jahrhundert*. Göttingen: Wallstein, 1998.

Weigel, Sigrid. "Der schielende Blick: Thesen zur Geschichte weiblicher Schreibpraxis." *Die verborgene Frau*. Ed. Inge Stephan and Sigrid Weigel. Berlin: Argument, 1983. 83–137.

Weigel, Sigrid. "Sophie Mereau." *Frauen: Porträts aus zwei Jahrhunderten*. Ed. Hans Jürgen Schultz. Stuttgart: Kreuz, 1981. 20–32.

Wellbery, Caroline Elisabeth. "Sensibility and Socialization: The German Sentimental Novel of the 1770s." Diss. Stanford University, 1981.

Wetzels, Walter D. "Schauspielerinnen im 18. Jahrhundert—zwei Perspektiven: *Wilhelm Meister* und die Memoiren der Schulze-Kummerfeld." *Die Frau von der Reformation zur Romantik*. Ed. Barbara Becker-Cantarino. Bonn: Bouvier, 1980. 195–216.

Widmer, Maya. "Amalie—eine wahre Geschichte?" Ehrmann, *Amalie* 499–515.

———. "Mit spitzer Feder gegen Vorurteile und gallsüchtige Moral—Marianne Ehrmann, geb. von Brentano." *Und schrieb und schrieb wie ein Tiger aus dem Busch. Über Schriftstellerinnen in der deutschsprachigen Schweiz*. Ed. Elizabeth Ryter, Liliane Studer and Doris Stump. Zürich: Limmat, 1994. 52–72.

Wiede-Behrendt, Ingrid. *Lehrerin des Schönen, Wahren, Guten: Literatur und Frauenbildung im ausgehenden 18. Jahrhundert am Beispiel von Sophie La Roche*. Frankfurt aM: Lang, 1987.

Wierlacher, Alois. *Das bürgerliche Drama: seine theoretische Begründung im 18. Jahrhundert*. Munich: Fink, 1968.

Wikander, Matthew H. *Fangs of Malice: Hypocrisy, Sincerity, & Acting*. Iowa City: University of Iowa Press, 2002.

Wild, Christopher J. *Theater der Keuschheit—Keuschheit des Theaters: zu einer Geschichte der (Anti-)Theatralität von Gryphius bis Kleist*. Freiburg iB: Rombach, 2003.

Williams, Simon. *German Actors of the Eighteenth and Nineteenth Centuries*. Westport, CT: Greenwood, 1985.

Winkle, Sally. *Woman as Bourgeois Ideal: A Study of Sophie von La Roche's* Geschichte des Fräuleins von Sternheim *and Goethe's* Werther. New York: Lang, 1988.

Wolff, Christian Freiherr von. *Vernünfftige Gedancken von dem Gesellschaftlichen Leben der Menschen und insonderheit dem gemeinen Wesen zu Beförderung der Glückseligkeit des menschlichen Geschlechts den Liebhabern der Wahrheit mitgetheilet*. 1732. *Gesammelte Werke*. Vol. 5. Hildesheim: Olms, 1975.

———. *Vernünfftige Gedancken von der Menschen thun und lassen zu Beförderung ihrer Glückseligkeit*. 1733. *Gesammelte Werke*. Vol. 4. Hildesheim: Olms, 1976.

Wurst, Karin A. "Elise Bürger (1769–1833) and the Gothic Imagination." *Women in German Yearbook* 13 (1997): 11–27.

Wurst, Karin A. "Negotiations of Containment: Elise Bürger's *Adelheit, Gräfinn von Teck* and the 'Trivial' Tradition." *Thalia's Daughters: German Women Dramatists from the Eighteenth Century to the Present*. Ed. Susan L. Cocalis and Ferrel Rose. Tübingen: Francke, 1996. 35–52.

———. "Spurensicherung: Elise Bürgers Einakter *Die antike Statue aus Florenz* (1814) als Beispiel dramatischer Experimente an der Jahrhundertwende." *Goethe Yearbook*. Ed. Thomas P. Saine. Vol. 8. Columbia, SC: Camden House, 1996. 210–37.

Zantop, Susanne. "Aus der Not eine Tugend: Tugendgebot und Öffentlichkeit bei Freiderike Helene Unger." Gallas and Heuser 132–47.

———. "The Beautiful Soul Writes Herself: Friederike Helene Unger and the 'Große Göthe.' " *In the Shadow of Olympus: German Women Writers Around 1800*. Ed. Katherine Goodman and Edith Waldstein. Albany: SUNY Press, 1992. 29–51.

———. "Nachwort." *Bekenntnisse einer schönen Seele*. By Friederike Helene Unger. Ed. Anita Runge. Vol. 9. Hildesheim: Olms, 1991. 385–416.

———. "Trivial Pursuits? An Introduction to German Women's Writing from the Middle Ages to 1830." Blackwell and Zantop 9–50.

Ziolkowski, Theodore. "Language and Mimetic Action in Lessing's *Miss Sara Sampson*." *The Germanic Review* 40.4 (1965): 261–76.

Index